Photographing the
Southwest

Volume 2 – A guide to the natural landmarks of Arizona

Second Edition

Laurent Martrès

This guidebook will take you on a grand tour of Arizona, starting with an in-depth discovery of the Grand Canyon, from the rim and from the river, exploring the superlative landscapes of Navajoland, including Monument Valley and Canyon de Chelly, amazing narrows and slot canyons such as Antelope Canyon, the incredible swirls of Coyote Buttes and its crown jewel: The Wave, the colorful area around Sedona, all the national parks and monuments of the Sonoran desert, and finishing with a foray into the adjacent southern tip of Nevada.

PHOTOGRAPHING THE SOUTHWEST (SECOND EDITION)
VOLUME 2 – ARIZONA

Published by PhotoTripUSA™
An imprint of

GRAPHIE
INTERNATIONAL, INC.
8780 19th Street, Suite 199
Alta Loma, CA 91701, USA

All photography by Laurent Martrès, Copyright © 2002-2006, except where noted.
Cover photo: The Last Shangri-La (Havasupai Reservation)
Title page: Yaki Point Sunrise (Grand Canyon Nat'l Park)
Overleaf: Sandstone Rhapsody (Lower Antelope Canyon)
End of book: Desert Pastel (Little Painted Desert)

Visit Laurent's web sites: **http://www.martres.com** and **http://www.phototripusa.com**

Also available in this series:
Photographing the Southwest – Volume 1 Southern Utah ISBN 978-0-916189-12-9
Photographing the Southwest – Volume 3 Colorado & New Mexico ISBN 978-0-916189-14-3

Printed in China

Disclaimer
Some of the locations described in this book require travel through remote areas, where footpaths and 4-wheel drive trails can be difficult, even dangerous. Travel at your own risk and always check conditions locally before venturing out. The author and publisher decline all responsibility if you get lost, stranded, injured or otherwise suffer any kind of mishap as a result of following the advice and descriptions in this book. Furthermore, the information contained herein may have become outdated by the time you read it; the author and publisher assume no responsibility for outdated information, errors and omissions.

Publisher's Cataloging-in-Publication

    Martrès, Laurent.
       Photographing the Southwest / by Laurent Martrès. --
    2nd ed.
       v. cm.
       Includes bibliographical references and index.
       CONTENTS: v. 1. Southern Utah -- v. 2. Arizona -- v.
    3. Colorado & New Mexico.
       ISBN-13: 978-0-916189-12-9 (v. 1)
       ISBN-10: 0-916189-12-0 (v. 1)
       ISBN-13: 978-0-916189-13-6 (v. 2)
       ISBN-10: 0-916189-13-9 (v. 2)
       [etc.]

       1. Southwest, New--Guidebooks. 2. Landscape
    photography--Southwest, New--Guidebooks.   I. Title.

F787.M37 2005   917.904'34
                      QBI05-200068

PREFACE
by Tom Till

I've often said that the Colorado Plateau is a place where two divergent forces, the world's best light and the world's most interesting landscapes, seamlessly combine to create a photographer's paradise. Having been lucky enough to travel worldwide in pursuit of landscape and nature imagery, and also lucky enough to have lived my entire adult life in canyon country, I believe I have the standing to make such a claim, although anyone who has spent much time here knows my words to be utterly true.

As I looked at the places mentioned in the text, I was flooded with a lifetime of memories of the great times I have had exploring, hiking, jeeping, river running and making photographs in the Four Corners area. I was fortunate, beginning in the 1970's, to be one of the first photographers to visit the Subway in Zion National Park, to cruise around the White Rim in Canyonlands without a permit, and to be the only photographer in Antelope Canyon for weeks at a time.

Photographers coming to the area now have a challenge I never faced in those early years: other photographers. Over the decades serious photography has become one of the major activities pursued by visitors to the region. As such, we have an increased responsibility to leave the land as we find it, behave ourselves around other photographers and visitors, and place the integrity of the land above our desire to create images. After you leave this magnificent place, you can also provide a valuable service and help insure its survival as a viable ecosystem by supporting national and local environmental groups who lavish a great deal of needed attention on the preservation of our spectacular deserts. These groups include The Sierra Club, The Grand Canyon Trust, The Southern Utah Wilderness Alliance, The Nature Conservancy, and The Wilderness Society.

I congratulate Laurent on the fine work he has done with these books, on his own wonderful photography, and on his mission to give many other photographers a forum for disseminating their great work. In this regard, he is unique among established western landscape photographers.

Photographing the Southwest will be a helpful tool for me when I return to many of my favorite haunts in the future, but I'm also glad that an infinity of canyons, arches, ruins, springs and secret places have been left out of this book. These places are the true heart of the wilderness desert southwest. They are available to all who push a little beyond the established scenic hot spots, and all who are willing to risk equipment, creature comforts, and at times, life and limb. It's all worthwhile in pursuit of the magical light that calls us onward around the next bend of the canyon.

Tom Till

ACKNOWLEDGEMENTS

As with any book of this scope, many individuals have contributed one way or another to a better experience for the reader.

My deepest gratitude goes to Philippe Schuler, whose careful editing of the manuscript and innumerable enhancements to its contents have resulted in a much better book. Philippe—who shares with me an intense passion for the Southwest—brought to these guidebooks a level of precision and excellence that I would not have been able to achieve on my own. He co-wrote several sections and contributed informative textual and pictorial content throughout the various volumes and chapters. He also spent countless hours verifying the relevance and accuracy of the practical information and helped immensely in restructuring the presentation of this Second Edition to make the three books a better read. Human error is always possible, but Philippe did everything he could to ensure that I provided the most accurate information about the locations.

Thanks to Kathi Muhlich for an outstanding editing job. Thanks also to Tony Kuyper who substantially edited and improved the Introduction and Photo Advice chapters; I'm very grateful for his help.

Tom Till's wonderful photography has consistently inspired me. Tom kindly wrote the Preface to *Photographing the Southwest* and some of his photography is also featured in this series.

Sioux Bally, of Heartstone Arts, lent her considerable artistry to designing the cover, as well as the anchor pages of each chapter.

Danelle Bell created the base map of the territory covered in this book.

The following individuals either contributed information or checked the manuscript: Julia Betz, Ron Flickinger, Bruce Fynan, Robert Hitchman, Robert McLaughlin, Sid Moore, Mike Salamacha, Isabel Synnatschke, Steffen Synnatschke, and Greg Vaughn.

My photography & hiking partners Vic Beer, Akira Kato, Tony Kuyper, Bob McLaughlin, Gene Mezereny, Sid Moore, Steve Peterson, Denis Savouray, Philippe Schuler, Steffen Synnatschke, Scott Walton, Charles Wood, as well as my wife Patricia accompanied me on many of my adventures in the Southwest and I'm grateful for their company.

Finally, I thank the photographers who have contributed their talent to enrich the pictorial content of this book: Sioux Bally, Vic Beer, Derek von Briesen, Alain Briot, Ron Flickinger, Tony Kuyper, Bob McLaughlin, Gene Mezereny, Denis Savouray, Philippe Schuler, Isabel Synnatschke, Steffen Synnatschke, Tom Till, Thomas Wiewandt, and Charles Wood.

ABOUT THIS BOOK

Welcome to the Second Edition of *Photographing the Southwest*. I like to think of this book as a resource for visitors and photographers to the natural landmarks of the Southwest. The present Volume 2 covers Arizona, Volume 1 covers Southern Utah and Volume 3 covers Colorado & New Mexico.

The purpose of these books is to document natural landmarks of the American Southwest from a photographic perspective. Some of these landmarks are well known; but, many are off the beaten track and seldom featured in more traditional guidebooks. Many are easily accessible and will provide you with unforgettable images and memories.

Some human activity is also covered in the books, but it is essentially limited to pre-Columbian dwellings and rock art of ancestral native Americans. This is due to the fact that cliff dwellings and rock art are tightly integrated into the landscape and can be interpreted as an extension of the natural world. I believe that most landscape photographers would agree with that.

On rare occasions, mention is made of more recent sites due to their proximity to natural landmarks. However, other forms of human activity which greatly contribute to the essence of the Southwest, such as architecture, modern native Americans crafts and rituals, rodeo, etc. are outside the scope of *Photographing the Southwest* and are purposely left out.

If you're not a photographer, you'll find in these books lots of information that more traditional guides leave out. The location of a hidden site, the most beautiful angle, and the best time of the day to view it are equally as valuable for seeing with your own eyes as for photography. These books are for everyone with a passion for the Southwest.

Each volume of *Photographing the Southwest* should be seen as a resource, rather than strictly a guidebook. It supplements other—more traditional—travel guides with specialized photographic information. The information is arranged by geographic areas. Locations whose photographic interest is particularly impressive are listed under these main headings. It also describes how to get there, as well as how and when to get the best shots. It purposely leaves out logistical concerns such as restaurant and hotel accommodations as there are already more than enough excellent travel books on that subject.

In addition to all the new areas covered in this Second Edition of *Photographing the Southwest*, all three volumes include a lot of new commentary and advice concerning previously visited sites.

The chapter on photography has been expanded, despite my initial reluctance to dispense this kind of advice. While I hope you'll benefit from my suggestions if you are a beginning photographer, my primary goal remains to provide you with a comprehensive location resource with which you can unleash your very own photographic talent.

In this series of guidebooks, coverage of pre-Columbian sites has been increased, reflecting the growing interest on the part of the public for exploring the heritage of native Americans and interpreting their rock art. As Val Brinkerhoff, photographer of *Architecture of the Ancient Ones* puts it: "Visit one ancient dwelling site and you're likely to be drawn to experience another, and another, and another."

With these three greatly expanded volumes, my goal is to give readers from all over the world the best practical information to discover and photograph the Southwest. I believe you'll enjoy experiencing the infinite photographic possibilities of the Southwest and make some truly amazing discoveries of your own in the course of your travels.

May this book bring you a slew of new ideas for your creative photography of the Southwest. ✿

—Laurent Martrès

KEEPING CURRENT

We live in a world where things change rapidly, this is particularly true of the Southwest, which has recently experienced an influx of tourism, as well as of special interests: trails become paved or deteriorate, road numbers change, some sites become off-limit to visitors while new ones open up, quota systems become mandatory, and new rules supersede all ones. The rapid pace of these changes is well beyond the capacity of a publisher to update their guides at regular interval, but the internet is our savior:

You'll find errors, omissions and updates to this book and others in the series on our web site at *http://www.phototripusa.com/updates.*

Conversely, should you notice an error or change in one of the descriptions of this book, kindly let us know about it by e-mailing us at *updates@phototripusa.com.* The entire community will benefit from it.

Thank you.

TABLE OF CONTENTS

Looking for the light

Chapter 1

INTRODUCTION

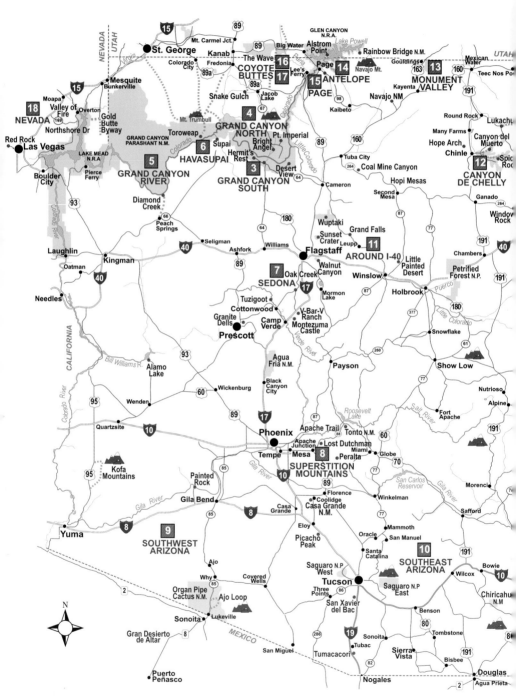

Territory covered in this volume

This chapter deals with the logistics of a trip to the Southwest. Some information concerning the geology, fauna & flora, and history of the Southwest can be found in *Chapter 1* of *Volume 1 – Southern Utah.*

Maps

You may find it surprising that this book doesn't contain any detailed maps other than the simple one to the left, which describes the general location of the chapters and some of the more prominent sections. The reason for this is that *Photographing the Southwest* has a different purpose than other guidebooks: I like to think of it as an illustrated location resource, providing ideas for discovering or expanding on your previous knowledge of the Southwest. Also, had I chosen to illustrate with numerous maps the locations covered in the three volumes of *Photographing the Southwest,* it would have dramatically increased the size, weight and price of the books, making them impractical to carry on a trip. Any number of small maps I could have included would still be no substitute for the real thing. The reality is that even with these books, you will need several different kinds of maps to effectively use the information.

Maps play a huge role in several respects. Large scale maps are necessary to get a global perspective of your trip and make initial decisions. Detailed road maps are necessary in order to follow the instructions in the *"Getting there"* sections of the book. You'll find a list of recommended maps in the *Appendix,* along with a short description of each. One particular map—the *AAA Indian Country* map—stands out as an excellent asset in the preparation and enjoyment of your trips. This remarkable map covers about 90% of the territory of *Volume 1* and about half the terrain of *Volumes 2* and *3.*

Additionally, since many of the locations I describe are off the beaten path, 7.5 minute US Geological Survey maps are necessary. Although the information on these maps is sometimes outdated, they are an indispensable tool for locating remote sites and navigating the backcountry. As it can become expensive and impractical to buy so many different topographic maps, I suggest that you purchase the remarkable *National Geographic Topo! State series* maps for your computer. These Digital Rasterized Graphics files allow you to print your own maps for specific locations. You can print only the portion of map corresponding to your needs, including markers and annotations. While the initial investment in the four *Topo! State series* maps covering the three volumes of *Photographing the Southwest* is sizeable, it will prove economical in the long run if you're going to make extensive use of the books.

The *National Geographic Topo!* maps become a powerful tool when installed on a laptop computer. Used in tandem with a GPS unit, you can track your precise location in real time on your monitor while driving on remote dirt roads. Consider this simple scenario: Driving back from your sunset shoot, you find yourself at a fork and do not remember which branch you came in on earlier. The digitized map and GPS combination makes it extremely easy to find your location and hence the correct turn in order to return home. It's true that you can do this with a mapping GPS alone, but tracking your progress on a computer screen with all the fine detail of a *Topo! State series* map provides a degree of accuracy and comfort that is not possible with the GPS' tiny screen. Entering waypoints from a computer keyboard is also easier and navigating the maps on the computer screen provides a better understanding of the topology—hills to climb, gullies to bypass, etc.—especially if you use relief shading or, better yet, three-dimensional viewing. If you haven't purchased these maps on CD-ROM, I suggest at least preparing your trips using the excellent *www.topozone.com* web site. Here you can access and print at no charge small-sized excerpts of topographic maps. There are also commercial web-based topographic services allowing you to print maps with various degrees of information for a fee.

So now that we've entered the realm of digital mapping, let's talk about this other useful tool: the GPS.

GPS considerations

In the previous edition, I considered it inappropriate to give away GPS points. My philosophy at the time was that readers needed to make their own adventure, performing a minor amount of effort in researching locations. I also considered, and still consider, GPS usage fraught with dangers in the hands of inexperienced users. Knowing GPS coordinates is one thing, but it is no substitute for a topographic map, particularly when it comes to understanding relief.

I have noticed that novice users tend to rely on the "GOTO" function of their GPS, without consideration for the topology. Rarely can one follow the straight line indicated on the GPS. Gullies too deep for crossing and vertical cliffs too high for scaling are common occurrences.

In the early 2000s, a majority of friends and government agency officials shared my concern. The consensus at the time was that giving away GPS coordinates could make things too easy and perhaps dangerous for novice users.

Circumstances have changed substantially since then. Today, GPS coordinates can be found on the Internet for just about any location of interest and the infor-mation is freely exchanged between peers with similar pursuits. In this rapidly evolving context, it would be counterproductive to force readers to seek GPS information outside of this book.

Therefore, in this edition, I have chosen to provide GPS coordinates very selec-tively. I do not want to entice readers to rely totally on their GPS unit. Instead, you'll find coordinates whenever they are truly useful or even indispensable.

I'll reiterate my warning, however. The GPS is no substitute for a topographic map and a compass, and in some cases for plain old instinct and navigational skills. Batteries eventually die, but the compass will continue to indicate your direction. You should always carry spare batteries, a compass and a map… and of course know how to use them.

If you are a novice user, I suggest that you attend a clinic. GPS clinics are available for free at many outdoor equipment stores in cities across the country.

One last bit of advice: do not walk with your eyes riveted to your GPS. Instead, try finding your way around by observing landmarks and following natural paths. Not only will you become a better routefinder, but you'll enjoy your surroundings a lot more. Your GPS is not a toy; use it only when necessary, to make sure that you are on course. Once you've mastered its use and are aware of its potential pitfalls, you may wonder how you got along without it.

The coordinate system used in this book is Degrees, Minutes, Seconds in WGS84 datum. It is the simplest to understand for novice users. It is also the best choice in terms of readability and ease of input: The popular UTM system may have some pluses, but it is not as immediately descriptive when comparing two waypoints. Coordinates expressed in UTM are also easier to mistype. Once typed into your GPS unit, *Topo!* application, or on-line web site, you can simply convert the coordinates to your preferred reference system.

Driving around

The question of the best vehicle to use may naturally arise when you visit an area as vast as the American Southwest. In this *Volume 2* of *Photographing the Southwest*, about 70% of the sites are accessible via paved roads or tracks adequate for passenger cars. An additional 12% of the sites can be accessed via rougher tracks that are still potentially passable by passenger cars if driven with caution in dry weather. The rest necessitate an SUV or some kind of high-clearance vehicle. In a number of cases—not the majority—use of a four-wheel drive (4WD) vehicle and some experience with this kind of driving is required. High-clearance is generally associated with larger tires than on the typical passenger car and is often necessary to negotiate the irregularities of a track, prevent damage to the undercarriage, and avoid becoming high-centered. Complementing high clearance, 4WD, especially in low-range, is useful on sandy or muddy tracks or tracks presenting rock steps and/or particularly steep angles—a small minority of locations in this book.

Road difficulty is examined in detail for each location in the text. Also, in the Ratings section at this end of the book, I rate the difficulty of vehicular access under "normal" conditions, i.e. always in dry weather and long after a rain. In wet conditions or after violent thunderstorms, a track rated accessible by passenger car can become impassable even to a high-clearance 4WD vehicle. The ratings provided should always be confirmed with visitor centers or local authorities, as track condition change frequently based on recent weather and the elapsed time since the last road maintenance. Don't take any unnecessary risks. Towing may cost hundreds or even thousands of dollars should you become stranded in some remote location.

Undoubtedly, using an SUV to explore the locations in this guidebook—even

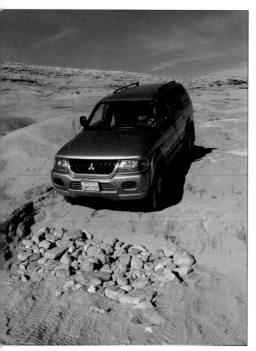

A bit of road building...

if it isn't 4WD—provides a degree of flexibility and comfort not offered by passenger cars and limits the risk of damage to your vehicle. If you are considering car camping on your trip, you may even be able to sleep in your vehicle. Assuming you have a flat surface after folding down the rear seats, a person of average height can usually sleep diagonally. If you own a pick-up, a shell will provide inexpensive and effective protection against the elements.

If you're traveling in your own SUV or pick-up truck, you should always carry a tow strap, a shovel and a small air compressor. The latter will allow you to reinflate your tires after airing down in particularly sandy terrain. If you fly in from another part of the country (or the world) and rent an SUV from a major rental company, be aware that it will rarely offer 4WD. Furthermore, your rental agreement usually prohibits taking the rental vehicle off paved roads, so think twice about where you want to go, as you'll be assuming a major financial risk. One last piece of advice concerning rental vehicles: Always verify the presence of an adequate spare tire and tools to change it. You don't want to be stuck on a remote road just because the crank to operate the jack is missing.

Hiking

I'm often asked about the level of difficulty of the hikes involved in visiting various locations. The answer depends on a plurality of factors. Many readers are not necessarily avid hikers. While a majority are probably content to carry a lightweight camera, some may be hauling heavy photographic equipment. At the other end of the spectrum, some folks prefer long hikes so they can "get away from the crowds". In *Volume 2*, about 60% of the locations can be visited and photographed with almost no hiking at all or else an easy stroll lasting less than an hour round-trip. An additional 23% of the sites should be accessible to most readers, requiring between one to three hours round-trip with moderate difficulty. About 16% are more demanding, as they require up to six hours round-trip and/or involve some kind of difficulty such as elevation change, orienteering, tougher terrain, obstacles or other risks. A small minority require longer, more strenuous hiking or backpacking (mentioned only marginally in this guidebook).

In addition to the descriptions in the text, hiking difficulty is summed up in detail at the end of the book, with ratings on difficulty of access on foot for each location. These ratings are done with the average hiker in mind, i.e. neither a person with mobility problems, nor a marathon runner, in average physical shape (exercising regularly, preferably walking) and having a reasonably good sense of orientation, under normal hiking conditions (in dry weather and average temperatures).

Reading this guidebook, you'll see that visiting the Southwest—even off the beaten track—is not the exclusive domain of hard-core hikers. You'll come to realize that ordinary city folks can find plenty of trips to satisfy their photographic pursuits with only a modest amount of effort. Obviously, you need to set reasonable goals for yourself. Begin your trip with easy hikes, increasing your mileage progressively and alternating hard and easy days. Pay particular attention to the duration of your hikes; some people tend to be overly optimistic, especially if taking lots of pictures.

Always heed the advice of park rangers and professional guides, even if it feels a little too conservative. This is particularly important when hiking in canyon country. Flash floods are a not so rare occurrence in all seasons, although they tend to happen much more frequently during summer. You don't want to find yourself trapped in a slot canyon when that happens.

Hiking equipment should also be considered carefully. It can make a significant difference in terms of security and comfort. Security should not be taken lightly as there is a very real risk of getting lost on backcountry hikes without trails. Although a minority, there are a few such hikes in this guidebook. Start with the Ten Essentials:

❐ A first aid kit
❐ Waterproof matches or a small lighter
❐ A pocket knife
❐ A headlamp (there are very small, lightweight LED models)
❐ Sunglasses (polarized types are nice for photography)
❐ A loud whistle (so you can be located by your party or a rescue team in case of mishap)
❐ High-energy food (trail mix or energy bars)
❐ A topographic map of the area
❐ A compass and if possible a GPS unit (always take a waypoint of your vehicle's location)
❐ Extra clothing in case of a sudden change in weather.

Your digital camera can also be a useful tool when hiking in the backcountry, where there is no trail or no obvious landmark and you'll be returning the same way you came. At each strategic location (such as a spot where you need to go down or ascend a cliff, an intersection of side canyons, or when leaving the course of a wash) turn around and take a snapshot, taking care to place the direction to be followed on returning in the center of the frame. If you have any doubt as to the correct course when you return, just examine the shots you took on your camera's LCD.

A good pair of hiking shoes with good ankle support is essential for hiking in the Southwest. You want good ankle support and soles with good traction on small pebbles and slickrock. Sneakers are definitely inadequate for the trail and should stay in your car. If you're going to wade inside streambeds—this book offers several opportunities to do so—a second pair of shoes, specialized for water activities, will come handy. This type of shoe usually has excellent anti-slip soles. Although not indispensable, they offer an additional level of comfort when hiking in water. Use them with a pair of wool socks or synthetic liners to avoid blisters. For pants, shorts, and shirts, the newer synthetic fibers work very well in the Southwest environment. They breathe well, transferring body moisture away from the skin, and they dry extremely fast (on you or after being washed). Don't forget the indispensable fleece jacket and/or windbreaker, which you should always have handy as temperatures can change radically throughout the day. Don't be fooled by the fact that the land looks like a desert; it can get cold very fast, especially at elevation, during the spring and fall months. When hiking in full sun—a common occurrence in the Southwest—consider a solar cap with a "legionnaire" attachment to protect your ears and neck. Also, frequent application of sunscreen to sun-exposed areas is recommended. Sunburn can hurt like hell and has potentially life-threatening health consequences.

There are many good daypacks and photo packs available. Consider one with sufficient capacity to carry not only your photo equipment but also your additional clothing, safety gear and, above all, plenty of water. In summer, dehydration may come easily and without warning. Some of the day-hikes in this book may require a full gallon of water. When hiking in the backcountry, I sometimes encounter photographers carrying "specialized" photo packs for their equipment and only a small hip-bag with just enough space for a couple of energy bars and two pints of water. Not having enough water places you at serious risk in case of unplanned occurrences. Taking the wrong turn or simply extending your visit because every bend of the canyon brings more captivating beauty requires additional resources, especially water. On long day hikes, I usually stash a water bladder behind a tree for the return trip. On some extended trips, I carry and use a water filter.

Trekking poles can be very helpful on hikes that involve lots of ascents and descents. They propel you forward going up and relieve pressure on your knees going down. Your poles can also aid in keeping your balance when wading rocky streams. Note that a trekking pole with a hole on top to screw in your camera is no substitute for a steady tripod!

A word about lodging

I provide no information or advice concerning accommodations, although I occasionally mention campgrounds. I have found that my readers have very different traveling styles depending on their individual goals, time constraints, and the level of comfort they require. There are excellent travel guides available that can assist the reader in finding the specific type of accommodations they desire.

Keep in mind, however, that you'll take many of your best photos during the so-called "golden hour", soon after sunrise and just before sunset. As many of the locations discussed in this book are on dirt roads far away from motels, you may have to camp close to the site to be present during the best light. Doing so, you avoid driving at night on backcountry tracks. What would pass as minor impediments during the day can become very dangerous when you discover them at the last second with your headlights. Depending on the situation, you may be able to opt for organized campgrounds, such as the ones found in many national or state parks (where camping is prohibited outside the official campgrounds). Alternatively, there may be primitive camping where you'll just pick your site in the middle of the backcountry if this is authorized, which is the case most on BLM-administered land.

Even if you're following a classic regimen of motels every night, you may want to carry in your car a small tent, a sleeping pad, a sleeping bag, as well as a stash of food and several gallons of water. Should some unforeseen circumstances prevent you from going back to town, you'll be able to improvise a night in the backcountry. You may even become addicted once you get a taste of it!

When to visit

Arizona can be visited year-round. Each season possesses its unique charm and presents various advantages and disadvantages.

Summer monsoon storms make for sublime skies, occasional rainbows, soft lighting due to the haze and spectacular sunsets, but there is a high price to pay for that. It's the busiest time of the year on the roads and in the parks. In the last two decades, foreign visitors en masse have also discovered the American West, in organized tour groups or as individuals, crowding the roads and parks, not to mention the motels. In the most popular places, reservations become indispensable and need to be made in advance to guarantee a place for the night. This can create a serious obstacle to the flexibility of your itinerary by imposing a measure of control on your evening's destination.   The intense heat is not generally a problem in the car or on short walks, but it is a factor on

Waterfall & Fall Colors

long hikes. Summer sees frequent afternoon downpours with all the risks they entail, especially when visiting the numerous canyons described in this guide. Additionally, dirt roads are sometimes closed by water runoff.

Insects can pose a problem in certain areas, particularly at the beginning of summer when deerflies and biting gnats or "no-see-ums" will attack your skin relentlessly. Unfortunately, it is impossible to predict when and where they will hang out in a particular year.

Finally, the days are at their longest; this allows you to cover a lot of ground and visit many sites. On the other hand, this can considerably limit your photographic opportunities during the day when the sun is high in the sky and your shots will be way too contrasty and without nuance. Bear in mind that the angle of the sun is at its highest in summer. There is no such thing as a "golden hour" at the height of summer, merely fifteen minutes of very good light after sunrise and before sunset. As a photographer, I find summer rather exhausting in Arizona and I'd recommend concentrating on Colorado and New Mexico at that time of year (see *Volume 3* of *Photographing the Southwest*).

Autumn is the best time to discover Arizona. It's still warm, but the heat is less ferocious. In the first part of autumn, days are still long but less grueling. Kids and the majority of grown-ups have returned to school and work after Labor Day. The motels empty out and prices lower to a reasonable level. The parks are less congested and parking near the panoramic vistas no longer requires you to drive around for ½ hour to find a spot. Hazy days become rare and insects no longer make your life miserable.

Fall colors begin in mid-October in the high country and in mid-November at lower elevations. October and November are absolutely marvelous in Canyon de Chelly and Grand Canyon as the foliage changes and a new, multi-colored palette of yellow, ocher and red appears with a much softer illumination than in summer. Strong rains are relatively rare, although at high altitude locations such as Sedona and both rims of the Grand Canyon, snow is possible. Finally, the sun rises and sets at a lower angle and the "golden hour" lasts quite a bit longer than in summer. This is my favorite season for general travel in the Southwest at large, as well as for photography.

Winter is the off-season and offers exceptional possibilities to enjoy the surrounding tranquility at incredibly low prices. Also, winter's short daylight hours, as well as the low trajectory of the sun on the horizon, are a real asset to the photographer.

With a bit of care to dress warmly, the dry cold is not disagreeable, though it can make camping less attractive. Winter storms often bring rain or heavy snow to the higher elevations and can last several days. However, a snowfall in Grand Canyon can be an absolutely magical experience when, with these alternate periods of beautiful weather, the air attains an unequaled purity and the sky is an intense blue. By the same token, there are few clouds in the sky and it can be tough to come up with spectacular photography including much sky. Nonetheless, unobstructed views such as those one sees in Grand Canyon reveal extraordinary distances when there is no pollution, as is rarely the case in summer. Large animals descend from the higher elevations and are frequently and easily observed in the valleys.

The main inconvenience is that certain sites become inaccessible, particularly the North Rim of the Grand Canyon and the Chiricahua Mountains (at least without adequate equipment, for these last two). Another negative factor is the lack of color in the vegetation. You'll have to be careful not to include bare vegetation in your images; bare branches and bushes don't make very nice foregrounds.

Spring is a magnificent season, although the weather can be very unpredictable. You are as likely to encounter stormy, wet days as warm and sunny weather. Precipitation is frequent in March and the rivers and waterfalls are at their highest. High peaks are still snowbound, greenery is sprouting, the trees are leafing out and wildflowers abound in wet years. It's a great time to visit Southern Arizona, when Mexican poppies explode with color and temperatures are still tolerable. However, beware of high water levels, which may make it impossible to drive inside washes and canyons.

Saguaro Twilight

The days are getting longer and prices are still not as expensive as during the height of the season. In late spring, insects can also be a great nuisance. No-see-ums, fond of blood and terribly annoying, as well as aggressive deerflies are to be found along watercourses and in washes.

Archeological Sites Etiquette

Rock art and ancient dwellings are a most precious heritage of Native American Indians and humanity at large. They are obviously extremely fragile and when not protected, are often the unfortunate subject of vandalism. When photographing rock art and ruins, the first and foremost rule is: Don't touch. Natural oils from human skin can and will affect glyphs and paintings. Even though a slight touch may only remove a minute amount of pigment or sandstone, when you multiply that by many years and many visitors it will eventually lead to irreparable deg-

radation of the art. Even worse than that is the use of chalk or crayon to enhance or highlight the art for photographs. It compromises the integrity of the art by becoming a permanent part of the design and paves the way for others to add their own mark, thus destroying the precious heritage forever. This is a sad and irresponsible act, which I have observed too many times on otherwise beautiful rock art throughout the Southwest. Another reprehensible practice is the wetting of rock art with water to accentuate contrast and

Ruins in Canyon de Chelly

texture. Needless to say, you should not cut, chip, or try to remove rock art. The Antiquities Act protects rock art and infractions are subject to very high fines. It is our responsibility as observers and photographers of our era to treat it properly so that it may be preserved as a testimony to those who came before us and for the benefit of future generations.

Please don't blame me as an author for disseminating information about public or lesser-known archaeological sites. Vandals don't read books such as this one, looking for information. In 99% of cases, rock art is defaced by teenagers, mostly males, often drunk, and happening to pass by in groups. The best way to prevent this from happening is through education, in school and at the sites.

Some of the best places to admire and photograph rock art and ancient dwellings in Arizona are Canyon de Chelly NM, Mystery Valley, Grand Canyon NP, Petrified Forest NP, the Arizona Strip, various locations near Sedona and Rock Art Ranch near Joseph City. The southeastern Nevada area described in this book also has some interesting rock art.

To visit hard-to-find panels and significantly increase your enjoyment and understanding of rock art, consider joining the American Rock Art Research Association, aka ARARA (see *Appendix*). ✿

Cobalt Waterflow

Chapter 2

SOME PHOTOGRAPHIC ADVICE

Photographing the Southwest makes no assumptions about your ability with respect to photography. Whether you are an enthusiastic beginner or a seasoned pro is irrelevant. While this book is essentially a location resource, it also provides specific photographic advice for almost every location to allow you to be better prepared for your visit. The advice is based on my experience in the field, having been at many of these locations several times and under different lighting conditions. In many cases, I have also checked my notes against those of knowledgeable friends or acquaintances.

After examining the indispensable photographic equipment, I'll discuss how to handle a number of generic situations you'll encounter in the field so you can create better images. I ask the more advanced photographers to be understanding if this advice seems trivial; drawing on the feedback from the past edition, many readers seem to appreciate having this quick photographic reference.

ABOUT EQUIPMENT

Terminology

The myriad of existing film and digital camera formats creates confusion when discussing lens focal length expressed in the metric system, i.e. millimeters. Since most people understand focal length based on the 35mm camera, I'll be using this as the reference camera throughout the book. Medium and large format photographers should have no problem recognizing the equivalent lens focal length. Newcomers starting with a digital camera, however, may find it more difficult. The digital camera's sensor size determines the angle of vision for a lens at a given focal length. The focal length inscribed on the lens simply reflects its effective focal distance from the sensor in millimeters. This is the distance the lens must be from the sensor in order to provide sharp focus for an object located at infinity. For each camera system with a different size image capture device, the inscribed focal length will provide a different angle of vision. A focal length that appears to be a very wide angle to a person using a 35mm system may in fact be a normal lens for a person using a digital camera. The difference is due to the size of the sensor in relation to the 24x36mm film size for a 35mm film camera. This size differential is known as the "crop factor". With a 1x crop factor—which exists only for the "full-size sensor" of some high-end digital cameras—the angle of vision is the same as on a 35mm film camera. Cameras with smaller sensors will have crop factors of 1½x, 2x or even larger. Take a 20mm lens for example. On a 35mm camera or a camera with a "full-size sensor" its angle of vision will be very wide angle. For a sensor with a 2x crop factor, the 20mm lens becomes equivalent to a 40mm lens on a 35mm film camera. Therefore, the 20mm lens is considered a "normal" lens on a camera with a 2x crop factor. On a digicam equipped with an even smaller sensor, this 20mm focal length could actually provide a small telephoto effect. Since the final angle of vision is what really matters,

I sometimes use additional terminology to describe what the lens does. A 40 to 50mm lens could be described as a normal lens, while 24 to 35mm is standard wide-angle range and anything below 24mm is considered super-wide angle. A 70 to 140mm lens provides a short telephoto effect and from 140 to 300mm is medium telephoto. Larger than 300mm is simply a very long telephoto lens.

Film vs. Digital

The technology of traditional film and camera equipment is very mature. There is little room for improvement, especially in image quality. Any further improvements in terms of lower grain or better color are likely to be trivial. Traditional film-based photography will eventually become obsolete, although, especially for landscape photography, it will coexist with digital for quite some time. For fine-art photographers, film retains definite advantages. It holds the edge in terms of color subtlety and smoothness, feeling of depth and presence, and the capacity to produce huge, incredibly sharp prints. This advantage is mostly limited to medium and large format cameras. In most regards digital has already equaled or surpassed 35mm in terms of quality and is knocking at the door of medium format.

My advice to newcomers is to go straight to digital. Digital camera technology, although already very usable, will see spectacular development in years to come. Having spent twenty years in the computer industry, I am a firm believer in "Moore's Law", which states that technological capacity doubles every 18 months. There is little doubt that we will see a similar rate of expansion in the digital camera industry, although perhaps not quite as rapid. For the most demanding users, there are still a few stumbling blocks. The shortcomings of sensor size, limited storage capacity, and short battery life will eventually be overcome. Current sensors are already able to produce digital files that are sufficient for most needs, including commercial photography. The last stumbling block to fall will be big enlargements of digitally-captured landscape scenes. However, it's only a matter of time until they compare to film. Economies of scale will keep driving prices down. After critical mass is achieved we will see miniature cameras capable of producing astonishing results at a very reasonable cost.

As of this writing, there are still a few problems awaiting better solutions. Storage, for example, is still an issue if you shoot lots of high-quality images during a long trip. Standalone devices are already replacing laptops to help you download, archive and review your images on the road. It is becoming increasingly easy to perform a quick review of your images "in-camera" almost in real time. At the end of the day and with the help of a large LCD display a more in-depth review can occur. Anything that isn't a "keeper" can be discarded to make room for more photographs. Battery life also presents somewhat of a challenge in the field. Digital photography requires a lot more energy to power the camera, store the image file, and pre- and post-visualize images on the LCD. This aspect is evolving rapidly and improvements in battery life are likely.

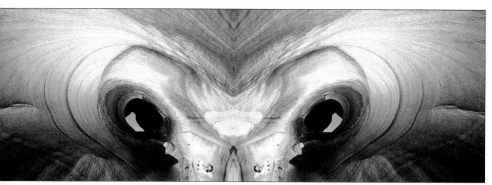

Sandstone Raptor - a simple digital manipulation

One side benefit of digital photography compared to film—at least with small-sensor cameras—is to allow telephoto lenses to act as if they were even longer. As I explained earlier, the source of this phenomenon is the fact that the footprint of a sensor is in most cases smaller than that of a 35mm film window. A 200mm lens may give you the magnification ratio and angle of view of a 400mm when used with a digital camera with a crop factor of 2x—although it won't provide the same nice blur in out-of-focus areas. While this is a tremendous boon for photographing wildlife, it is not necessarily so for landscape photography where a wide angle and its associated depth-of-field are more useful. In the case of a digital camera with a crop factor of 2x, you'll need to use a 14mm lens to get the actual angle of vision provided by a 28mm lens on a 35mm film camera. To minimize distortion, a digital lens must be built to very high standards, which means additional costs. This explains why a majority a digicams do not have wide-angle lenses and also why quality wide-angle lenses for digital SLR cameras are so expensive. On the other hand, for an equivalent angle of vision, digicam lenses with a short focal length offer remarkable depth-of-field, which is perfect for landscape photography.

Digital files are also much more practical than film for creative manipulation. Since no scanning is required for digitally-captured images they are more easily made available for computer management. This naturally enhances the photographer's capacity to interpret his work in new ways and to share images with others for fun and to garner feedback.

One final aspect where digital shines is in the area of noise, which is equivalent to grain in film. High-end digital cameras are able to produce clean images with very little noise, up to 400 ISO or more. This allows you to shoot handheld while preserving quality. Even when noise is present, it can be almost entirely removed without degrading detail using specialized noise reduction algorithms. The images produced by digital cameras can also be more easily enlarged than those that come from film. Because images from digital cameras are inherently clean, they can be more easily "up-rezed," a computer method for increasing the file size, to produce larger prints with excellent results.

The Middle Way

For a few more years, there is an excellent alternative to all-digital by combining traditional film-based photography with digital scanning. If you own several quality lenses for a film camera—sometimes incompatible with newer digital bodies—you can use them to shoot film, scan the film, and then print your pictures at home using the new generation of photo-quality printers. High-end scanners are capable of extracting every bit of information from a medium or large format transparency or negative to produce stunning prints. This method works extremely well as long as you stay away from low-cost consumer scanners. If you only want to produce a small quantity of large prints, send your film to a professional lab to be scanned on a high-end scanner. Drum scanning by these labs yields the best quality but at a very high cost. Consumer film scanners have improved tremendously and are very usable for enlargements in the 11"x14" to 16"x20" range. They remain difficult to use for negative film, however, and are downright hopeless for B&W film. Mid-range "prosumer" scanners—although cheap in comparison to drum scanners—are still out of reach for most people. Flatbed scanners with transparency adapters are cheap and convenient, but adequate only to a certain extent. Their advertised resolution and d-max is often a bit optimistic and they do not yield razor-sharp scans despite what the ads would like you to believe. I find them unacceptable for making exhibit-quality work. Based on my own experience, unless you can afford a professional-grade dedicated scanner, you will get better results at a very economical rate by sending your film to a pro lab with a non-drum high-end scanner.

Prints vs. Slides

This question is now almost obsolete, eclipsed as it is by the film vs. digital debate. Still, for film purists and owners of high-end film-based equipment, it is worthy of a brief discussion. Print film has largely overcome the handicap of poor quality it had compared to positive film, also known as transparency film or slides. The capacity of print film to forgive exposure errors and keep high contrast in check can be useful in certain circumstances. That said, print quality ultimately depends for the most part on your photo lab, unless you scan and print your own negatives. If you use print film, 400 ISO is the way to go for shooting handheld and getting good depth-of-field. The grain of these fast emulsions is barely noticeable even with big enlargements. However, one has to raise the obvious question: Why shoot film for small prints when you can shoot so cheaply and practically with a digital point-and-shoot camera and have so much more control over the printing process in your digital lab? Print film will certainly be the first to go as digital technology continues to mature exponentially.

Transparency film, on the other hand, yields high quality results and saturated color but also imposes more constraints than color negative film. First and foremost, correct exposure is absolutely critical. This effectively excludes using point-and-shoot cameras that do not allow for manual exposure compensation. In addition with transparency film you lose at least one stop exposure range compared to negative film. You must constantly concern yourself with keeping the contrast between light and dark areas to a minimum. Finally, although slow color transparency emulsions have almost no grain, it does become an issue at film speeds above 200 ISO. All these factors make it necessary in a number of circumstances to use a tripod if you want to shoot transparency film. It can be a nuisance for many who are on a pleasure trip, but it will go a long way toward high-quality results.

One other advantage of transparency film is that you can see your results easily on a light box. It's easy to determine which images are going to be "keepers". Slide film also scans extremely well, which can't be said of negative film.

In my experience and that of most serious photographers, Fujichrome Velvia is the transparency film of choice to photograph the Southwest. Velvia's high saturation and pleasing colors are particularly well suited to capture the warm light of the Golden Hour on sandstone. Even under very difficult circumstances the results can often be surprisingly good. In fact, there is a well-known saying in landscape photography circles: "Never underestimate the power of Velvia." All this leads me to believe that transparency film will continue to co-exist for quite some time with digital technology in order to satisfy the needs of discriminating users and fine-art photographers.

Printing your Images

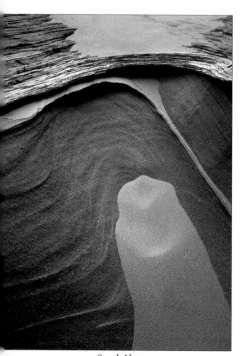

Sand Abstract

Having processed my own film and prints since I was eleven-years-old, I'm thankful for the memories of my early years in photography, but I'm also glad I no longer have to deal with the "chemical lab". In the mid-seventies I was using the Cibachrome system to process my own color prints. I have been producing inkjet prints for several years now and I have never looked back. The combination of state-of-the-art advancements such as archival inks, fine resin-coated or cotton rag papers, and miniaturized nozzles allow you to create stunning enlargements from digital files at a surprisingly low cost. Print longevity is no longer an issue as state-of-the-art papers rival traditional color prints for permanence. For small prints, a large number of consumer-grade photo printers do an excellent job. For big enlargements, wide-carriage inkjet printers are becoming affordable to acquire and economical to use and maintain. I am personally very satisfied with inkjet prints, but others still prefer laser or LED printers such as the Lightjet and Chromira brands.

There are many option for printing, all of them very good to excellent. The main thing you need to do is to profile your scanner and printer and color-calibrate your monitor. If you are not sure, buy yourself a book or attend a workshop dealing with color management. This is the best investment you can make toward getting high quality results for your prints.

What to take on your Trip

You will notice that I do not talk much about equipment throughout the book. That is essentially because gear is not a decisive factor in the quality of your photography. Light, the ability to "see", and an eye for composition are much more likely to affect the results than simply pointing an expensive camera at a well-known landmark and shooting.

❐ The camera body is at the center of your photographic equipment, although it is not the most important component in terms of results. Modern camera bodies offer a tremendous number of functions—too many in my opinion. Some of these functions are nonetheless useful, if not indispensable, if you want to go beyond simple snapshots. Single-lens reflex cameras (SLR or dSLR in the case of the digital SLR) have through-the-lens viewing capability which is helpful for precise framing, although many people are just as happy with a rangefinder, optical or electronic viewfinder. Note that the optical viewfinders in digital point-and-shoot cameras usually show only about 70% of the image forcing you to use the LCD for accuracy. This can sometimes result in fuzzy pictures shot with extended arms.

In traditional photography, aperture-priority mode is essential to maximizing depth-of-field. You'll be able to preview the depth-of-field if your camera has depth-of-field preview. Some sophisticated cameras have special modes allowing you to maximize depth-of-field automatically. While this is fine for non-critical shooting, it is no substitute to setting the depth-of-field manually.

Aperture compensation allows you to manually correct exposure under difficult lighting circumstances. Exposure bracketing is very useful to guarantee correct exposure for those critical shots. An all-metal lens mount is also recommended over polycarbonate if you're planning to change lenses often.

One function that has completely vanished on entry-level film cameras is mirror lockup. This is sad because it has been scientifically demonstrated that pictures taken with the mirror up have a higher count of lines per millimeter, producing sharper enlargements. Fortunately, manufacturers have resurrected this functionality on affordable dSLRs. Rangefinder cameras eliminate the mirror shock problem completely, but they come with their own set of limitations.

❐ Lenses are the most important component of your camera system. High optical quality glass is crucial for producing quality results. Single focal length lenses used to be better than multi-focal length zooms, but high-end zooms are now equally as good and are extremely practical, both in terms of speed, weight and protection of the mirror and internal mechanism from dust and wind. Stay away from low-cost consumer zooms; they yield disappointing results. Digital sensors are even more demanding. High quality lenses are absolutely essential if shooting digitally. A bright zoom covering 28mm to 105 or 135mm works well in the Southwest. If you take a digital or analog point-and-shoot camera, be sure not to settle for 35mm or 38mm at the wide end. It will be not be sufficient in the field. You'll find yourself using the wide angle range most of the time. Needless to say, a super wide-angle (24mm or less) and a long telephoto (200mm and above) will significantly enhance your potential for original shots.

Wide-range zooms (28-200mm and 28-300mm) are deservedly popular as versatile lenses for travel photography, but be aware that they are usually soft at the telephoto end. They are adequate for small prints up to 5"x7", but do not expect high-quality enlargements.

One new development offering great value to the photographer is the emergence of in-camera stabilization systems and gyro-stabilized lenses. This technology allows you to gain at least two stops, which may be enough to forego a tripod in non-critical 35mm or digital landscape photography. While this doesn't completely obviate the use of the tripod, especially to maximize depth-of-field, it offers greatly improved sharpness at speeds in the 1/30th and 1/60th range and with telephotos. It allows you to quickly capture those fleeting moments—a furtive ray of light or a rainbow—with increased chances of getting good results.

As for teleconverters, which generally come with a 1.4x and 2x magnifying factor, only use prime models in conjunction with high-quality lenses in order to get good results. A factor of 1.4 is less radical and less detrimental to overall picture quality.

Whatever lenses you decide to buy, don't be frugal. Too many people buy an expensive body, only to equip it with a mediocre zoom lens. Major manu-

facturers always have two or even three lines of lenses: a consumer line, a so-called "prosumer" line, and a high-end more expensive line. My advice is to buy a cheap body and the best possible lens you can afford. It will result in sharper, higher contrast pictures, with better color.

❐ I do occasionally recommend the use of filters to enhance and compensate for the shortcomings of film. A UV or Skylight 1B filter will protect your lens without

Dawn on the Buttes

diminishing image quality, but use them with caution on a zoom lens. Zooms, due to their complex optical construction involving the use of many elements and groups, are particularly prone to flare—the phenomenon of light entering the lens and causing unwanted reflections. I do not personally use these filters, relying instead on my lens shade to protect the lens, but this advice is not for everybody.

A graduated neutral-density filter (or ND Grad) is an essential piece of equipment, especially if you shoot transparencies. It will help keep contrast in check and open up shadow areas. Split neutral-density filters work great when the separation line between lit subject and shadow is very obvious, but these instances are rare in Canyon Country. By all means, use a high-quality filter. Cheap ND grad filters are not neutral and will give a nasty color cast to your skies. In my opinion, you'll be better served by a two-stop filter than one with three stops. Also, a model you can slide up and down in a holder is more flexible than a simple screw-in filter.

A mild warming filter such as an 81a, KR 1.5 or Nikon A2 is also an important filter. It is useful under many circumstances, but most particularly in the shade to remove the blue cast from the sky and when photographing under a strong sun. It adds a slight warmth to your images, without introducing a color cast. These filters work very well in the Southwest.

Most books and articles enthusiastically endorse the use of a polarizing filter, or "polarizer", as a vital piece of equipment to carry in your bag. I am not so enthusiastic and recommend that you use your polarizer with moderation with anything other than print film. This advice also applies to digital cameras. If you have high-quality, high-contrast lenses and shoot on a highly saturated film, such as Fuji Velvia, you won't need one most of the time. Used indiscriminately a polarizer may create skies that are too dark. Also, in combination with a wide-angle lens, the polarizing effect can become too strong, resulting in light falloff in one or more corners of the image. I use my polarizer mostly to eliminate glare on foliage, streams or various textures, but generally keep it in the bag during broad daylight unless the sky is full of fluffy clouds. If you use a rangefinder, carry a pair of polarizing sunglasses and look straight into the lens to see the effect of the filter. Then, based on your experience, apply the proper amount of exposure compensation for your particular filter, usually 1½ to 2 stops. It is also not too hard to use an ND grad with a rangefinder with a little practice.

❒ A lens shade is helpful in preventing flare. Be sure it is designed for your lens to avoid the phenomenon of vignetting, which is light falloff in the corners of your image. This is particularly nasty with blue skies.

❒ Now we come to what I consider the second most important piece of equipment after your lenses: the tripod. A tripod is nearly indispensable for landscape photography, particularly if you shoot transparencies. Good slide film is inherently slow and doesn't lend itself to handheld photography. A tripod also allows you to compose your images more carefully and to keep the horizon straight. Unfortunately there is also price to pay when you need to carry a four-pound tripod on long hikes, especially if some scrambling is involved. Carbon fiber tripods are a good alternative albeit quite expensive. They can shave a couple of pounds from an otherwise heavy piece of equipment. I recommend buying a headless tripod and purchasing your own ballhead. I personally use a combination carbon-fiber tripod and magnesium ballhead. There are now smaller, lighter-weight, and less expensive tripods that do a great job with small digicams and lightweight dSLRs. If you have never used a tripod before when shooting landscapes, you'll be surprised at how much it can improve your photography.

❐ The natural companion of the tripod is fortunately very lightweight: a cable release. It is useful in avoiding camera movement when releasing the shutter, even when the camera is mounted on a tripod. A good quality one costs only a few dollars more than a small flimsy model and is much nicer to use. If you don't want to bother with one, you can also use your camera's built-in timer release. There is one potential pitfall with the timer technique on entry-level cameras: someone may walk right in front of your camera just when it's taking the picture. I can almost guarantee that this will happen in highly visited places, such as Antelope Canyon. Most digital camera manufacturers offer remote control devices, which take care of this problem.

❐ You shouldn't carry your camera and lenses without some form of protection. It is risky to switch lenses in an environment where dust and sand are present, especially with a dSLR. Be sure to protect your camera from the wind when changing lenses and to blow away dust every time you load a new roll or sheet if you shoot film. It's amazing how many frames can be wasted by dust-induced streaks. Consider Antelope Canyon again. There is always a fine dust suspended in the air, although you might not see it. If this lodges in your camera when you change lenses or film, you run the risk of having lines etched across your entire roll. A single speck of dust can ruin all the frames when you rewind. You should also carry a soft airbrush with which to blow away dust from the lens and from the inside of the camera between rolls. Obviously, digital point-and-shoot cameras, also known as digicams, with their permanently attached lenses are almost impervious to this type of misadventure. It's exactly the opposite with a dSLR, which are extremely prone to dust problems. Some dSLRs incorporate vibrating sensors to shake the dust off, apparently with very good results. Dust can also cause malfunctioning of the storage media.

If you carry several lenses, consider a photo backpack. It will also take your tripod and, hopefully, your water bottles. For reasons I explained in Chapter 1, I think it is essential to use a backpack capable of carrying your water. If you are going to venture into wet canyons when the water level is high, you should carry your photo equipment in sealable plastic bags. If your photo adventure involves swimming, a dedicated dry bag is a must to protect your equipment..

❐ If you use expensive, bulky or slow-to-operate equipment, such as medium or large format, I recommend that you take along an auxiliary digicam with a good lens. It will prove invaluable for photographing difficult sections of trails or narrows. A small digicam is also useful for shooting test images before exposing large-format film. Finally, as noted in Chapter 1, a digicam can prove very useful in helping you "remember" your way while hiking in the backcountry.

IN THE FIELD

In the following sections, I'll discuss how to handle a number of common situations you'll encounter in the course of photographing the Southwest. This advice is based on what has consistently worked for me in the field. It doesn't replace a good book specializing in lighting and composition, and it certainly is no substitute for a workshop with an experienced instructor. If you are a novice user wanting to explore the locations in this guidebook without bothering too much about learning photography, I hope this advice will come handy and will help you bring home better pictures.

Using Reflected light

I'll start this discussion with what is arguably the quintessential element of photographing the Southwest: reflected light. Let's define reflected light first. Reflection involves two rays of light. One incidental ray strikes a given surface, which in turn sends out a reflected ray. You can immediately guess that the reflective properties of the surface in question impact the quality of the reflected rays. This is where the second ingredient comes into play: sandstone. People often ask me what I consider so special in the Southwest. My answer is that it has the greatest body of sandstone on the planet and that this sandstone comes in a great variety of flavors. The combination of sandstone and reflected light is what sets the Southwest apart. When light strikes sandstone directly, the reflected light has a much warmer color. If the reflected light happens to reach another patch of sand-

Golden Light (photo by Denis Savouray)

stone that is not illuminated by direct light, it will cause it to glow with warm colors ranging from deep red to soft yellow. Reflected light is the main ingredient of the best photos of the Southwest. It should always be given priority over direct light.

Photographing Scenics including close Subjects

If your scenic composition includes a close subject, it is often necessary to work with the smallest possible aperture, i.e. the highest settings such as f/22, or often less if you shoot digital, to guarantee maximum depth-of-field. It is very disappointing to view a "grand scenic" photograph in which some parts are not razor-sharp. This is even worse if you enlarge the photo.

If you use a sophisticated SLR or dSLR, you may be able to visualize depth-of-field in the viewfinder. For critical landscape work, it is preferable to work with the manual focusing option and to set the distance not as the exact focus when viewed through the lens, but by using the depth-of-field marks of your lens to maximize sharpness within the particular range of distance pertaining to your shot. Unfortunately many modern lenses, particularly zooms, lack depth-of-field marks so it is often necessary to improvise. Another way to guarantee sharpness and to maximize depth-of-field is by using the hyperfocal distance method. As an example, a 35mm lens focused at 10 feet at f/16 yields a sharp image from 5 feet (which is half the hyperfocal distance) to infinity. There are some handy charts you can find on the web or buy for a few dollars for every camera format. This method is a sure bet to create a sharp-focused image from close range to infinity. In certain cases, you may want to purposely blur the background to isolate your foreground and create an artistic effect using *bokeh* (a Japanese term signifying the out-of-focus area of a photograph).

Photographing on River Trips

Your primary concern on a rafting trip is to keep your camera equipment dry. This includes not only the body but also your lenses, batteries, film and/or storage devices. It's one thing to have a splash-proof camera, but you'll need to protect your lenses too and take all precautions to avoid immersion. Some cameras are designed to survive a short immersion in clean water, but few will resist dirty water full of tiny particles of sediment. Your film would not like it either.

To keep your camera and small personal items dry, you'll receive a supposedly waterproof "ammo can". Ammo cans work well as long as the rubber gasket in

the lid is in good condition; they tend to deteriorate over time after being repeatedly drenched and cooked in the sun and few clients bother reporting leaks at trip's end. If possible, I suggest you test it in a bathtub prior to your departure. Another concern with ammo cans is that your gear risks being knocked around badly when your craft is tossed about in the rapids.

Serious photographers have to look into more secure alternatives for their gear.

Oar boat float

Waterproof camera bags work well but it can be difficult to keep the sand out when handling the bag in camp, which is always a sandy beach.

Personally, I use a Model 8 waterproof, transparent Sealline bag while on the boat, in which I carry a small digital camera equipped with an image stabilizer. When crossing rapids, the bag quickly clips to the top strap of my life jacket and the camera can be stored or retrieved in a matter of seconds. The digital camera is the only thing I need to shoot from the boat, when movement and speed preclude anything else than snapshots and require you to work fast. Meanwhile, my main equipment is safely stowed in my camera backpack, which is itself hermetically sealed in a waterproof Pelican hardcase strapped on deck. My tripod is also strapped until we land, but can be retrieved immediately. Upon landing for a hike, the camera bag goes directly from the Pelican case to my back. Admittedly, this setup will only work with a relatively small bag.

If you have a large amount of gear, the specialized waterproof photo backpack is the best solution. I recommend using a solid carabinier to strap the pack somewhere on deck so it's not constantly in your way. If you do go with only one camera and one zoom lens, consider taking only a Sealline bag; it is highly practical and perfectly adapted to the rigors of rafting the Grand Canyon.

Additional advice can be found in *Chapter 5*.

Photographing Running Water

Waterfalls and running water are great subjects for photography. Many people wonder how to create the so-called "angel hair" effect of soft water. It is actually quite simple: use a long exposure. To get the smooth flowing look but also retain a bit of detail or "texture" in the water, try shooting at 1 to 3 seconds. It's not always possible to achieve such slow shutter speeds under normal circumstances and chances are you'll need a bit of help from some extra equipment. Your first option is to use the lowest ISO possible. If you have a polarizing filter, you can use it to further reduce the aperture by 1½ to 2 stops, thus almost quadrupling the exposure. In most cases, this is still not going to be enough. To get a truly beautiful effect you'll need to resort to a neutral density filter (non-graduated). The most common ND filter adds 6 stops to a scene, so what was a 1/30 second exposure at f/8 now becomes a 2 second exposure—enough for

Raging River

a wonderful image of nicely blurred water. Obviously, you'll need a tripod and some kind of mechanical or electronic shutter release. If you are using an SLR or dSLR, I can't emphasize enough the benefit of mirror lockup.

In some cases, a bluish cast can enhance the beauty of running water. To add a bluish cast, photograph the water in indirect light with the high color temperature of the blue sky providing the illumination. A film such as Fujichrome Velvia, which is optimized for warm color temperature will produce some truly exquisite enhanced blue. Using a digital camera, you may have to experiment a bit with the white balance to achieve the results you're looking for.

Photographing Water Reflections

There are several key elements to obtaining great reflections on a body of water. First you need side light or backlight—the latter works great as long as it is not directly in your field of vision and you're using a shade. The light should be soft, so as not to overwhelm the scene, eradicating details and creating nasty shadow areas. Next, you need the ambient air to be perfectly still. The slightest trace of wind will agitate the surface and create ripples that will mar your subject's reflection. If the wind shows no sign of abating, try using it to your advantage and concentrate on playing with colors in the reflection. You'll also need some strong foreground element to anchor the composition and add depth, making the viewer feel immersed in the scene.

Lake Reflection

In most cases, the reflection will be significantly less bright than the actual subject. If it occupies a large portion of the frame, such as in the case of a reflection in a lake, you'll need to use a split or graduated neutral density filter to compensate the exposure and keep some detail in what would otherwise be a shadow area in an uncorrected photograph.

An example of using a neutral density filter to preserve detail in a reflection can be found in my Cottonwood Reflection photograph in the Canyons of the Escalante chapter of *Photographing the Southwest – Volume 1*. In that image I used a graduated filter diagonally to open up the shadows in the lower left part of the image. Arguably the most photographed lake reflection in the Southwest is the famous Maroon Bells scene near Aspen Colorado (see *Photographing the Southwest – Volume 3*).

Photographing Snow & Ice

If you shoot in winter and spring on the Colorado Plateau, you're bound to encounter snow and ice and you may want to integrate them into your compositions, either as part of a scenic landscape or by themselves.

Your camera's built-in meter is programmed to render everything a neutral grey, which is of course not what you want with snow and ice. To avoid this, you need to compensate by opening your aperture between 1 and 2 f/stops depending on how bright the scene is. Exposing snow and ice correctly is tricky because you don't want to lose detail in the highlights. In broad daylight, I usually start with a +1½ stop compensation in order to expose the snow so it will be white. If snow is just a background, you'll want to expose your main subject correctly, particularly if it's a person, and let the snow be overexposed.

As with any ordinary scene, shooting snow during the golden hour creates nice shadows, making your photos more interesting. I usually prefer a fair amount of sunlight to make the snow shine.

A bright sunny sky will create a strong blue cast in the shaded areas, especially when your subject is extremely bright. If you don't want the blue cast, use an 81a or 81b filter to provide warmth but making sure that the snow or ice don't look reddish.

A polarizing filter can accentuate the contrast, eliminate glare and restore proper exposure for the sky if the latter is somewhat hazy. If the sky is already very blue, be sure not to overdo the polarizing effect or your sky will be too dark; even more when the sun is at a 90° angle.

An overcast sky during a clearing storm can also work to your advantage by filtering the light, making the snow act as a soft reflector.

Digital cameras have a strong advantage over film as you can fine-tune the white balance by checking for immediate results on your LCD. Print film is also quite forgiving on snow and ice, but transparencies must be perfectly exposed.

Icy river

Photographing Dunes and Lava Beds

Sand and lava are two subjects that can easily fool your built-in meter and you may get unpleasant results if you use it. Many new automatic cameras have programs that supposedly compensate for specific lighting conditions; however, you will get better results by compensating the exposure manually based

Golden Dune (photo by Denis Savouray)

on the lighting conditions. For brown and red sand, you should bracket your exposure in small increments of ½ to 1 f/stop based on the effect you want to achieve. For deeply saturated red sand in the evening sun, try ½ f/stop underexposure, as well as whatever your meter says. For extremely white sand in bright daylight 1½ f/stops overexposure works best; in early to mid-morning, late afternoon or when it's overcast, try ½ f/stop overexposure for scenics and 1 f/stop for white sand patterns.

Depending on the light, lava usually doesn't need as much correction, as it is more gray rather than pure black. However, if you want to make it darker, underexpose by ¼ or ½ f/stop.

I do not recommend that you shoot sand and lava using print film—or any other bright or dark texture for that matter—unless your goal is to have them scanned professionally or to have custom enlargements made.

Photographing Slot Canyons

The range of perception of film is greatly limited in comparison with the human eye, and it is impossible to reproduce on film all the nuances that we perceive. Variations of 5 or 8 f/stops are the norm in slot canyons and choosing the best exposure is not easy. Your task consists of perfectly exposing the part that most interests you within the limitations of the film. To do this, carefully select your composition to avoid too many highlights and to minimize large areas in deep shadow. The shadows risk appearing completely black, especially on transparency film, and the highlights can be completely blown out to pure white. Avoid photographing sunlight directly hitting a canyon wall as this is a sure way to exceed the contrast range of the film or sensor. Exposure can be determined by making an intelligent compromise between the various spot measurements obtained on those parts of the wall for which you want to preserve detail. In practice, I find that it is very difficult to overexpose in slot canyons. By increasing the exposure, either purposely or by accident, you will still get good images, albeit with a different gamut of colors. Short exposures yield a lot of yellow as well as deep rust, orange and red, while very long exposures introduce light and deep purple into the palette.

If you do not have a spot meter, either handheld or in your camera, be ready to bracket heavily: Easily said when you shoot 35mm or digital, but almost out of the questions if you carry a view camera. You'll often have to carefully add 1½ to 2 f/stops overexposure to bring out the detail on the darker surfaces without overexposing the lighter walls. If you add too much, what could be a beautiful yellow light could end up totally white.

Try to find compositions that restrict the EV range to the smallest possible value. Avoid the brightly lit areas, concentrating instead on reflected light. Take plenty of time to frame your shots and even more time to take them. Use a very small aperture and long exposure in order to let the beautiful reflected light seep onto your film. If you use an automatic camera, a fast ISO and a steady hand can simulate a spot metering technique. Close in on an interesting detail that is not too brightly lit and lock the exposure by pressing the shutter release half-

Antelope Tapestry

way. Then move back, recompose, and take your picture. Don't use a flash if you want to preserve the texture of the walls and the nuances of color created by natural light.

Knowing your equipment well is a must. Not only must you be able to operate it without hesitation, but you should also be able to anticipate how your images will look. If there is one thing I have learned from my many visits to slot canyons such as Antelope Canyon, it is that experience can play an important role in increasing the number of high-caliber "keepers" that you'll bring back from your visit.

In popular slot canyons, be prepared to deal with a steady traffic of visitors who are not necessarily interested in photography and will be in your way. Just be courteous and don't take yourself too seriously and you'll find that people will give you a wide berth. One consequence of such intense foot traffic is small particles of dust pervading the air, a phenomenon exacerbated by some photographers purposely throwing dust in the air to add dimension to the shafts of light hitting the floor around midday. Be sure to protect your equipment as best you can, especially if it's a dSLR, and give it a careful cleaning after your visit.

Photographing Wildflowers

Superstitions Wildflowers

The two most important factors in photographing wildflowers are the presence of soft, diffused light and the absence of wind. In the case of the light, one thing to avoid is direct illumination by the sun. A cloudy, overcast day always works best. Partly cloudy conditions may provide intermittently suitable conditions.

If you are really serious about your wildflower photography, you may need a diffuser and/or reflector for the light and a small tent for the wind (and light) if you do macro photography. An acquaintance of mine has built a wonderful little tent/diffuser using a cheap laundry bag, so it is definitely possible to improvise.

Two filters are essential for wildflowers. A warming filter will always come in handy to remove the blue cast, particularly at higher elevations and if you shoot during the day. An 81a warming filter works best. A polarizing filter is also very useful to remove glare.

I find that high-end digital cameras work well for close-ups of flowers against a blurred background. I still prefer film with medium and large format, however, to shoot scenes involving large fields of flowers, On the other hand, this point may be moot by the time you read this.

When shooting fields of wildflowers, avoid placing your camera too high. You'll get more dynamic results if you shoot at the flower's level. Large format cameras with tilt and shift movements have an enormous advantage. They allow you to concentrate on a close group of flowers while keeping the background in focus to infinity. Digicams with small size sensors can also do the same thing but at a tremendous cost in terms of detail and sense of three-dimensionality.

One common mistake is to be in too big a hurry to take pictures when arriving on the scene. Instead, scan the field for the best flowers, making sure you have an interesting background and paying attention not to include any white or grey sky. Don't be overwhelmed by the color alone; be sure that the flowers you are photographing appear fresh and are wide open. Some older flowers may still look good to you in the viewfinder but may not look their best on a large print.

Arizona is usually great for shooting wildflowers from mid-March to late April, particularly poppies. There are some great online resources for monitoring wild-flowers' bloom, such as *http://www.desertusa.com/wildflo/wildupdates.html*.

Photographing Cacti

While traveling through the Sonoran Desert, you'll be hard pressed not to want to photograph cacti over and over again, during daytime as well as at day-break and sunset. The most common cacti are the saguaro and the cholla, found in abundance in every corner of the Sonoran, often interspersed with the beauti-ful ocotillo. Less common are the senita and the organ pipe, which are restricted to the Mexican border area. As you cross the border toward Puerto Penãsco and the Gran Desierto de Altar, you are greeted by the magnificent cardon and the tallest saguaros you'll ever see.

The two Southern Arizona chapters contain some typical examples of cacti photography. Here are a few guidelines for successfully photographing cacti: One of the most fun and interesting way is to photograph them with a backlight, creating a beautiful halo effect. In the case of a group of saguaros, this works best against the dark background of a mountain side. Fields of backlit saguaros can look great when compressed by a telephoto. On the other hand, chollas make a good foreground to a wider scenic, using a wide angle lens and using either a back light or a side light. If you shoot backlit to bring out detail in the shards, make sure you bracket your shots and use a lens shade to protect against flare, this is particularly important with zoom lenses. For twi-light and sunset shots, also bracket your shots, but it is always better to err a little bit on the side overexposure. In direct light, it is better to concentrate on one indi-vidual cactus, bringing out color and texture in interest-ing compositions. Saguaros come in so many shapes, they are sometimes downright funny. Use your imagination, looking for suggestive shapes. In Spring, close-ups of short cacti in bloom can also be a lot of fun to shoot. One last bit of advice: be sure to have a small pair of twee-zers handy to remove shards from those nasty "jumping chollas". They have an almost eerie ability to painfully embed their shards deep inside your skin at the slightest brush.

Shards

Photographing Fall Colors

Photographing fall colors in the Southwest is an exhilarating experience. While the Southwest may lack the red foliage of autumn in New England, it adds the incredible yellow and rust colors of cottonwoods and aspens to the grandiose backgrounds of canyons and snowy peaks. Many outstanding fall color locations in Colorado are discussed in greater detail in *Volume 3*.

Autumn colors

One filter you absolutely need for fall colors is a warming filter. Once again a Skylight or 81a filter is usually sufficient to get rid of the bluish cast, which is particularly noticeable at higher elevations. A polarizing filter may also be useful when used in moderation.

Film, particularly medium and large format transparency film, will continue to give better results than digital for a number of years, not necessarily in terms of sharpness, but for tonality, overall smoothness and three-dimensionality. Fujichrome Velvia 50/100 is the classic film for shooting fall color. Fujichrome Velvia 100F does a better job with the reds and is a little tamer when it comes to controlling contrast. Kodak film usually does a better job with subtle orange hues.

Photographing Rock Art

Rock art tends to be quite contrasty; therefore it is prone to color casts when photographed with highly saturated films under strong reflected light. Puebloan ruins, often tucked inside deep alcoves, bring the danger of reciprocity failure, particularly for those who shoot large format.

If you shoot under strong reflected light, you are bound to have an exaggerated amount of red on films such as Fujichrome Velvia and Ektachrome VS. If you shoot in dark areas, Velvia will tend to give you an excess of green. In both cases, a slightly lower contrast film such as Fuji Provia will serve you better. The latter offers the finest grain of any slide film as of this writing and it is well suited to accurately reproduce the delicate textures and subdued golden browns of rock art. With large format, an exposure of 30 seconds is common in low light situations. With an additional one stop, you can reduce this to fifteen seconds, thus limiting the color shift.

Large format photographers have the advantage of being able to change plates to match a particular lighting situation. 35mm and medium format photographers must be more careful with the kind of film they load before shooting rock

Finely drawn pictographs on alcove ceiling

art and small ruins. If you shoot negative film for paper prints, these problems do not really affect you. If you shoot digitally, it might be a good idea to take a custom white balance measurement on the panel, especially if you shoot Jpeg. If you shoot Raw, it doesn't make much difference as you'll be able to adjust the white balance when post-processing your file.

More on Exposure

If you are working with transparency film and wish to obtain the best results without concerning yourself too much about determining the right exposure, take five different shots at ½ stop intervals—i.e. two on either side of the setting you think is correct. In the case of negative film, this is unnecessary since the density of the highlights and shadows can easily be altered during the printing process. Negative film tolerates up to 2 stops of overexposure fairly well, but does poorly with underexposure. If you are a perfectionist, you can always take a second shot with one stop of overexposure—it is useless to try more. If you are using a digital camera, you have the advantage of seeing the results immediately on your LCD. While this is not very precise, it at least gives you a starting point. Also, the more advanced digital cameras have the ability to display a histogram, which allows you to check exposure with a high degree of accuracy

Attention should also be paid to the reciprocity failure characteristics of your film, especially if you are using a tripod and slow transparency film. With exposures of several seconds, certain slide films display a tendency towards incorrect exposure and you risk underexposing the film. There are reciprocity failure tables for the major brands of film on the market. Unless you are taking exposures of four seconds or more, you shouldn't have to worry about this.

Some Advice on Composition

Composition is fortunately not an exact science or else it would be the domain of engineers. Rather, it is a subtle blend of classic established rules, specific properties of your subject and, perhaps most importantly, your own artistic sensibility. While I can't help you with the last two, this short refresher course might help you remember and use "the rules" during your visit to the Southwest.

❒ Before you think about composition, remember that lighting is everything in landscape photography. An image is rarely attractive without interesting light.

❒ Remember the "rule of thirds" to avoid an unaesthetic horizon line in the middle of your picture or a main subject that is too centered. Visualize your image overlaid by an imaginary grid dividing it into thirds horizontally and vertically. Try placing your key elements at the bottom left or right intersections of the grid, or at the upper left or right intersections if there is an interesting foreground, but avoid the middle of the picture.

❒ Be sure to check that the horizon doesn't appear tilted in your viewfinder. Using a tripod and taking your time is the best way to avoid an unpleasant surprise. If you're having trouble, use a small level in your camera's hot shoe.

❒ Resist the urge to squeeze too much of a grand panorama into a small picture. Results are almost always disappointing due to the lack of a center of interest, unless the sky is particularly exciting. Your image will usually be more interesting if you zoom in on a small portion and include some of that nice sky. Fill most of the frame with your main subject. Too many secondary subjects create clutter and become indistinguishable in a small picture, even though they look good to the naked eye.

❒ Include an interesting foreground and put your main subject slightly off-center when it is distant. This will create depth in your image and reinforce the feeling of presence. Make sure the foreground is not just empty fill-in space, however. If this is the case, it is often better to give the distant subject more prominence rather than having the bottom two-thirds of the frame filled with a boring subject. Always think depth and presence. Some imposing formations may appear

Lil' Oliphant Arch

smallish in your image if you do not include a reference object, such as trees, a trail or a human silhouette, to provide a sense of scale.

❏ Thoughtfully consider the benefit of telephoto lenses. Long telephoto lenses serve three purposes: extracting details from the landscape, making a subject stand out through creative use of *bokeh* (the unsharp area in a photograph) and compressing the perspective. The compression effect makes your photographs appear rich and dense by allowing several planes to cohabit in one image.

❏ Super wide-angle lenses give excellent results with very tightly-framed close subjects by accentuating—or even esthetically distorting—the graphic, geometric or even abstract properties. Rocks with interesting colors or texture, shapes in sand dunes or badlands, and trees and bushes are examples.

❏ Be mindful of shadows, especially when using slide film, and make use of a graduated neutral density filter if necessary. So called "golden hour" photography is great, but what appears to you as a simple shaded area may look completely black on film.

Crossbedding

❏ Above all, be constantly on the lookout for photogenic details around you—rock texture, natural elements with abstract shapes, uncommon colors, reflections, transparent views, interesting vegetation, or tracks and leaves on the ground. Using these elements, you can create some wonderfully original compositions. Not all of them will be keepers, but some will yield beautiful compositions that are a welcome departure from the common "grand scenic" images.

Photographing in National Parks

Most people carry some form of camera and are eager to capture memories of their trip using the recognized icons of the West as a background. National Parks have become incredibly recognizable through movies, advertisements, park literature, and coffee table books, not to mention guidebooks such as this one. No wonder people want to show that they've been there. The glorification of the West creates a desire to accumulate photographs as trophies, and cheap film and easy-to-use digital cameras make this almost effortless. In view of the massive onslaught of people in relatively concentrated areas, we must be mindful of our collective impact on the land.

So far the National Park Service has maintained the view that photographers—whether amateur or professional—should be treated like any other visitors. While there are no specific restrictions imposed on us, we are also expected to obey the rules. Some large-format photographers talk of a stigma attached to carrying a tripod and bulky equipment in remote places. I carry a tripod at all times and I have never felt singled out in my interactions with park rangers. So should we worry? I personally don't think so. The National Park Service once floated the possibility of requiring permits for professional photographers, but the idea was abandoned. My credo is that we, as privileged visitors to pristine areas, should act as good citizens and be mindful of the environment in order that our impact on the land not force more closures of sensitive areas.

One area where some closures may be unavoidable is backcountry roads. There is little doubt that vehicular access off paved roads has the potential to cause substantial damage—not only when vehicles are driven irresponsibly, but also because of sheer numbers. Let's face it, fifteen years ago the term SUV wasn't part of our vocabulary. Today, light trucks and SUVs form the largest segment of the automobile market and they are the vehicles of choice for visiting the Southwest. We must do everything we can to tread lightly, on foot and on the back roads, to avoid damaging the land and to preserve it for generations to come.

Parting Shots

There is another less palpable, but no less essential ingredient to good landscape photography: an unbridled love for nature and strong emotional connection to the land and your subject. The act of photographing should be an extension of that love, to record the memories and share with others the joy of being there. If your fascination with camera equipment or the physics of photography take precedence over your love of nature in an unbalanced way, it is doubtful that you'll ever achieve great results. Your craft may become technically excellent and you may acquire a nice portfolio to show friends, but you won't be able to communicate emotions if they weren't present when you took the picture. Most people I know who seriously pursue photography of the Southwest have this love of the land within them. Sometimes, however, I meet folks who are more interested in the act of photographing than in enjoying the beauty around them. Over the years I have taken pleasure in asking people whether they would do a particularly strenuous hike to a beautiful spot if they had to leave their camera at home. I have had a few people flatly—and honestly—tell me that they wouldn't. This isn't necessarily a criticism; photography doesn't have to equate to love of nature to be enjoyed as a hobby. I do say, however, that simply being there, quietly enjoying the place and the moment, is far more important than bringing back a few pictures.

Another important axiom of good landscape photography is that it rarely happens by accident. In all probability you'll need to visit a location several times,

Opposite page: Furry Feet

to see it under different light and in different seasons—perhaps even a few times without a camera—to start pre-visualizing your image. As you observe, think and feel during your time there, you will learn to refine your past experience to anticipate a change of light or a break in the clouds. Your best images—those which carry the most emotional content—will be the result of careful planning and pre-visualization.

Finally, with your pre-visualized image in mind, you'll rise early—very early—and drag your sleepy body inside a freezing car. You'll drive on the edge of your seat to the now familiar location, peering at the darkness to spot deer on the road through the partially frozen windshield, nervously glancing at the clock and worrying about the changing light on the horizon. Perhaps you'll be chewing on a hard power bar between nervous sips of coffee to warm you up a bit and get your mind in gear. You will walk to your location briskly, plant your tripod firmly, ready-up filters and lenses. You'll wait, floating in a dual state of serene peace and nervous anticipation. And then, the momentous event you came for will happen: sunrise. The land will be bathed in hues of yellow and red and you will understand the reason you must take this journey.

But there is little time for reflection. There is a job to be done—photos to be taken. The adrenaline kicks in and you are totally focused. You shoot like a maniac, oblivious to everything else but your subject, annoyed if someone else suddenly shows up. You shoot and shoot until the incredible light finally becomes a little too bright, a little too crude. When you're done you smile and bask in the deep feeling of joy that overtakes you as you feel one with this place that you love so much. You linger a while to make the feeling last, letting the sun warm you up, your body still weary from lack of sleep. As you walk back to the trailhead you let your mind wander and play like a puppy. You're proud and ecstatic at having experienced this cosmic moment. You suddenly become part of the great brotherhood of early-rising nature lovers, and, unbeknownst to you, you've just bonded with the fly fisherman in Montana, the ice fisherman in Minnesota and the deer hunter in Idaho!

Months later you sit in your living room looking at the big, majestic enlargement hanging on the wall and you grin happily at the beloved landscape basking in the morning sun. But you also feel something deeper—a special connection. The memories that you bring back from such incredibly poignant and precious moments are treasured as much as the print itself. You may not have the words express it, but that's okay. The picture will speak for you. ❀

Mather Point at sunrise (photo by Tom Till)

Chapter 3

GRAND CANYON — SOUTH RIM

Yavapai Point Sunset

GRAND CANYON — SOUTH RIM

The Grand Canyon of the Colorado River is by any standard one of the great wonders of the world. Visiting this extraordinary geological phenomenon is something I wish everyone could have a chance to do during their lifetime. Still, some people come back from the Grand Canyon somewhat disappointed, mostly because what they get to see with their own eyes doesn't hold a candle to what they saw in print or in a theater. There are some reasons for this: first and foremost, the vast majority of people see the canyon during the day, when the light is crude and crowds of people mob the viewpoints. While this doesn't diminish the grandeur of the canyon, it fails to convey the quasi-mystical feeling one can experience during the best moments of a good day. Another reason is that the sky is often a uniform blue and devoid of clouds. The canyon is basked in uniform light, offering precious little nuance to tease the eye. These circumstances are often a source of disappointment to keen photographers. The fact of the matter is that the Grand Canyon only reveals its true splendor when atmospheric conditions are just right. If you are lucky enough to have nice fluffy clouds or a dark stormy sky, the whole scene takes a magical turn, and your camera will capture a subtle palette of tonalities. Beams of sun light up the formations and give a fantastic sense of depth. If, on top of that, you are lucky enough to find yourself on the rim after rain has cleansed the air from the almost permanent haze, you will be hard-pressed not to experience that mystical feeling.

While there isn't much you can do about atmospheric conditions, you can at least avoid the feeling of disappointment by adopting a proactive attitude. Instead of simply hanging out at the often crowded rim overlooks, take a short 3 to 4-hour walk inside the canyon. The trail under the rim will radically alter your mood and perception of the Grand Canyon. Do so early in the morning or late in the afternoon. It will allow you to relate more intimately to the grandeur and beauty and you'll emerge with the feeling of having experienced something truly unique and very personal.

Mather Point & Yavapai Point

Coming from the south via Tusayan, Mather Point and Yavapai Point are the first two overlooks you'll encounter.

Mather Point is an excellent sunrise location with its very open view down into the canyon. Views of Wotan's Throne and Vishnu Temple are awesome and so are the views looking down into the canyon. A standard lens or short telephoto works well in the morning. Be aware, however, that in the early morning O'Neill Butte may appear as a large blob of black on your image. Mather is also great at sunset when you can go all out from wide-angle to telephoto. If you'll be hiking into the canyon to Phantom Ranch, this is the best place to catch a distant view of your destination.

Yavapai Point is a great all-around location at any time, sunrise or sunset. The view west is quite open. The Plateau Point Trail is visible down below and a sheer cliff with juniper trees also makes a good foreground looking west.

The trouble with these two viewpoints, especially Mather Point, is that they are extremely crowded due to their permanent accessibility to private vehicles. At times, it can be difficult to find a parking spot. For photographers, it can be a zoo in any season and you'll be jockeying for position at sunrise and sunset. If you want a prime spot for sunrise at these viewpoints, you must be there at least a half hour before dawn, regardless of the season. For sunset, it's better to arrive one hour before dusk to "claim" a spot and enjoy the good light before the canyon is entirely in the shade.

Hopi Point & Hermit's Rest Road

All the viewpoints along the 8-mile long Hermit's Rest Road, heading west from Grand Canyon Village, are good sunset locations. The fact that private vehicles are not allowed on this road most of the year helps greatly with crowds during the high season. A shuttle service is available close to the Bright Angel trailhead. However, from December through February, Hermit's Rest Road is open to private vehicular traffic and the shuttle is not mandatory.

Hopi Point is one of the best sunset locations on the South Rim. You have an excellent, albeit distant, side view of Wotan's Throne and Vishnu Temple.

Mojave Point and Pima Point offer nice open views of the Colorado River downstream as it enters the Granite Gorge rapids. Hermit's Rest is the trailhead for the Hermit Trail, which many Grand Canyon aficionados consider one of the most rewarding backpacking trip into the Inner Canyon, with its relatively moderate access to the river via the Tonto Trail and Monument Creek (*see Chapter 5*).

Back at the shuttle departure station, there is a nice view of Lookout Studio after dark from the rim path behind the Bright Angel Lodge cabins. Otherwise, the view of the canyon is very restricted around the lodge.

Yaki Point

Yaki Point Sunrise

Along with Mather Point, Yaki Point is the prime destination for sunrise photography. The view is very open, with miles of canyon toward the west, offering layer upon layer of depth to play with light and shadow. Many a picture shot at Yaki Point makes use of that naked little tree sticking out in the foreground. Like everyone else, I have shot that same nice, but "academic" image. However, I am happier simply concentrating on the canyon. My advice at Yaki Point, and on the canyon rim in general, is not to feel compelled to frame your images with shrubbery in the foreground or on the side. If the light is acceptable, there is absolutely no need for that to convey the depth of the canyon. If the light is great, the show is right in front on you. Don't mar it with unnecessary distractions.

Getting to Yaki Point for sunrise requires that you catch the shuttle at the Canyon View Information Plaza at least ½ hour before sunrise (from December to February you can still use your car). During the week in winter and spring, you might find yourself alone; but, there will be guaranteed competition in summer. The first shuttle leaves one full hour before sunrise. You may want to catch that one if you shoot large format and need plenty of preparation time. The next shuttle leaves a ½ hour before sunrise, which works well for most photographers as it takes less than 15 minutes to get there. You'll still have 15 minutes to catch the pre-dawn light, which is often ethereal over the canyon. If you miss the shuttle, you can park your vehicle at the rim parking located on the Desert View road, close to its intersection with the Yaki Point spur and hike from there. It's about a mile to the viewpoint.

The Inner Canyon

In my view, the descent into the canyon from the south rim offers much more personal satisfaction than photographic opportunities. It is a great way to experience firsthand the awesome depth and three-dimensionality of the canyon. You can do so from the South Rim with much less effort than from the North Rim, whether you only have a few hours or a couple of days.

South Rim trails are less exposed to the sun than those of the North Rim. There are sometimes shady spots protecting the hiker from the relentless heat of the sun. Also, shooting in the direction of the canyon is never against the sun.

Several backpacking trails lead down the canyon, requiring extensive preparation and backpacking experience. Specialized guidebooks will help you prepare for these trails. For the purpose of this book, I'll concentrate on the most popular trails: the South Kaibab Trail and the Bright Angel Trail.

If you only have a few hours, the first part of the South Kaibab Trail (which requires that you take the Kaibab Trail Route shuttle also leading to Yaki Point) is without question a better choice than a descent of the Bright Angel Trail. The Bright Angel Trail is always busy with hikers going to Indian Gardens for the day (9.2 miles round-trip, 3,060 feet of elevation loss). Indian Gardens is merely a rest stop for hikers coming from the river and has no views. You'd have to continue on the plateau for a 3-mile round-trip in full sun to reach Plateau Point where you can see and photograph the river.

The South Kaibab Trail, on the other hand, has several good vantage points where you can take pictures. There is a lovely viewpoint—appropriately named Ooh-Aah Point—only 0.75 mile from the trailhead (880 feet of elevation loss). After another 0.7 mile you arrive at Cedar Ridge (1,140 feet of elevation loss from the trailhead)—the goal of many day hikers. There, leave the trail and walk

South Kaibab Trail (photo by Philippe Schuler)

level to an outcrop at the far end of the ridge for a good view into the canyon. For more privacy in season, continue about 0.5 mile past Cedar Ridge until you reach a small platform just before the foot of O'Neill Butte, from which you have great views on both sides. At this point, you may want to turn back; otherwise, it will take 2.6 more miles and 1,850 feet of elevation loss to reach the Tip Off and your first good glimpse of the Colorado River. Count on nearly 4 hours to tackle the 4-mile round-trip and 1,500 feet of elevation to the foot of O'Neill Butte. This is best done in the second part of the afternoon.

If you have two days to devote to the canyon and are a seasoned backpacker in good physical condition, you can have an unforgettable time going all the way and back to the Colorado River. Here is a short description of such a walk. The recommended route is to descend by way of the South Kaibab Trail on the first day and ascend by the Bright Angel Trail on the second day. The trail down is about 7 miles to Phantom Ranch and needs three or four hours to accomplish. It is extremely steep and there is little shade and no water. The temperature rises as you descend and it is imperative that you carry a good-size water container. There are few hikers past Cedar Ridge and you are free to experience the euphoria surrounding such an experience. At almost Mile 5, you come to a platform with a good, unimpeded view of the river and the suspension bridge leading to Phantom Ranch. On the bridge, you are but a few feet above the Colorado River, that indefatigable architect of this majestic work. It's an unforgettable experience.

Buddah & Deva Temples

The personnel at Phantom Ranch will wake you up before sunrise on the second day and after a hearty breakfast you'll be on the trail an hour later. The distance to the rim is about 10 miles, with an elevation gain of about 4,400 feet. You begin your walk by following the River Trail for 1.7 mile alongside the Colorado River until it connects with the Bright Angel Trail. In the early morning, the first part of the Bright Angel Trail is mostly in the shade. When you get to Indian Gardens, you can drink from the springs and rest before continuing to the top. The second part is in the sun—unless you start walking after 3:30 PM in summer—and is much more difficult to hike, despite the fact that you'll find water every 1.5 miles. The hiking time estimate given by the National Park Service to complete the ascent is a bit conservative. At a relaxed pace, you should be able to finish it in six or seven hours from the bottom. This time may vary depending upon current circumstances.

Yavapai Dusk Panorama (photo by Alain Briot)

If you are a very strong hiker, it's possible to do the whole circuit in one day by starting the hike at sunrise. After reaching the river, start your hike up as soon as possible in order to reach Indian Gardens before the hottest part of day. There, you'll rest for several hours before continuing your hike in mid-afternoon, walking mostly in the shade until you reach the rim. The Rangers will strongly discourage you to do the hike in one day. In fact, it may even be impossible. When temperatures are extremely high, access to inner canyon trails may be restricted to early morning and evening (See *Appendix* for information on trail restrictions and trail closures). I do not recommend the one-day trip either, particularly to photographers. For photographers, who don't want to be constantly in a hurry, two days is definitely the best option, with an overnight stay at Phantom Ranch either camping or in dormitory-style accommodations. A few cabins are available for couples.

Getting there: Catch the Kaibab Trail Route shuttle at the Canyon View Information Center and get off at the South Kaibab Trailhead, one stop before Yaki Point. There is also a Hikers Express version of the Kaibab Trail Route leaving from the Bright Angel Lodge, stopping at the Backcountry Information Center (close to the Maswik Lodge and parking lot E), then going directly to South Kaibab Trailhead. There are 2 or 3 Hikers Express trips each morning, with departure times depending on the month (from 5 AM to 8 AM).

Practical advice: Take plenty of water and plenty of snacks (salty food or an energy drink will prevent loss of electrolytes if you drink a lot.) Staying properly hydrated is your most important task. You can be an athlete and still succumb to cramps and fatigue for lack of hydration. If you have ever experienced the phenomenon in person, perhaps by prolonging a hike beyond your original intent, you know how debilitating it can be. Avoid hiking in the heat of the day, from about 10 AM to 4 PM in the hot season, by planning a very early start. Rest often and snack every time you do so. If hiking during the day, stop in the shade whenever the opportunity arises. Try wetting your shirt and neck to cool your upper body. I personally love the neck coolers that you dip in cold water for a few hours to get a chemical reaction. I usually let mine sit overnight in cold water at the bottom of the ice chest and it keeps me remarkably cool for many hours. A wet bandanna will also work, albeit less effectively. I also wear a cap with a reflective liner on the inside and legionnaire sides protecting my ears and neck. Be sure to have some protection against UVs on this long trip and make liberal use of lip balm. Using a long-sleeve shirt and long pants protects your skin and can also protect your body from the heat. Obviously, you'll need good hiking boots, preferably a pair that you've worn before and know to be comfortable. The Grand Canyon is no place to test new boots. Needless to say, river sandals don't belong on these trails. Don't forget the moleskin or second skin to prevent blistered feet. Hiking poles will relieve a lot of the pounding on your knees, especially going downhill. You'll be happy to have them.

One final thought to ponder: over 250 people have to be rescued from the Canyon each year. The best way to avoid becoming a statistic is to prepare your trip carefully, ensuring that you are in tip-top condition and mentally prepared for the effort and potential pitfalls. An emergency helicopter evacuation is very costly and puts a lot of people at risk trying to rescue you.

Clearing storm on Desert View

The Desert View Road

The Desert View road follows the rim for about 22 miles from Grand Canyon Village to Desert View and the East Entrance of the park. If you are coming from Cameron, Desert View will be your first stop. What an introduction! The view is stunning, very open, with a large stretch of river in open view. There is a close foreground to show the depth of the canyon. It is a terrific sunset location. Overall, it is one of the best locations in the park, although not a "classic" view. A medium to wide-angle lens works best here. A very wide angle will allow you to photograph the reconstructed Hopi tower and part of the canyon.

Heading west, Navajo Point and Lipan Point offer vistas similar to Desert View. Further west, Moran Point and Grandview Point are the closest locations to two of the most recognizable landmarks of the canyon: the stunning Vishnu Temple and Wotan's Throne. Both are also good late afternoon locations.

The Little Colorado River

Outside the eastern boundary of the park on Navajoland, there are a couple of viewpoints on the north side of AZ 64 between Desert View and Cameron, that are worth a stop. The main viewpoint, between Mile markers 285 & 286, gets the most traffic and there are numerous Navajo jewelry stalls on the parking area. A small fee is charged to enter. A 0.2-mile trail leads to several platforms offering a strikingly close view of the Little Colorado River as it forms a bend below. The other, less-crowded viewpoint, is located less than a couple of miles east and offers a rectilinear view from a high cliff. With good light, there are some good shots from both viewpoints, ranging from super-wide angle to telephoto.

Nearby location: Although these viewpoints are interesting, neither offers a view of the turquoise waters of the Little Colorado River, which occurs only in the lower gorge, from Blue Spring to the confluence with the Colorado River.

Adventurous hikers and backpackers can hike down into the canyon from several dirt roads and unmaintained trails. Finding the trailheads is difficult and most trails involve considerable risk from falling or twisting and breaking an ankle. These trails are only for the most experienced of hikers and backpackers and should not be undertaken solo and without preparation. They usually require a Navajo Backcountry Use Permit and even a Park Service backcountry permit if you enter the Grand Canyon Park boundary.

Two of these trails, which stand out for their historical and scenic interest, are mentioned here only for reference, thus no directions are given; however, good information can be found on the web.

On the south side of the Little Colorado River, the Blue Spring Trail leads to the spring of the same name and to beautiful turquoise waters. Most hikers do this trip as a very long day hike. The upper part of the trail has substantial exposure so only hikers with some climbing skills should tackle this trail.

Little Colorado River (photo by Denis Savouray)

The Salt Trail leads to the Little Colorado River down a steep scree gully from a trailhead located on the north rim of the canyon. The river is visible from about 1.5 to 2 miles past the trailhead so you'll know whether the water is turquoise-color or muddy, sparing you a dangerous 5-hour descent. The Salt Trail is a historic initiation route for the Hopi people on route to the salt mines located at the confluence with the Colorado River (*see the next two chapters*). This trip is best done as a multi-day backpack; you'll need to carry plenty of water down as the river's water isn't drinkable.

For more information, inquire at the Cameron Visitor Center or at the Navajo Parks and Recreation office in Window Rock (*see On the Go Resources in Appendix*). ✿

Looking into the Grand Canyon from Toroweap

Chapter 4

GRAND CANYON — NORTH RIM

Sundown at Bright Angel Point

GRAND CANYON — NORTH RIM

On occasion, I have heard some people express disappointment with the South Rim upon returning from the Grand Canyon. The main culprits seem to be the overflowing car parks and the endless stream of tourist buses disgorging visitors at the viewpoints. On the other hand, I have yet to hear of someone coming back unhappy from the North Rim.

Many people never visit the North Rim and that's a shame. The North Rim of the Grand Canyon offers similar extraordinary beauty but exhibits none of the sometimes carnival-like atmosphere of the South Rim. In any event, the North Rim offers a different and complementary experience due to its remoteness, higher elevation (a thousand feet higher than the South Rim), more frequent rainfall and denser forested area. The views are quite different because of the longer distance separating the rim from the Colorado River (with the exception of Toroweap Point). They are less precipitous, with more side canyons in the foreground. On the other hand, the North Rim is harder to visit as there are no visitor services outside the short summer season from mid-May to mid-October. The very scenic main access road (AZ 67 from Jacob Lake) may even close early after a heavy snowfall. Also, lodging near the rim is very limited during this brief window of opportunity and must be reserved well in advance to avoid a long drive back to Jacob Lake or even Fredonia or Kanab.

The various hikes from the North Rim to the banks of the Colorado River are longer and have more elevation gain than their South Rim counterparts. However, the additional work is compensated by a much greater abundance of really great tasting water, making the logistics of hiking and backpacking a lot easier. That's because the continental drainage is southward. The exposed south-facing north side of the canyon allows groundwater to spill forth, year round, in such wondrous places as Bright Angel Creek, Tapeats Creek and Thunder River. These waters are the sweetest you will taste anywhere. There is another major distinction between North and South Rim hiking. Except for sections close to the Rim, North Rim trails are almost always fully exposed to the sun, especially the long and demanding switchbacks through major formations such as the Esplanade and the Redwall. Also, photographers beware that on the North Rim trails and at the viewpoints many photo opportunities will be "into the sun" towards the south.

Bright Angel Point

The views are superlative from right behind the lodge and get better as you move deeper into the canyon. A short trail leads to a series of viewpoints overlooking Bright Angel Canyon, bordered to the east by a spectacular ridge leading to the Zoroaster Temple. From the last couple of viewpoints on this trail, the view to the south is a must in late afternoon.

About a mile before the lodge, you'll find the trailhead for the North Kaibab Trail on the left side of the road. The North Kaibab Trail offers a range of possibilities for day hiking and photography. The easiest dayhike is to the Supai Tunnel (3.6 miles round-trip, 1,415 feet elevation gain) and the longest is to Roaring Springs (10 miles round-trip, 3,055 feet elevation gain). A good intermediate hike is to Redwall Bridge (6 miles round-trip, 2,193 feet elevation gain). The views on this trail are not as open and photogenic as on the South Kaibab Trail, its counterpart on the South Rim (*see previous chapter*); but, they are greener and quite different.

Photo advice: The views from the various vantage points around Bright Angel are fantastic in late afternoon and should not be missed. A 35mm lens to short telephoto will work very well here. Avoid very wide angle lenses, unless there is a particularly attractive sky. The trail to Bright Angel Point is exposed and the wind is often very strong in late afternoon. If that's the case, be sure to hold your tripod firmly or weight it.

Getting there: Via AZ 67 from Jacob Lake, midway between Kanab and Page on US 89 A. It is 43 miles from Jacob Lake and the road is very scenic.

Time required: A long half-day at the least from Jacob Lake.

Nearby location: If you are traveling between mid-fall and mid-spring, you'll find the road closed even if there is no snow. However, it's relatively easy to reach

Indian Hollow and Crazy Jug Point, two other viewpoints on the canyon rim, by taking the gravel road that parallels AZ 67 on its west side (see *Getting there* in the Deer Creek section later in this chapter).

Point Imperial

Like its Desert View counterpart on the South Rim, the view at Point Imperial—the highest in the park—embraces an area as vast as you'll ever encounter, but not in the classic Grand Canyon style that one so often sees in pictures. You look far to the other side of the Colorado River into the Painted Desert, past Nankoweap Creek, with spectacular Mt. Hayden in the foreground. The sunrise view at Point Imperial is a classic, one of the great sunrise views of the Colorado plateau. You are unlikely to find more than a couple of other photographers on any given day. Be sure to allow plenty of time for the drive. You should be on location at least 15 minutes before sunrise. If you miss sunrise, don't despair; Mt. Hayden can also look pretty in the evening sun.

Mt. Hayden sunrise

Getting there: From Bright Angel Lodge, backtrack for almost 3 miles on AZ 67 and make a right on the marked paved road. Follow it for about 5 miles and turn left on the side road leading in. It is less than 3 miles to Point Imperial.

Cape Royal

If you were to imagine the Grand Canyon as an ocean, Cape Royal would be the prow of the Titanic. It juts out deep into the vastness of the canyon, allowing you to photograph on all sides in early morning or late afternoon. Right in front of you is the awesome Wotan's Throne and the Vishnu Temple, to the right is Thor Temple and to the left is Apollo and Venus Temples. Far below, the Colorado River is visible in the vicinity of the Unkar Rapids. The Hopi Tower at Desert View is also visible on the South Rim and so are the San Francisco Peaks in the background. The best views from Cape Royal are at or soon after sunrise, which requires a very early start from wherever you decide to spend the night.

Wotan's Throne (photo by Denis Savouray)

Getting there: 5 miles after leaving AZ 67, leave the Point Imperial road to your left, bearing right and continuing for almost 15 miles until the road dead-ends at Cape Royal.

Nearby locations: Along the way to Cape Royal, views from Vista Encantada, Roosevelt Point, Walhalla Overlook and Cape Final are closer to the Colorado River and you can see the confluence with the Little Colorado River near Cape Solitude. However, they lack a close and spectacular formation, such as Mt. Hayden, to attract the eye.

Point Sublime

Point Sublime is a fantastic destination with a great open view of the canyon from a high vantage point. The view is framed by the Scorpion Ridge to the right and the Confucius and Mencius Temples to the left. Although the Colorado River is almost 4 miles away as the crow flies, it is clearly visible just past Crystal Rapids, arguably the most awesome rapids on the river. As with every vast panorama, it is difficult to photograph especially during the middle of the day; but the sheer beauty of the place, coupled with relative solitude due to the long drive, makes it easy to linger and soak in the grandiose view.

Getting there: There are two ways of getting to Point Sublime. Coming on AZ

67 from Bright Angel Lodge, turn left on the marked dirt road located 0.2 mile south of the Cape Royal/Point Imperial turnoff and follow this road through a forested area for about 17 miles to Point Sublime. At about Mile 11, you'll pass an unnamed overlook with an obvious car park close to the rim. It offers nice views of Crystal Creek with beautiful white rock formations at the edge making an interesting foreground. Shortly after that is the junction with the dirt road heading north to the Kaibab Lodge (on AZ 67) via Kanabownits Canyon. This is the second, and preferred, alternative to reach Point Sublime if you are coming from Jacob Lake. In that case, on AZ 67 turn right on the marked dirt road about 0.5 mile past the Park's entrance station and follow it westward for about 7.5 miles. Turn left at the fork continuing southward for 2.5 miles to the junction with the southern road coming from Bright Angel Lodge. From this point, it is another 6 miles on your right to Point Sublime. If you're coming from this northern route, be sure not to miss the very short side trip to the east to the previously mentioned overlook above Crystal Creek on the southern route. Both dirt roads are usually in relatively good condition, requiring a high clearance vehicle. You should check first with the Rangers at the Bright Angel Lodge station. Deep snow or muddy holes can still be present in May when the North Rim road opens. These roads are very narrow in places and offer little room to pass oncoming vehicles. Due to the maze of forest roads and complete absence of signage, do not leave without the proper USGS 7.5' maps.

Deer Creek/Thunder River Trails

This 25-mile loop trail is a very rewarding backpack with fewer crowds than on the North Kaibab Trail, although the lower part is popular with rafters hiking up from the river. It allows you to photograph two Grand Canyon landmarks—Thunder River Falls and the Deer Creek Narrows—without joining a lengthy rafting trip.

The trail starts at the Bill Hall trailhead, just east of Monument Point, descending through the sandstone to Monument Point where it sharply turns north for about 0.5 mile before switchbacking down through a scree-covered drainage. After another 0.5 mile, it connects with the Thunder River Trail which undulates over and through drainage after drainage for almost 4 miles across the Esplanade to the Redwall. From there, it rapidly switchbacks down to Surprise Valley. In another 0.5 mile, it meets with the trail connecting Thunder River/Tapeats Creek (left) and Deer Creek (right). Go left for about 1 mile. The trail suddenly spills over the ridge into steep switchbacks. The Thunder River oasis, at the bottom of the falls, is visible down and to the north, nestled below the ridge. A final 0.5 mile and you're there. A pair of crystal-clear falls cascade magically over boulders through a fantastically lush stand of trees and shrubs. After miles of arid desert hiking, this is an incredible respite from which you will find it hard to part. This is a great spot for photography; so, you'll want to take your time. The remainder of the trail is resplendent with vegetation and water and, after another 0.5 mile of hiking along the Thunder River drainage, you'll arrive at Tapeats Creek which will take you to the Colorado River, 2.5 miles below. Tapeats Creek is very much like a mountain stream—very uncharacteristic of most Grand Canyon side canyons.

To get to Deer Creek, you have the choice of returning to the Surprise Valley junction, or you may follow the river trail which is well-defined and offers many opportunities for photos from river-level perspectives not found elsewhere.

The river trail passes through a number of minor side canyons that offer interesting features. Finally, the trail rises over a ridge, offering a panoramic view of Deer Valley. Keep a sharp eye out for the tell-tale signs of Ancient Puebloan granaries. The ruins are to the right and left but are hard to spot. As you go down, watch the slope west of Deer Creek as you face north. That area, too, has several ruins.

Deer Creek Narrows

The real treat, however, is the spectacular narrows that modest little Deer Creek has carved into the fragile red sandstone and on to the inner gorge of the Colorado River. When it reaches the river, it spills out in a spectacular hundred-foot high waterfall. At river level, a side trail leads to a lagoon under the falls, offering great swimming. Don't fail to get into the falls for a special thrill of the power of water.

The walk through the Deer Creek Narrows is an easy 0.3-mile stroll, first climbing up to a high point above the Colorado River with spectacular views up and down its wandering way. The trail then enters the narrows following a level ledge above the gorge with some minor exposure in a couple of points. The narrows progressively recede until you come out onto an open area known as the Patio. If you follow Deer Creek for a hundred yards, you'll come to a lovely little cascade. From the Patio, a trail follows the right bank of Deer Creek for a little over 0.5 mile to a nice backcountry campsite. Here the trail angles right, heading northeast to Deer Creek Spring, which you can spot on the ridge above. The 0.5-mile climb to the spring is moderately strenuous if you carry a backpack; but, you'll find the 30-foot waterfall very refreshing and just the right amount of force. Just past the falls is the awesome Throne Chamber where hikers and backpackers have built a couple of spectacular thrones out of sandstone slabs. From here, you start the long trudge back east toward Surprise Valley and follow the endless switchbacks of the Redwall on your way back to the Esplanade and the Bill Hall trailhead.

Deer Creek Falls

Photo advice: Although this is a backpacking trip, water is readily available along the trail. You'll have more room for your camera(s) than on comparable South Rim trips. Be sure to protect your lenses from the spray near the falls.

Getting there: From Jacob Lake, head west for almost 5 miles on Forest Road 461. At the fork, continue westward to the right on FR 462 for 3.2 miles until you meet FR 22. Turn left and head south for 11.6 miles. Turn right at the fork on FR 425 and continue for 8.5 miles until you reach the junction with the road leading to Indian Hollow campground to the right. Turn left instead and continue for another 1.7 miles to Crazy Jug Point, then turn right, heading west on FR 292A, which leads in another 1.3 mile to the marked Bill Hall Trail.

As you can see, finding the trailhead is not exactly easy. It is essential that you navigate your way on the forest roads using the Kaibab National Forest/North Section map, available at the Jacob Lake Lodge.

These forest roads provide access to the North Rim year-round, if you have an adequately equipped 4WD vehicle and the snow is not too deep. In summer, most forest roads are passable by passenger cars. Indian Hollow Campground is right on the rim and makes a good base.

Time required: 3 days to thoroughly enjoy this beautiful area.

Toroweap

For an exceptional view into the canyon and the Colorado River, which is rectilinear in this spot with walls almost 3,000 feet high and only 1 mile apart, Toroweap has no equal. It is one of my most favored views in the Southwest. The Toroweap viewpoint and picnic area is actually located on the edge of the rim and is different from the actual location of Toroweap Point, which sits in between the rim and the Tuweep Ranger Station.

From a pure photographic standpoint, Toroweap is a dream location with fantastic compositions available in both directions from the rim, at sunrise and sunset. Granted, it takes a while to get there and you need the proper vehicle; but, you can literally walk less than a hundred feet from your car to get this awesome view—the best rimside view of the Colorado River inside the Park—and there is a very nice campground close by.

Toroweap also has several interesting attractions outside of its superlative overlook. With a pair of binoculars, you can scan the sheer walls of the canyon which are truly spectacular on both the National Park and the Hualapai Reservation sides. Far below, you can spot Vulcan's Anvil, a lava pinnacle rising bluntly from the Colorado River. To the southwest, you can see rafters preparing to tackle the huge rapids of Lava Falls in season. Driving back less than 2.5 miles from the rim toward Tuweep, a dirt road on your left leads through the dry bed of former Toroweap Lake to the base of Vulcan's Throne and the trailhead to the Lava Falls Trail, dropping a sheer 2500 feet to the river—an extremely difficult and dangerous trail for experienced hikers only.

Photo advice: From the overlook, the view northeast is a classic at sunrise with the first rays of the sun casting a warm red glow on the vertiginous sandstone walls. Try using a person on one of the outcrops for added perspective and fun. The view westward is more open and allows you to frame several miles of the Colorado River vertically. Numerous compositions are possible.

Getting there: There are three ways to come to Toroweap. From AZ 389, you'll find the most popular road, CR 109, 8 miles west of Fredonia. This mostly well-graded dirt/gravel road, also known as the Sunshine Road, is about 60 miles long to the rim and is passable year-round; but; it is also rocky in places. Drive slowly to avoid tire punctures and be attentive for herds of deer and antelope milling around at night and in the early morning. Coming back from Toroweap, you can leave the road almost 20 miles from the rim to take CR 5, the Clayhole Route,

Chasm

leading northward in another 40 miles to Colorado City. As its name implies, it is a clay road, which means it will be easier on your car—not to mention your back—but it can become impassable for days on end after a hard rain. This road can be a bit hard to find from Colorado City; so, it's best used to come back from Toroweap. The Main Street Route to and from St. George is by far the most scenic. It is about 30 miles longer and is often closed because of snow in the winter in the vicinity of Mt. Trumbull. Get off I-15 at Exit 8 and take River Road, passing the Arizona State line, continuing south on BLM Road 1069 and following the signs to Mt. Trumbull. Alternately, you can get off I-15 at Exit 4 in Bloomington and head east on Brigham Road to River Road and south into Arizona. Follow BLM 1069 (which turns into CR 5) for about 72 miles until it merges with CR 115. Eventually, all three aforementioned roads merge into CR 115 and follow the beautiful Toroweap Valley southward. The track deteriorates badly for the 5 miles past the Tuweep ranger station and the last two miles are on very rough slickrock, with some moderate steps in places. From here on, high-clearance is required and 4WD is recommended.

Time required: A minimum of a very long half day is required, as you have at least 60 miles to go in each direction. A full day is required if coming from St. George. Time permitting, I recommend that you camp overnight to catch sunrise. A very pleasant campground is located just shy of a mile from the rim.

Nearby locations: About 60 miles southeast from St. George, on the way to Toroweap on CR 5, you'll come to the lovely Mt. Trumbull Pioneer Schoolhouse. The schoolhouse was built in 1918 for the children of a few hardy Pioneer families making a harsh living raising cattle. Eventually, the last remaining members of the community left in the early 60s. After a first restoration was burned down to the ground by vandals in the year 2000, a replica of the schoolhouse was built over the old one, thanks to a joint effort between the BLM and private citizens. The immaculately clean and freshly painted structure is very endearing; but, it lacks the nostalgic charm of the original and is a bit too perfect for most photographers. It will delight black & white photographers, however.

Another interesting viewpoint of the Colorado River is Kanab Point. It puts you just above Kanab Creek, close to its confluence with the Colorado River. Although not as spectacular as Toroweap, it's nonetheless very impressive. The track (BLM Road 1058) requires high-clearance and things get a bit bumpy past the National Park boundary. Unfortunately, it is hard to follow due to lack of signage. Consult with the BLM in St. George before embarking.

Parashant

Southwest of Mt. Trumbull is the recently-designated Grand Canyon–Parashant National Monument. It is almost totally undeveloped and has no paved roads. The Monument is arguably one of the largest stretches of sparsely developed lands in the continental United States, incorporating vast tracts of public lands as well as four wilderness areas. As there is a network of dirt roads—formerly used for cattle ranching—and very few signs, it is imperative that you obtain the Arizona Strip Visitor Map before venturing inside the Monument. You can do so at the BLM office in St. George, located close to Exit 6 on I-15 (follow the signs). While you're there, inquire about current road conditions. Backcountry rangers and a network of volunteers working at the BLM office provide remarkably accurate and up-to-date information on this part of the Arizona Strip.

If you come to Toroweap from St. George via CR 5, you'll pass briefly through the eastern section of the Monument shortly after leaving the Mt. Trumbull Schoolhouse. Several trails with varying degrees of length and difficulty offer access to the Colorado River. The most accessible is the Whitmore Trail, 90 miles from St. George, which has great views of the canyon and river. Do not attempt to drive this road in a passenger car because the last 7 miles are on lava, which is extremely hard on small tires built for highway driving. Even with thick tread, you'll be facing a real danger of multiple tire punctures. The road to Whitmore leaves from the Mt. Trumbull Schoolhouse via BLM 1063, then BLM 1045. As there are a number of side roads along the way, you'll definitely need your map to follow the road. A 7.5' USGS map is also required to find the trailhead. To monitor your progress in real time, I recommend the use of a mapping GPS loaded with the appropriate map, or a standard GPS feeding your position to a laptop running a program such as *Nat'l Geographic Topo! State Series*. It's easy to take the wrong turn in Parashant, even if you've been there before. At the end of the road, cross the barbed-wire fence to find the trailhead. It's an easy 1-mile descent to the river with a moderate 900 feet elevation loss.

A good base to visit the Whitmore area of Parashant is the Bar 10 Ranch, located on private land inside the Monument. It sees a fair amount of traffic from visitors flying in from Las Vegas as well as from rafters picked up by helicopters for a 10-minute flight to the ranch before being bused back to civilization. You can rent an ATV and drive yourself to the Whitmore Trail, thus avoiding driving your own car over the lava field.

Whitmore Point (photo by Bob McLaughlin)

Close to the CR 5 road and just 4.5 miles before the junction with CR 115 to Toroweap, BLM Road 1028 branches off to the southwest. Follow it for 1.1 miles to the sign indicating the Nampaweap Rock Art Site. From the car park, a 0.75-mile trail leads to a large number of classic abstract and anthropomorphic petroglyphs pecked on rocks on the north side of the canyon. Some of the glyphs are quite photogenic.

Snake Gulch

Easily combined with a visit to the North Rim area, Snake Gulch is a very rewarding and easy hike or backpacking trip in a pleasant canyon, offering an opportunity to see abundant and colorful rock art. The first two miles are in a wide valley and not especially rewarding; but, the trail is almost flat and in excellent condition so you'll make very good time. The canyon becomes very pretty between Mile 2.5 and 6 and makes for a pleasant half-day outing. A first panel of petroglyphs is located at mile 2.5. After that, you'll see mostly pictographs. Almost all of them are located on the north side, close to the trail and can't be missed because of the well-trodden spurs that lead to them. After Mile 5 some

Masks

pictographs also appear on the south side. Some of the panels are badly faded while others show surprisingly good color, with some yellow and black in addition to the ubiquitous ocher. As of this writing, the areas around the panels are not fenced.

Photo Advice: The best panels are located between Mile 4.5 and 6 just before and after Toothpick Canyon and near the confluence with Table Rock Canyon to the south.

Getting there: Take CR 22 from US 89A just southeast of Fredonia for almost 23 miles. Turn right on Forest Road 423, less than 2 miles past the intersection with the road to Jacob Lake. There is a signpost marking the Kanab Creek Wilderness. Drive 1.3 miles to Forest Road 642 and follow the latter for a little over 2 miles until it dead-ends at the trailhead.

Time required: Thanks to the flat terrain and the good trail, you'll have no trouble maintaining a pace above 3 mph so don't be alarmed by the 12-mile round-trip distance of the suggested hike. Count on a half-day outing from the trailhead. More time is of course even better. Snake Gulch is a prime location for a leisurely 2 or 3 day backpacking trip. Many people use Snake Gulch as a trailhead for longer backpacks into Kanab Creek and on to the Colorado River. ❧

Elves Chasm

Chapter 5

GRAND CANYON — THE COLORADO RIVER

Havasu Canyon

GRAND CANYON — THE COLORADO RIVER

No in-depth experience of the Grand Canyon could be complete without an intimate look at the canyon from the river level. After visiting the various viewpoints on both rims and hiking the canyon's many trails, you'll find floating the river a truly remarkable experience: geology, wildlife, birdwatching, history, whitewater, combining with adventure, group dynamics, friendships and bonding. True, it does require a substantial amount of free time and money to float the Canyon; but, it is an unforgettable, "once-in-a-lifetime", experience and you won't regret the effort and financial sacrifice.

Although hiking down the canyon is very rewarding, you can only cover so much territory due to limitations such as trail and water availability. Extended hiking trips into the canyon with photography as the main goal can only be targeted at one small area. A rafting trip, on the other hand, offers a much broader perspective of the inner canyon and a greater variety of scenery.

Rafting trips fall into two broad categories: private and commercial. A private expedition requires a clear understanding of the challenges and risks involved, as well as, adequate skills and preparation. It is—or should be—the exclusive domain of experienced rafters and kayakers. The waiting list for private trips is a legendary 10 years. As of this writing, the NPS is in the process of modifying the rules to reduce the backlog of over 7,000 people on the waiting list. There are about 260 private trips authorized each year. Private rafters currently have

18 days to complete their trip inside Grand Canyon Nat'l Park and most groups take advantage of their full time allotment. This book assumes that you'll be taking a commercial trip run by one of the sixteen concessionaires authorized by the Park Service. Although commercial trips can also last up to eighteen days, the vast majority last four to seven days.

Commercial rafting trips offer many advantages to the casual visitor. They eliminate complex logistics, as almost every aspect of the trip is taken care of by the outfitter. They are very safe—river guides are regulated by the NPS, and most have spent several seasons on the Colorado River and other North-American rivers. Finally, there is little or no waiting time compared to private trips. Commercial trips do not ordinarily have waiting lists. Some of the outfitters usually have availability for the current year's season or, worst case scenario, the following season. If you have some flexibility with your schedule, there is also a high probability of getting a spot from a waiting list.

Some outfitters offer trips specifically designed for photographers. These trips are advertised on the web or the back pages of photography or outdoor magazines. If you are serious about photography, I strongly encourage you to sign up for a photography-centric trip or you may be otherwise disappointed. Ninety-five percent of the 55,000 people rafting the Grand Canyon every year do so for a fun, relaxing experience, the thrill of the rapids, the joy of playing in the water and kicking back at the stops, most of the time enhancing the experience with a liberal amount of beer and liquor. Booze has been a long-time tradition on Grand Canyon rafting trips. In many cases, it arguably helps make perfect strangers feel like family after the third day. The fact is that such a rafting trip is heavenly and an extraordinary antidote to the stress of everyday life. So, if you are here for the experience and only in passing for photography, you'll be very happy. On the other hand, if you are a serious photographer, you'll find it almost impossible to be productive on a regular trip and I encourage you to join a photography-centric trip.

The advantages of a photographic trip are many: first, and foremost, all participants march to the same drumbeat, with everyone focused on photography, thus creating a very productive environment. On a regular trip, people are primarily interested in taking pictures of themselves with the canyon as a pretty background. Next, you're pretty much guaranteed to hit a good number of scenic sites along the way, which is not necessarily the case with a regular trip where priority is given to recreational activities. Also, within limits, most photography trips try to take advantage of the golden hour. If you shoot film, your precious rolls will be kept cool in an ice chest instead of cooking in 120° heat on deck. They will be available during the day instead of being buried deep inside a dry bag. If a landing beach is already occupied by too many other boats, your boatman will wait for a spot. On a regular trip, a boatman is more concerned with keeping things moving and chances are you'll get going.

Rafting trips are costly; this is due in part to the fact that they last much longer than the average week-end of fun. Obviously, rafting the Canyon is no day trip, although short powerboat excursions are available from Lee's Ferry and Diamond

Creek. A non-motorized rafting trip—in an oar boat or paddle boat—lasts anywhere from six to eighteen days depending on how far you go. Motorized trips last 4 to 8 days. All commercial rafting trips put in at Lee's Ferry. The shorter trips put out at Phantom Ranch, involving a hike out (*refer to Chapter 3 - Grand Canyon South Rim*). Longer trips continue on to Diamond Creek, on the Hualapai Reservation—a 225-mile journey or Pierce Ferry, on Lake Mead—a 277-mile journey. The trips ending at Phantom Ranch take a new set of clients—who have hiked or ridden down from the Rim—and continue downriver to Diamond Creek or Pierce Ferry. Time and budget permitting, I recommend that photographers take the entire trip. Trips for photographers usually cost quite a bit more, especially if chaperoned by a big name professional acting as your guide and lecturer. Shop around on the internet before signing up for your trip. I can say one thing for sure, however: you'll improve your skills and come back with better photographs by choosing a photography-centric trip.

The Colorado is a powerful river—power that comes mostly from depth. In some places the river is more than 100 feet deep. This results in a huge volume of water channeled through steep and narrow spots, sometime under 100 feet wide, creating very unpredictable rapids. The volume of water is regulated by the release from the dam at Glen Canyon and is usually much higher at the height of the season in July and August. This is due to the fact that more water is needed downstream for electricity, irrigation and other water needs. On the other hand, less water is released at the end of the season, creating a different set of problems: protruding rocks, sand bars and eddies. Rapids then take on a very different character and boatmen have to adapt to these different sets of circumstances. Some rapids that are dangerous in high water become tame, while others that are normally easy can become tricky to negotiate.

Quiet moment on the River

At any time, even the monster 36-foot motorized rafts are at risk of hitting a rock, being caught in an eddy and flipping over, and dumping everything in 55°F water. Needless to say, your equipment will have to be well protected, not only from the water but also from the sand. Refer to the *Photographing on River Trips* section of *Chapter 2* for equipment logistics.

Here are just a few brief suggestions for your Grand Canyon trip, that you'll not necessarily find in outfitters' literature.

❐ Don't bring too many clothes. Most people take way too many. You will bathe in the river in the evening, where you can wash the day's garments and they'll usually be dry in the morning. For a week-long trip, three T-shirts will easily do. You'll most likely live, swim and hike in your swim trunks. You'll get wet all the time anyway, whether on the boat or at the numerous swims holes encountered during the day. A comfortable pair of synthetic swim trunks, with pockets is perfect. A rafting trip is an adventure, not a fashion show.

❐ Don't bring heavy-duty hiking boots. You won't be needing them and they would stay wet and uncomfortable the whole trip. Most people prefer sandals for the boat and camp and running shoes for the trails. Personally, I prefer wearing specialized river shoes at all times; I just add a pair of thin synthetic liners for hikes. None of the hikes are long enough to generate blisters, as long as you've worn your river shoes before. Also, I carry a pair of running shoes for camp, in case it gets cold. Some people like to wear Crocs, which are comfortable and offer good protection; but, they aren't suited for trails. Aqua Sox are also fine for the boat and at camp.

❐ Bring a cotton or silk sleeping bag liner. They weigh nothing, take very little room and are more than enough on warm summer nights. If it gets cold, they add some warmth and a measure of comfort to the outfitters' sleeping bag.

There are many photographic highlights along the trip, including dozens of side canyons, waterfalls, ancient ruins and granaries, beautiful canyon walls, spectacular alcoves and, of course, the exhilarating whitewater. You'll soon discover that rapids are loads of fun. They are tremendously exciting but never really dangerous in a large motorized craft. You'll quickly learn to love them and take your turn in the front of the boat, where you'll be thoroughly drenched. If you find out that you don't enjoy "wave punching" the whitewater up front, you can ride the "Cadillac section" at the back of the boat, where all but the meanest rapids feel like a mild amusement park ride.

The following is a summary of the highlights of a full 277-mile float of the Grand Canyon, as far as Pierce Ferry. I will not go into too much detail as you'll find these in two excellent specialized publications: the *Guide to the Colorado River in the Grand Canyon* and the *Grand Canyon River Guide (see Appendix)*.

For practical purposes, the information is broken down in two logical sections: the Upper Grand Canyon from Marble Canyon to Phantom Ranch and the Lower Grand Canyon from Phantom Ranch to Lake Mead.

First, I'll go quickly over some of the highlights. From a photographic standpoint, the numerous waterfalls are one of the highlights of the trip. Vasey's Paradise, a superb waterfall cascading off the canyon wall, is encountered on your second day out of Lee's Ferry. This waterfall is best photographed from the boat or, occasionally, from a small sand bar in the middle of the river should your boatman decide to stop the boat there for a while. Elves Chasm is a lovely little cascade located just a short walk from the river. There are a couple more waterfalls higher up the same canyon as Elves Chasm, requiring some scrambling. The powerful Deer Creek Falls, further down canyon, are also spectacular (*see the*

Grand Canyon – North Rim chapter). And then there is Shinumo, Clear Creek, Saddle, Deer Spring and so many others. The Nankoweap Granaries are also a highlight of your trip, combining interesting Indian ruins and a very photogenic view of the Colorado River.

Another major benefit of a floating trip, to the photographer, is easy access to two remarkable tributaries of the Colorado River. Hard to reach on foot are the Little Colorado River and Havasu Creek (*see Grand Canyon South Rim* and *Grand Canyon Havasupai chapters*). Both feature turquoise waters and beautiful travertine formations—at least when there hasn't been any rain. Make sure your outfitter allows plenty of time at the confluence of both rivers so you can hike and photograph upstream.

Marble Canyon to Phantom Ranch

After putting in at Lee's Ferry, you'll enter Marble Canyon. You'll leave Cathedral Wash to the right (*see Chapter 15, Around Page*) before passing under the twin Navajo Bridges, the last sign of civilization for the next few days.

Many non-motorized trips stop at North Canyon for the first night. It has a nice sandy beach and the small canyon is extremely photogenic. Unless your

Vasey's Paradise

trip starts unusually early, Vasey's Paradise is usually reached on Day 2. Most regular trips don't stop here because of a rampant problem with poison ivy; but, photography-centric trips usually do. The rapids in this upper section of Marble Canyon are collectively known as the Roaring Twenties. Despite the name they pale in comparison to the monster rapids of the Granite Gorge, encountered during the second half of this trip. Your next stop will be the massive Redwall Cavern, made famous by Major Powell's boast that it could hold 50,000 people. If that was ever possible, it no longer is the case due to the Glen Canyon Dam preventing floods from upstream. As a result, sand accumulation has greatly reduced the cave's volume and I doubt that it could fit more than three or four thousand folks, unless you'd pack them like sardines. Nevertheless, the cavern is huge and very impressive, definitely the biggest alcove I've seen in the Southwest.

Your next stop is the short but steep trip to the Notiloid Cave. Most of the time, only two-week trips or geology-centric trips stop here. Photographically, the nautiles are not so interesting.

Next come two interesting sights on the right side: the Royal Arches and, at the next bend past the good President Harding rapids, the Triple Alcoves. I find both quite spectacular, although they fall in the category of "documentary photography".

Saddle Canyon is your first venture into one of the many side canyons that make a river trip so attractive. It leads to a lovely slot canyon and equally nice waterfall. The hike is relatively easy until you enter the slot after 0.75 mile. After a bit of hip-level wading, you'll need to pull yourself up a short chimney. With the help of knowledgeable boatmen, most people are able to reach the waterfall.

Your next major stop will be the fantastic Nankoweap Granaries—one of the highlights of the trip. The light is best in mid- to late afternoon. Be sure your boatman stops here around that time. There are large sandy beaches close by and many trips stop here on their second night. The path to the granaries is extremely steep. Be sure to pace yourself. Although morning light is nowhere near as good for photography, the view is just as impressive. Beyond the sheer historical interest of the granaries, this is arguably the best place of the trip for a great perspective shot of the Colorado River, winding its way far below.

Little Colorado Confluence

Next, you'll be stopping at the Little Colorado River confluence. This is a great place provided conditions are right. You have to hope for turquoise waters (*see Little Colorado section in Chapter 3*) and sufficient flow. Most people are content to float in inflatable rubber boats in shallow rapids located 0.3 mile from the confluence. Photographers can usually wade the river just upstream from the first small rapids and ascend a bit of the Beamer Trail to photograph the tall ridge of the Desert Facade.

Past the Little Colorado River, the canyon opens up, revealing more distant vistas and you'll be able to spot Desert View's Hopi Tower (*see Desert View section in Chapter 3*) between Lava Canyon and Tanner Rapids. Some boatmen pull over on the right bank above Tanner Rapids to let you see and photograph the petroglyphs.

After passing the Unkar Puebloan settlement on the right and the rapids of the same name, the real whitewater fun begins and you'll ride a succession of three

Overleaf: Nankoweap Granaries

fun rapids marking the beginning of the Upper Granite Gorge: Nevills, Hance and Sockdolager.

Just before reaching Phantom Ranch, get ready for the classic shot of hikers or mules crossing the bridge above the Colorado River.

Phantom Ranch to Lake Mead

If you're joining the trip at Phantom Ranch (unlikely if you are part of a photography-centric trip), you'll be exposed in short order to a series of excellent rapids: Horn Creek, Salt Creek, Granite, Hermit, and Boucher. Just before the Granite rapids, there is a good sand beach next to Monument Creek, whose drainage provides access to and from the South Rim via the Hermit and Tonto trails. You'll probably see some backpackers here. A little while later, you'll hit the most feared whitewater of your trip: the Crystal Rapids. By now, you'll be used to the whitewater and relaxed enough to enjoy the saddle bronc ride they'll give you.

Most trips stop for the Shinumo Creek Falls, a very short hike leading to a big blob of a waterfall, not great photographically, so save your film or memory card for the next waterfall: Elves Chasm. A short hike up Royal Arch Creek leads to this exceptionally beautiful cascade, arguably the finest on the river.

Next comes the longest straight stretch of Colorado River in the Grand Canyon: the 3-mile long Conquistador Aisle. It is a spectacular spot with remarkable cliffs on both sides. As the river angles north, you'll be passing just below Enfilade Point and entering the Middle Granite Gorge.

A must for all trips is the lovely Blacktail Canyon, which serves as a prime example of the geological phenomenon called the Great Uncomformity. It exemplifies a 1.2 billion year gap in the geological formation of the earth. Some serious food for thought, and great material to mull over on sleepless nights.

After the Deubendorff Rapids, you'll reach Tapeats Creek and a chance to hike up the creek to Thunder River if you are on a two-week trip.

If you've ever backpacked the Bill Hall Trail loop to Thunder River, Tapeats Creek and Deer Creek (*see Deer Creek section in Chapter 4*), you'll be able to catch a glimpse of the faint path above the river.

Deer Creek is arguably the longest and most popular stop on a Grand Canyon float trip, beating the Little Colorado Confluence and Havasu Canyon (still to come) by a nose. Swimming and relaxing in the lagoon at the foot of the great waterfall is a wonderful experience and you can hike the narrows to the Patio and Deer Spring from the River (following the path described in the *Deer Creek section in Chapter 4*).

Two great canyon hikes come next: Kanab Creek to the right, a wide canyon offering great hiking for as long as you wish or have time for (*see Toroweap section in Chapter 4*) and Matkatamiba Canyon to the left. The latter is usually visited only by photography-centric trips, as it is very scenic but quite difficult to hike.

Soon after leaving Matkatamiba, you'll come to Upset Rapids, the location of one of my most favorite stories in Grand Canyon lore. There, Emery Kolb—of the famous Kolb brothers, whose photography studio was located on the South Rim—boasted to the party who had come seeking his help to tackle the rapids: "Follow me, boys, and I'll show you how it's done". Unfortunately, he soon proceeded to capsize at this difficult spot, which also saw the death of a boatman in the seventies.

Next is a highly anticipated moment. You're approaching famous Havasu Creek. The mouth of Havasu Creek is very narrow and could be too low or too crowded for your boatman to moor in. In this case, you'll moor a couple of hundred yards downstream where you'll be jostled by the strong current. The lower part of Havasu Creek is quite beautiful; but, don't expect to go much further than the large swimming holes located 0.5 mile upstream if you are on a regular tour. If you are on a two-week trip, you'll probably have enough time for a hike. The trip to Beaver Falls takes 4 to 5 hours round-trip and reaching Mooney Falls and Havasu Falls is a full day endeavor. You'll be much better off hiking down from Hualapai Hilltop on a separate trip to spend a leisurely couple of days in Supai, enjoying these beautiful falls (*see Chapter 6 – Havasupai*).

Resuming your trip, you'll arrive at Tuckup Canyon on the right, then National Canyon on the left. National offers good hiking and most photography-centric tours stop here.

After passing below Toroweap Point (*see Toroweap section in Chapter 4*), you'll stop by the interesting volcanic plug of Vulcan's Anvil jutting out in the middle of the river before reaching the vaunted Lava Falls. These falls are often touted as the hardest of the trip, neck to neck with Crystal Falls. Lava Falls can be particularly daunting for boatmen whenever the river

Conquistador Aisle

is full. Toward the end of the season, when less water is released from the dam, the furious wall of water is quite a bit tamer. Nevertheless, these big falls will give you an unforgettable ride.

After passing Whitmore Point and the moderate switchbacks of the Whitmore Trail (*see Parashant section in Chapter 4*), the gorge opens up quite a bit and you'll gain excellent views of highly-photogenic Diamond Peak.

For some tours, the take off is soon after Lava Falls, where helicopters pick up clients and whisk them in less than ten minutes to nearby Bar 10 Ranch. Many tours continue to Peach Springs Canyon/Diamond Creek on the Hualapai Reservation. If you signed up for a full descent to Pierce Ferry, you'll pass

Colorado River Sunset

several smaller, but very enjoyable rapids before reaching Separation Canyon. In the days of Major Powell, Separation Rapids used to be the biggest and meanest rapids of the entire trip. Today the rapids are non-existent, submerged by the waters of Lake Mead. Powell named this canyon for the fateful event that took place here during his first trip. Powell had originally planned on ending his trip here; but, he decided to continue. Three fellows, however, chose to leave the expedition here and took off with provisions to hike up to the plateau and find their way back to civilization.

After successfully navigating the huge rapids, Powell fired his gun to let his three companions know that they had made it and he continued downriver. He found out later that they never made it out of the canyon. Months later, Powell led a search party in vain. Their bodies have never been found.

Shortly after Separation Canyon, you reach the Grand Canyon Nat'l Park boundary, entering Lake Mead Nat'l Recreation Area. At this point, most float trips transfer to a faster jet boat to finish the remaining 40 miles of the Colorado River, now submerged under the waters of Lake Mead. ✿

Travertine terraces in Havasu Creek

Chapter 6

GRAND CANYON — HAVASUPAI

Navajo Falls (photo by Derek von Briesen)

GRAND CANYON — HAVASUPAI

Havasupai may well be the closest thing to a Shangri-La in North America. Its superlative waterfalls have been photographed over and over, but not yet to the point where it is cliché. A popular rite of passage for groups of young people and a favorite of church groups, it is a must for anyone who loves the sidecanyons of the Colorado River.

This idyllic place is located inside the Havasupai Reservation, home of the "People of the blue green water". Only 450 people inhabit the reservation, the majority of whom reside in the village of Supai. Although there is some small scale farming, the reservation's income is essentially derived from tourism.

Photographing the Falls

Before arriving at the falls located inside the reservation, you'll pass by the village of Supai. To get there, you'll follow an 8-mile trail leaving from Hualapai Hilltop—unless you decide to take the helicopter. The last 2 or 3 miles before Supai are the most spectacular, with beautiful views and great sandstone walls. I find this trail at least as interesting as the South Kaibab and Bright Angel trails. The village proper is located in a spectacular bend of the canyon, dominated by high walls and interesting rock shapes. The twin rock formations called the Wigleeva by the Havasupai are revered by them as guardian spirits of the tribe.

It takes another 1.5 miles past the village to get a glimpse of your first falls: the Navajo Falls. These falls are less spectacular than the next falls, which are the highlight of Havasupai; but, they do deserve a stop. Although not very high, they form a massive 200-foot wide wall consisting of a network of small falls alternating with green shrubbery, somewhat like in a Central or South American landscape. They are not easy to photograph, unless you get close by walking inside the stream and look for an appropriate foreground.

Next comes the crown jewel of the reservation: the Havasu Falls. The falls are located 0.5 mile past the Navajo Falls, just before the campground. Less than a mile further are the Mooney Falls, at the far end of the campground. Both falls are extremely photogenic during an extended period of time throughout the day, with Havasu more exotic looking and Mooney starker.

For the classic view of Havasu Falls from the top, as depicted on page 89, mornings work fine with the canyon in the shade. In mid-morning, the sun will be somewhat against you or to the right depending on the season. I suggest that you crop the falls tightly to avoid overexposing the background. At midday and until mid-afternoon, the falls will be directly illuminated by the sun. Although it will create contrasting colors on the canyon walls behind the falls, the water can look spectacular. In mid-afternoon, the right side of the falls will be in shadow and it's best to wait rather than tinker with a ND Grad filter. In late afternoon, the falls and the canyon behind and to their left are no longer lit directly but have plenty of soft and even illumination, making it ideal for foolproof photography. For a photo encompassing the falls, surrounding vegetation and travertine, just use an average reading. You will not need to compensate exposure to keep the water bright white, unless you crop extremely tightly. In early evening, the light is still soft and pleasant; but, a slight warming filter will give a more pleasant color to the turquoise pool and green vegetation.

At the bottom of the falls, you will want to include pools and travertine in the foreground of your compositions; however, the flash flood that rampaged through the area in the early nineties destroyed almost all the cascading travertine pools. These have been artificially reconstructed. Although they seem to look better and better with time, they still haven't achieved the wonderful virgin look of the old days. The nice tree that was on the shore to the left

Travertine Pools

of the falls is now submerged in the pool. Photographing Havasu falls from above or from the bottom requires a 28mm to a 50mm lens.

Mooney Falls can be easily photographed from above, from a small platform

Mooney Falls

located next to a bench. Photographing Mooney Falls from the bottom is a much more difficult proposition, requiring sure footing, no fear of heights and adequate equipment—preferably hiking boots with good traction and definitely no flat-soled sandals. Exercise extreme caution if you are planning on taking heavy photo equipment with you to the bottom of the falls. There are ample warnings of the inherent danger of venturing past the top. If you choose to descend to the bottom of the falls, you do so at your own risk.

Right past the edge of the campground, the trail drops in a series of switchbacks, leading to the first of two steep tunnels dug into the travertine. This area is about one-third of the way down the height of the falls and offers excellent perspective, with a travertine stalactite in the foreground. Past the second tunnel, the trail drops down vertiginously and you'll be descending almost vertically using a series of old ladders, assisted by anchors and chains. This area requires great caution. Take your time, watch your foot placement carefully, wipe any sweat from your palms, relax and everything will go well. Also, take comfort in the fact that going up is much easier than going down.

At the bottom of the falls, you have several good compositions with pools of travertine in the foreground. The best require that you wade into the creek.

Mooney Falls is basked in soft and even light in the morning and in late afternoon. The drop is higher than Havasu Falls and the surrounding walls of deep red travertine are spectacular. You can use a 24mm to 50 mm lens.

After photographing Mooney Falls from the bottom, you may want to continue toward the Colorado River. This is a long and difficult 12-mile round-trip and it would be wise to set a more reasonable goal for yourself, such as reaching Beaver Falls, which is a 5-mile, 4-hour round-trip. The footpath—sometimes hardly a trail—is not easy and you'll be fending off brush most of the time. You'll need to ford Havasu Creek three times, once in thigh-high water. You'll also need to negotiate a 12-foot rock wall, using a knotted rope. Your reward is solitude in a luxuriant canyon—wilder and greener than the trail to Havasu Falls. A few

Opposite page: Havasu Falls, the Last Shangri-La

minutes beyond the rock wall, you'll come to a small ridge overlooking Beaver Falls in the distance. The falls are actually a succession of small cascades, linked by beautiful travertine pools. This is a good spot to photograph the falls.

Logistics for Havasupai

Time to go: Despite the high temperatures, the vast majority of visitors come to Havasupai during spring break and in summer. Havasupai is very popular with school kids and college students, as well as with visitors from Europe—all demographic groups that traditionally travel mostly in spring and summer. You may want to consider the off-season for your visit to Havasupai. Temperatures are still pleasant and the cottonwoods very colorful in the middle of autumn, enhancing your pictures. Seasons have no particular effect on the water level of the falls as Havasu Creek is perennial and doesn't depend on meltdown. To properly photograph the falls and enjoy yourself in Havasupai, you'll need at least two full days.

Getting there: First, you should be aware that Havasupai is far to the west of the South Rim of Grand Canyon. You'll most likely spend the night in Seligman or Peach Springs—or even in your car at the trailhead—in order to be on the trail early. There are no other towns around and you must drive about 60 miles

on Indian Route 18 between Route 66 and the trailhead at Hualapai Hilltop. From there, you can go to Havasupai in a variety of ways. You have a choice of making it easy on yourself—at a hefty price—or very demanding (the price is still hefty).

Assuredly, the easiest way is to catch the helicopter from Hualapai Hilltop, stay at the comfortable lodge in Supai Village and return the same way. At the other extreme,

Beaver Falls (photo by Philippe Schuler)

you can hike down carrying all your food, camping and photographic equipment and just walk back up. If you have a lot of equipment and a heavy tripod, it will be a long, punishing hike especially on the way up. It is 10 miles from the campground and a fair amount of it is in the sun unless you leave extremely early. Many people start hiking up from the campground as early as 4:30AM in summer. You'll need a minimum of two quarts of water if you hike with a daypack, more if you backpack. The average person should be prepared to walk 4 to 6 hours each way from the campground, depending on whether they carry a backpack or not. The trail is mostly flat, except for the 1.5-mile section close to Hualapai Hilltop, which is very steep.

You can combine different logistics to make getting there a pleasurable rather than painful experience. Some people choose to walk back up but send their packs on a mule. This is a very sensible solution for many folks. Others ride the mules back up and a few ride the mules both ways. If you stay at the lodge and eat your meals at the cafe in Supai, it's easy to walk both ways carrying just a light daypack. This also allows you to shave an hour off the walk from the campground on the way back. However, take into consideration the fact that you'll need to walk 4 miles round-trip from Supai to Havasu Falls and 6 miles to Mooney Falls. Taking the helicopter on the way back is also a good compromise if you're willing to pay the money. I understand that it gives you a different sense of the canyon and an awesome feeling of exhilaration.

Limited food supply is available in Supai, at the store and at the cafe. Camping can be a wonderful experience if you are well prepared. The campground has plenty of good sites, with good shade, on both sides of pristine Havasu Creek. There is spring water available; but, it is recommended that you treat it before drinking. Regardless of the season you'll have to reserve accommodation (lodge or campground) and transportation (mules, as needed) well in advance. Don't forget that you'll have to pay a $30 entrance fee per individual (as of this writing). You do so at the Tourist Office in Supai, unless you stay at the lodge, in which case it is automatically added to your bill.

On Route 66

If you go to Havasupai coming from Flagstaff, you will pass by the small town of Seligman, a well-known stop on what has become the longest section of historic Route 66 still in service. Route 66—first immortalized in print by John Steinbeck's *The Grapes of Wrath*, then in song by Bobby Troup—used to link Chicago to Los Angeles; in its heyday, it saw the historic migration of hundreds of thousands of unemployed who had come to seek work in the West during the Great Depression.

Seligman itself was founded in 1886 and became an important hub for the railway. However, the town practically died following the opening of I-40 which bypasses it a mile to the south.

Fortunately, Seligman managed to preserve its old days' atmosphere and even sprang back to life when it became the birthplace of the Historic Route 66 Association of Arizona, founded by two emblematic figures: the Delgadillo brothers.

There is almost always something going on in Seligman on weekends. As a photographer, you may be interested in taking a few snapshots of some of the buildings, as well as of the grand old Chevys parked on Main Street.

To the visitor bound for Havasupai, Seligman is the most practical gateway.

Grand Old Chevys (photo by Sioux Bally)

There are some very nice diners as well as half a dozen motels, catering to a variety of budgets. Most of them will allow you to store your belongings while you hike the canyon. This is a good alternative to letting your belongings cook in your car for several days in the intense heat of Hualapai Hilltop.

Nearby locations: Peach Springs, with its modern lodge, can also serve as a base for your Havasupai trip. The Hualapai Tribe offers jeep tours, raft trips and permits to go camping on the Colorado River. Without rivaling the Granite Gorge rapids, some of the whitewater between Diamond Creek and Separation Canyon is very substantial, making for fun rafting day-trips. The canyon itself is tall and spectacular until it meets the calm waters of Lake Mead.

Grand Canyon West, which is the closest Grand Canyon destination for small aircraft and helicopter traffic from Las Vegas, has been extensively remodeled to accommodate an influx visitors. It now harbors a new "Indian Village" and most notably the surprising "Skywalk", a glass walkway extending 70 feet from the rim and ¾ of a mile over the Grand Canyon's bottom. The thrill factor and the attraction of the high-tech structure built of space-age materials is enough to draw throngs of visitors from Las Vegas.

Unfortunately, it will cost you dearly to visit what is now billed as the "West Rim" by tour operators. As of this writing, you'll have to pay a fee of $49 to see the viewpoints and the Skywalk. Walking on the Skywalk proper will cost you an additional $25. The Skywalk is not extending over the canyon as far as the brochures would lead you to believe and the view is over a side canyon. Photography is strictly prohibited on the Skywalk (you will even be searched prior to entering). Cameras must be checked in lockers, for a fee!

The great majority of visitors come by air, but if you're driving from Las Vegas or Kingman, plan on about 5 hours round-trip travel time and a couple of hours at Grand Canyon West. A high-clearance vehicle is necessary. ❖

Red Rock Crossing

Chapter 7

SEDONA

Kokopelli Live at Cathedral Rock (photo by Philippe Schuler)

SEDONA

Introduction to Sedona

In a not so distant past, Sedona was a place one went through on the way to Grand Canyon and other attractions of northern Arizona and southern Utah. Today, Sedona sees more than 4 million visitors each year, with a growing number making it their main destination or a base to visit the area. Add to that the large number of people who settle here every year. All put together, Sedona has grown tremendously. Every time I pass through, I am amazed and quite distressed by the rapid pace of its expansion.

There are many good reasons for this growth. The town and its superlative surroundings have a lot to offer to people with all sorts of interests. The list is long. New-age folks see Sedona as a center of metaphysical energy, or vortex. Artists look for inspiration. There are seekers of art galleries and followers of music festivals. Affluent travelers look for luxurious golfing resorts and fine dining. Tourists visit natural and archaeological sites in jeep tours or fly over them in helicopters or hot air balloons. Outdoor sports enthusiasts abound. Amateur and professional photographers are attracted by Sedona's beauty and exceptional light.

If you are able to disregard the crowds and the unabashed commercial exploitation, Sedona is still a wonderful gateway to outstanding scenery. So-called Red Rock Country, of which Sedona is the center, is among the most spectacular sights of the Southwest and would have more than justified National Park status if it hadn't already been encroached upon by mankind. Movie makers, ad agencies and calendar makers have jumped on the bandwagon and rare are those who haven't seen a view of Sedona and its red sandstone monoliths in print or video.

What makes the area so special is the amazing contrast of green and red, heightened by an intense sun and blue sky, accentuating colors even more. There is an abundance of pine, juniper, bushes and even cacti in front of every colorful spire, cliff and mesa dominating the town and surrounding canyons. Sedona is at the edge of two ecosystems. You've barely left the Colorado plateau a few miles to the north; but, you can already feel the presence of the Sonoran desert, farther to the south. On some winter days, you can wake up to several inches of snow covering saguaros and agaves.

The increasing number of visitors has resulted in many outdoor activities and housing encroachment wherever there is still space, threatening the fragile ecological balance. To counteract this, local authorities—Chamber of Commerce, Coconino Nat'l Forest, etc.—have introduced the Red Rock Pass Program. It is financed by a mandatory fee for each vehicle parked alongside roads and tracks outside downtown and on all trailhead parking lots. You can get a Red Rock Pass from one of the four Visitor Centers in and around town as well as from automated tellers located at the major trailheads. Their laudable goal is the restoration and conservation of natural sites, as well as increased public awareness. Yet, at the same time, one keeps seeing more and more jeeps with flashy colors on the trails, carrying hundreds of tourists daily on accredited commercial tours. Likewise, some years ago the entrance to Boynton Canyon was marred by a huge resort and recently the entrance to Long Canyon has been leveled off to build yet another golf course. Note that if you have an "America the Beautiful" Interagency Annual Pass, Senior Pass, Access Pass or Volunteer Pass from the National Park or U.S. Forest Service, you do not have to purchase a Red Rock Pass. Just place one of these cards in view on your windshield.

As a photographer, after having shot the ubiquitous west face of Cathedral Rock, most of your time in Sedona should be devoted to exploring the 124,000 acres of federally designated wilderness areas surrounding town towards the east, north and northwest. There are over 200 miles of well-marked hiking trails running a full gamut of length and difficulty rating and most of them are usable year-round. This is definitely a hiker's paradise. Another factor that makes hiking so great in Sedona is that you can pick your trail according to weather conditions. Pick shady trails when it's hot and sunny trails when it gets colder. For a good in-depth description, I recommend the well-documented *Sedona Hikes: 130 day hikes and 5 vortex sites* by R. & S. Mangum. If you have only a few days in Sedona, try the much shorter *Sedona's Top 10 Hikes* by Dennis Andres. It is nicely illustrated and contains good maps (see reference to both in *Appendix*). There is a large number of sights to see around Sedona. In this guidebook, I will discuss what I consider the main attractions from a scenic and photographic standpoint.

Getting there: Whatever access road you use to reach Sedona, the landscape becomes superlative as soon as you reach the outskirts of town. Coming from Flagstaff on US 89A through Oak Creek Canyon is a striking sight. A couple of miles before entering town, the canyon suddenly opens up in dramatic fashion after keeping you confined for miles on end. A great alternative way to come to Sedona from Flagstaff, if you have a high clearance vehicle, is from Exit 320 off I-17 over the Schnebly Hill Road. This graded dirt/gravel road has outstanding panoramic views (*see the Munds Mountain section below*). Coming from Cottonwood on US 89A, you'll encounter a series of monoliths with evocative names such as Chimney Rock, Sugar Loaf and Coffeepot Rock. From the south, take AZ 179 at exit 298 off I-17 and you'll discover the famous Bell Rock, Courthouse Butte and Cathedral Rock after passing Oak Creek Canyon village. In town, the intersection of US 89A and AZ 179 is commonly referred to as the "Y" and serves as a reference point for all mileage.

Time required: A minimum of 3 days is needed to get a good overview of Sedona and its three principal sectors: Munds Mountain, Oak Creek Canyon and Red Rock–Secret Mountain. However, you can easily spend an additional 4 days for a more relaxed pace. Use Sedona as a central location to visit the nearby locations described in this chapter, as well as some of those described in the Around Interstate 40 chapter, which are located within 70 miles of Sedona.

In Sedona

Before you venture out of town, there are a few sights you shouldn't miss in town or its outskirts.

Next to the Sedona Bridge on Oak Creek is the Tlaquepaque commercial center, with its numerous stores, restaurants and galleries—including the interesting Eclectic Image photo gallery. What makes this charming pedestrian-only place worthy of mention is its Spanish Colonial style modeled after a suburb of Guadalajara, Mexico. On its grounds, you'll find pretty plazas with shady fountains under grand sycamores, graceful archways with iron gates and flowers everywhere. To photograph Tlaquepaque, it's best to get there during lunchtime or outside opening hours (10 to 5 PM) to avoid the crowds.

Sunrise from the Huckaby Trail

Another modern building

that is highly recommended is the Chapel of the Holy Cross. It is located at the end of Chapel Road, off AZ 179, about 3 miles south of the Y. It is wedged inside a rock overlooking the area. Its sober modern architecture is well integrated in the environment. A huge glass wall behind the altar offers a great view from the inside. From the terrace, there is a superb view of the Two Nuns, Courthouse Butte, Bell Rock

Chapel of the Holy Cross & Two Nuns (photo by Phil Schuler)

and Cathedral Rock. There are several angles to shoot the Chapel from below, using a wide angle to include some red rocks, nicely lit during the golden hour.

Surprisingly, one of the most spectacular views of Sedona is right in town, on Airport Road, south of US 89A and about 1 Mile west from the Y. Take this road up about 0.5 mile and park at the small pullout on the left. If it's full, which is often the case in late afternoon, you'll need to park 0.5 mile further and walk back down. Walk to the knoll located to your left and you'll reach a flat summit with a wonderful panoramic view of the area. This spot works just as well for early morning and late afternoon photography. Don't expect to be alone, as it is also well known as Sedona's most accessible vortex. Across from the parking lot 0.5 mile higher is a viewpoint offering an awesome birds-eye view of the northwest of town and surrounding rocks. This is a popular spot for sunset.

Cathedral Rock

Sedona's most photographed landmark is also one of the most photographed of the entire Southwest. It's the west face of Cathedral Rock across Oak Creek.

This photo spot is located in its own park, called Red Rock Crossing–Crescent Moon. Crescent Moon Park is the actual name of the park and Red Rock Crossing is the name of its famous landmark. It is a favorite of families who come here to picnic and play in the water. Photographers are also here in great numbers every evening.

To get there, take US 89A west for about 4 miles from the Y. Turn left on Upper Red Rock Loop Road (FR 216). Drive about 2 miles on this scenic road offering good distant views of Cathedral Rock from pull-outs. Make a left onto Chavez Ranch Road for about 0.5 mile and turn right onto the access road to the park. There is a fee and your Red Rock/Eagle Access Pass is not valid here. You can also reach the other side of the creek from Oak Creek Village, south of Sedona. Off AZ 179 in the Village, follow for 4.6 miles Verde Valley School

Road, which turns into a good gravel road leading to a car park near the creek.

Once in the park, a short walk along the river bank leads to several vantage points offering open views of the fantastic buttes of Cathedral Rock. Although this classic photograph has become just as cliché as, say, Delicate Arch, you'll find tremendous enjoyment in just sitting there quietly, admiring the view and of course photographing it. Still, it is better to see it in the off-season and on a weekday. Show up from late afternoon to sunset, when the rocks are best lit. During the fall, spring or early summer on a clear day, you'll be jockeying for position with many other photographers, all vying to get their trophy picture. Start by walking upstream on the north bank, toward the red rock flats. This is where most people tend to gather as there is more water and turbulence, which makes for a good foreground to the buttes. When shooting there, use a long exposure to accentuate the silvery veil of the stream. Afterwards, you may want to walk downstream to the so-called "Footbridge"— sometimes consisting of a few planks, but often nothing

Cathedral Rock Sunset

more than a relatively shallow ford. Cross the creek and follow the trail on the south side, looking for an area where the water is perfectly quiet with a good reflection of the buttes. Be very careful when looking for a spot in the streambed, as there are many patches of very slippery slickrock. It is much better to just step on the rocks.

To eliminate clutter in your photograph, especially in late fall and early spring when there is no foliage, use a focal length close to 70mm.

Near Red Rock Crossing, there is a mildly interesting spot before sunset, where crowds won't be in your way. Coming from Upper Red Rock Loop, continue straight on Chavez Ranch Road for another 0.6 mile instead of turning right toward the park. On top of the hill, park to the right. Opposite Cathedral Rock, there is a distant view of the well-lit monoliths to the northwest of Sedona, which you can photograph with a long telephoto.

The Red Rock Crossing-Crescent Moon site should not be mistaken with Red Rock State Park, which is located 2-1/2 mile further when continuing on Upper Red Rock Loop (which becomes a good gravel road). This park is a center for environmental education and a nature wildlife preserve with a few short hiking trails such as the Eagle's Nest Trail, which offers good views over the surrounding rock formations, including Cathedral Rock. However, from a photographic perspective, these views don't compare with what you see from Red Rock Crossing.

The classic photo of Cathedral Rock's west side isn't the only one you can take. From the east side, you can reach the saddle between the two main buttes in less than 45 minutes. Up there, you gain a totally different perspective. To reach the trailhead, take AZ 179 for 3.5 miles south of the Y. Turn right at the Back-O-Beyond sign and follow this road for 0.7 mile to a small parking lot on your left. The 1.2-mile round-trip route is marked by cairns and crosses a dry wash before ascending 600 feet on a slickrock slope to the saddle. The slope is steep but is manageable all the way by most people, provided you have good gripping soles. Don't risk climbing, however, if there is a chance of rain or ice.

Views from the saddle are spectacular east and west, so you can plan on being there in the morning or late afternoon. Walking alongside the cliff to the right of the saddle, you reach a small ledge with a great view to the west. Back at the saddle, follow the cliff to the left for about 150 feet, then carefully climb to another small saddle located at the foot of a tall needle. This is a good spot for late afternoon photography. Plan on being there about 1 hour before sunset. Looking west, you'll see the silver thread of Oak Creek glistening in the distance near Red Rock Crossing. But the view east really steals the show, with Cathedral Rock's W-shaped shadow slowly extending toward Courthouse Butte while the rocks all around you take on a dramatic golden hue. A 28mm is just right to include the needle.

Munds Mountain

Located east of Sedona and AZ 179, the 18,000-acre Munds Mountain Wilderness has its share of beautiful red rock formations typical of the Sedona area. It offers a mix of canyons and summits that are accessible through day-hiking, as well as famous landmarks such as Bell Rock and Courthouse Butte, which are located along the highway.

The Schnebly Hill Road marks the northern border of the wilderness area. It is also the most impressive of all the access roads to Sedona. Approximately 12 miles long, it began as a cattle trail before turning into a "farm to market" road at the onset of the 20th century. To reach the road coming from Flagstaff, leave I-17 at Exit 320 and take Forest Road 153 heading west. The first part of Schnebly Hill Road traverses the flat top of the Mogollon Rim, going through a nice ponderosa pine forest interspersed with open meadows. It's a good dirt road but it can be closed in winter due to snow. In its more interesting second half, the road descends 2,000 feet on the western flank of the rim toward Sedona. Shortly after the beginning of the descent, you'll reach the Schnebly Hill Vista, one of the most beautiful overlooks in the area, and a staple of all jeep tours, that deliver their endless cargo of tourists. All for good reason, because you'll find a breathtaking panorama of the valley, surrounded by cliffs and monoliths. The best light is during the first part of the morning. During springtime, some cacti in bloom near the rim's edge can make a good foreground. However, the cliffs are very distant and it's hard to make an eye-catching photograph. Most people reach the Schnebly Hill Vista coming directly from Sedona, taking the Schnebly Hill Road close to the east end of the Sedona Bridge on AZ 179. The beginning of the road is paved for about a mile, but the remaining section to the Vista is no longer graded; in recent years, it has become very rocky and hard on the tires and it is no longer suitable to passenger cars.

During the descent from the overlook, you'll find several open views allowing you to shoot at closer range. In particular, there is a good spot—known as the Merry-Go-Round—about 1.6 miles past the Vista, where you can climb on two little buttes to the right of the road. If you are interested in hiking in this area, stop 0.5 mile higher at a small car park located near an interpretive panel, 1.1 miles from the Schnebly Hill Vista. A path leaves about 100 yards lower on the road, ascending slowly along the mountainside with views that become more and more interesting and photogenic as the different ranges come into view toward the west. A wide-angle lens or a telephoto (to compress the perspective) will both work well here. The trail angles left after about 30 minutes and you can either turn back or take an easily-missed side trail leaving to the right. It is marked by a sign indicating Munds Jack Hot Loop. Winding pleasantly through the forest, this trail leads in about 30 minutes to several photogenic viewpoints; the final viewpoint is located about 500 yards past the second cattle gate. The trail goes on; but, views become less interesting after that.

Continuing the descent on Schnebly Hill Road, as you hit the asphalt, you'll see a large parking area to your right for the Huckaby Trail (# 161) trailhead. The trailhead is less than a mile from downtown Sedona and offers one of the finest views of town in the early morning. It would make a superb panoramic photograph, but for the prominent water tower to the right. From here, the moderate hike is a 6-mile round-trip going north toward Oak Creek Canyon. It is mostly in full sun, with good views over Steamboat Rock and Wilson Mountain before descending toward Oak Creek. At the creek, you'll find a few swimming holes somewhat reminiscent of Slide Rock State Park.

At the Sedona Bridge on Oak Creek, take AZ 179 south to visit the other highlights of the Munds Mountain sector. About 1.4 miles south of the Y, before milepost 312, make a left on Morgan Road (aka Broken Arrow Estate) and follow it for 0.6 mile to a small car park, which fills up quickly. This is the trailhead for the popular Broken Arrow Trail, an easy under 4-mile walk. It is a mild 300-foot elevation gain and is mostly in full sun. After passing the Devil's Dining Room, a natural sinkhole, you'll reach a spur trail to your left at about Mile 1. This short trail leads to Submarine Rock, a long flat slickrock butte with a 360° view in the center of a very scenic basin with chaparral-type vegetation. It is surrounded all around by red rock cliffs. It's a surprising sight, so close from the hustle and bustle of Sedona. To the southwest, you can see the Twin Buttes and Chicken Point, your next destination after rejoining the main trail. Walk toward Chicken Point, which offers great views all around and is best in the morning. Unfortunately, you'll also have plenty of company here, because this a favorite stop for the ubiquitous Pink Jeeps which have territorial exclusivity over the tracks that go around the hiking trail. On the other hand, you may be interested in photographing the jeeps going down in low gear at very steep angles over the slickrock. Retrace your steps from Chicken Point, which allows you to admire the area from a different perspective.

Vortex

About 5 miles south of the Y, east of AZ 179, you'll find some of the most picturesque and photographed forma-tions around Sedona: Courthouse Butte and Bell Rock. Bell Rock, in particular, is considered a vortex by New-agers, and as such attracts quite a bit of attention. There are a few parking spots along the road, just north of Bell Rock, but the largest car park is farther to the south. The easy 4-mile loop around these two formations is nice and allows you to get different angles; but, it is in full sun. You'll probably see people climbing the sandstone slope on the north face of Bell Rock to gain a better view or reach its attractive summit. With good soles, you can climb fairly high from here, but not to the summit as access to the platform near the top is from the west face. It follows a very steep slickrock slope. Although the view from the top is far-reaching, I don't recommend this ascent which can be risky and is not particularly rewarding photographically: The area around Bell Rock is extensively developed and the other landmarks are too distant.

If you only have a short time in Sedona, there is a way to photograph both Bell Rock and the famous west face of Cathedral Rock (*see previous section*) during the evening's golden hour. To do so, come to Bell Rock approximately 1½ hours before sunset. If you hurry a little bit, you can easily climb partway on Bell Rock until you find a suitable location. Take some photographs in a very decent light and be back at your car in less than 45 minutes. Next, you can drive the back way to Red Rock Crossing. You'll find the road by driving toward Oak Creek Village and turning right on Verde Valley School Road. Continue on this road for 4.6 miles until you find a large car park on the left side almost near the end of the road. The drive should take you no more than 20 minutes. From here it's a 10-minute walk to the aforementioned "Footbridge", which leaves you with about ½ hour before sunset for the best shots.

Oak Creek Canyon

Leaving Sedona toward the north on US 89A, you'll soon encounter the vaunted West Fork of Oak Creek. However, before entering this superb canyon, stop about 2 miles past the Y at the parking lot northeast of Midgely Bridge. From the well-marked vista point, you can get an excellent open view of the well-known formation called Snoopy Rock by walking down and under the bridge to a small promontory.

Shortly after the bridge, US 89A winds its way for about a dozen miles through a lush riparian environment following the clear waters of Oak Creek at the foot of colorful cliffs. This is a superb road, particularly in autumn, when the stunning color on the big trees lends additional majesty. As is the case with every great fall color area, the display brings an even bigger influx of visitors than spring and summer do. Great campgrounds and picnics areas are peppered along the road and there are several trailheads for day hikes or water holes. By far the most popular water hole is Slide Rock State Park, about 7 miles north of the Y. It's not rare to be denied access in summer when the park gets seriously over-crowded. It's an area of shallow pools and smooth rock acting as a natural water slide. It's a very pleasant place if you have children and don't mind the crowds. There are some lovely and peaceful sights with good photographic opportunities upstream from the main slide rock area.

About 3 miles further north or about 10.5 miles from the Y, between mileposts 384 and 385, you'll reach the large "Call of the Canyon" parking site where your Red Rock pass is not valid and you need to pay a fee. This is the trailhead for

the West Fork of Oak Creek Trail (# 108), which is arguably one of the most famous day hikes in the United States. It is an exquisite hike, in a dense riparian area, with beautiful views and endless photographic opportunities under the right light, particularly during fall. It's only a 6.5-mile round-trip requiring 3 hours or more if you linger on the extremely pleasant but crowded trail. The nice thing about this hike is that persons of all ages and physical condition can do it. There are no difficult passages or slippery rock. It has a few fords, easily crossed on well-placed stepping stones. The path is mostly wide, marked with large cairns and distance markers every half-mile. It is often well above the perennial creek with its shallow pools and tiny cascades. Toward the end, it becomes somewhat rougher and harder to follow.

Luminous Canyon (photo Alain Briot)

The canyon is deep but not very narrow

Oak Creek Canyon in winter (photo by Tom Till)

so it is basked in a lot of light, making photography difficult during the middle of the day. The abundant vegetation makes the task of photographing the colorful canyon walls a bit difficult and you'll find the best photographic opportunities at creek crossings or by venturing in the riverbed. In some places, the canyon is remotely reminiscent of Taylor Creek and in others of the Subway walk, both in Zion National Park—albeit in a much more relaxed way. At about 2.5 miles in, there is a tunnel-like rock overhang on the right side that is particularly photogenic. Views are excellent in both directions at this point.

The official trail ends after a bit over 3 miles when the canyon closes in and the stream occupies its entire width. With some initial easy wading you can continue up into the canyon and have the place to yourself. The canyon goes on for about 11 miles, deep into Coconino National Forest. It becomes progressively more difficult and requires some boulder hopping and swimming of deep pools. The complete crossing of the canyon is in a totally different league and must be done starting from the rim with a shuttle at Call of the Canyon. Access to the rim is via FR 231 south of Flagstaff.

Back on US 89A and continuing north, the excellent road turns into a steep grade with many switchbacks before reaching the Mogollon Rim at 6,400 feet. Take a break at the large Oak Creek Vista car park, to the right, which has a superb view over miles of Oak Creek Canyon. From this point, only a dozen miles through beautiful forest separate you from Flagstaff.

Red Rock – Secret Mountain

This extensive wilderness area, stretching from Oak Creek Canyon to several miles northwest of Sedona, isn't really as secret as the name implies. In fact, it is fairly accessible and it sees a large number of visitors. On the other hand, it does harbor several canyons and a lot of red rock formations of all shapes and sizes in an often green environment. It's an outstanding area for photographers eager to do a bit of hiking, as most of the local trails are well-built, relatively short and never very difficult. You can easily spend an entire day hiking, moving from one trail to another with only a few short hops in your car in between. To keep things simple, I'll present this section's highlights as a circuit. Just keep in mind that you'd need at least two full days to cover the entire territory presented here.

The main access to the wilderness is via paved FR 152C, aka Dry Creek Road, off US 89A, 3.1 miles west from the Y. There is a tremendous panoramic view of a large part of the Secret Mountain area from a high point on Dry Creek Road, about a mile north from the US 89A turnoff. From this vantage point, you can catch superb early morning light on the Cockscomb, Chimney Rock, Capitol Butte, Sugar Loaf and Coffee Pot Rock with a medium-range telephoto.

About a mile further, you'll find the turnoff for FR 152, aka Vultee Arch Road, to your right. It leads to several interesting hikes, among which are Devil's Bridge, Brins Mesa and Vultee Arch. In dry weather, this rough road is passable by most passenger cars, with some careful driving.

The Devil's Bridge trailhead (# 120) is to the right, 1.4 miles from Dry Creek Road. An easy 2-mile round-trip with only 350 feet elevation gain leads to a very photogenic bridge, which you can photograph from above, with the green valley and red rock cliffs in the background. This is a good mid-morning shot, when the contrast between the bridge's opening and the sunny valley is high. The span is wide enough that you can carefully walk on it.

About 2.5 miles from Dry Creek Road, you'll find the western trailhead for the Brins Mesa Trail (# 119) to your right. It's an easy 6.5-mile round-trip to the overlook above Mormon Canyon and Sedona, with Wilson Mountain to the left and Soldier's Pass to the right. When you reach the mesa top after 2.4 miles, take the unmarked path along the rim to your left. After about 15 minutes, the flat rocky outcrop forming the overlook comes into view. A bit of easy scrambling leads you to this high vantage point where you'll marvel at the spectacular bird's eye view. Count on 3 hours round-trip. Most people now do the Brins Mesa trip from its new southern trailhead closer to town. From uptown Sedona, 0.3 mile north of the Y on US 89A, take Jordan Road then turn left until Park Ridge Drive and follow it past the cul-de-sac and onto the dirt road until you reach the large car park. From here, the good Jim Thomson Trail climbs steeply, reaching the rim in only 1.4 miles. Take the trail to the right, following the rim, until you reach the overlook. The round-trip is only 4.6 miles, taking only 2-1/2 to 3 hours and can incorporate a side trip to the Soldier's Pass Arches, which I'll describe at the end of this section.

Back on our trip from Dry Creek Road, at the very end of the Vultee Arch road (or about 5 miles from Dry Creek Road), you'll come to a sandy turn-around with the trailhead for Vultee Arch (# 22), east of the parking lot. It's an easy 3.5-mile round-trip ascending slowly along Sterling Canyon under a dense canopy, making this a great summer destination. As you can imagine, this trail is heavily frequented by families during the high season. After about 1.5 miles,

Devil's Bridge

go left at the junction, leaving the Sterling Pass Trail to your right. Soon after the junction, you'll reach a slickrock area with a little bronze plaque dedicated to the Vultee couple, who died nearby in a 1938 plane crash. You'll see the Vultee Arch natural bridge to your left, high up on the north face of the canyon. The angle and distance are less than ideal for photography and you'll be tempted to get closer. To do so, cross the dry streambed to the northeast and look for a faint path heading toward the right of the arch. This path is very narrow and steep and you'll need to pull yourself with branches and do a bit of scrambling to reach the arch. Walking on the arch is not recommended as it is only about four feet wide. The best angle to photograph the arch lengthwise, including the span and Sterling Canyon, is from a small rocky outcrop with a cairn on it, just above the east side of the arch. However, it's difficult and rather dangerous to get there, especially with photo equipment. On the way back from the arch, climb the slickrock slope close to the plaque for a good westward view of Sterling Canyon and the mountains below. The best light from this spot is in the morning.

Back on paved Dry Creek Road, continue north for 0.8 mile until you reach a T (about 2.8 miles from US 89A). Going left at the T, follow Boynton Pass Road for about 1.6 miles to another junction, where you'll turn right and drive another 0.2 mile to a car park close to the entrance to a resort. This is the trailhead for Boynton Canyon (# 47), one of the most popular hikes in Sedona due to its beauty, its moderate difficulty and easy access, without forgetting its reputation as a vortex. As you can imagine, both the car park and the trail tend to get busy, especially on week-ends and during the high season. Photographers will love this 5-mile round-trip scenic trail, taking about 3 hours at a leisurely pace.

Close to the trailhead, you'll pass the Boynton Canyon Vista Trail to the right. It climbs to a saddle between two spires supposed to form the center of the vortex. The main trail skirts around a resort that proclaims to be enchanting but that, in many people's opinion, disfigures what used to be a beautiful entrance to the canyon. As the trail bears left after skirting the resort, just before entering a wooded area, notice an unmarked spur trail to the right. If you choose to do this short detour, you'll climb in less than 15 minutes to small Indian ruins nestled under a rather vast alcove that you can photograph with a wide-angle lens.

The end of the main trail is signaled by a marker on a platform at the base of a slickrock slope. To reach a more photogenic spot, continue on mostly level ground, skirting the platform to the right until you reach a short steep slope with gray markings. Ascend the slope until you reach the foot of a tree that will assist you in reaching a ledge to the right. Follow this ledge for about 300 feet to a platform with a great view of Boynton Canyon, which is best photographed in the second part of afternoon.

Drive back about 0.2 mile to the last junction leading to the resort and continue southwest on FR 152C aka Boynton Pass Road for about 0.5 mile. This road is now paved and accessible to passenger cars. Park on the left side for the trailhead to Fay Canyon (# 53). This trail is a pleasant 2.2-mile round-trip, practically flat and in a mostly shady canyon. However, its the spur trails that make it truly interesting. About 0.5 mile past the trailhead, look for an unmarked steep and rocky path to the right. It climbs on the side of the cliff to a voluminous arch that only reveals itself at the last moment, because it's so close and parallel to the wall. It's almost impossible to photograph; yet, it's so striking it warrants the short 0.5-mile round-trip detour. At about 1.1 miles from the trailhead, the official trail ends at a fork at the base of a large formation. Climb about a hundred feet on the loose slickrock butte, keeping slightly to the left, until you reach a sort of small terrace with an excellent perspective of the canyon and distant monoliths. With a few interesting clouds and mid- to late afternoon light—before the canyon bottom is in shadow—it makes an excellent photograph using a moderate

Fay Canyon (photo by Philippe Schuler)

wide-angle. Back at the base of the rocky formation, take the path to the north, leading toward the forest. In less than 0.5 mile, it climbs progressively, then very sharply through some dense vegetation, to a ledge under a small alcove. Leave the ledge to your right and, staying level, cautiously follow the base of the cliff as it angles to the left until you reach a small isolated promontory overlooking the box canyon. You'll find yourself surrounded by eroded cliffs with interesting shapes and colors in a setting feeling extremely remote.

Back on FR 152C, continue southwest on the paved road for 0.7 mile and park to the left at the car park serving both Doe Mountain Trail and Bear Mountain Trail, just before the road becomes unpaved. Doe Mountain Trail (# 60) takes you to the top of a flat mesa from where you have a superb view over Sedona and many surrounding landmarks. Climb 0.75 mile of switchbacks on the north face of the mesa until you reach the top, 400 feet higher. Make sure you remember exactly where you came in on the mesa so you can find your way back, especially at dusk. Except near the rim, the mesa is covered with small trees and cacti. There is a network of not so obvious paths on the mesa and it's not necessary to walk the complete circle along the edge—about 1.3 miles—as the east and south rims offer the best views especially in late afternoon to early evening. Count on about 2 hours for this hike, which sees few visitors.

Bear Mountain Trail (#54), which begins on the other side of the road, is a much more strenuous hike as you need to follow cairns on a steep rugged trail during 2.5 miles one way with an elevation gain of about 2000 feet. However, you're rewarded along the way with superb panoramic views of colorful mesas, buttes, cliffs, canyons and a vast expanse of red rock country. At one point, you encounter surprising swirls of beige sandstone. After several false summits, the trail ends at the edge of a wooded summit where you have a startling view of Red Canyon. As usual, distant views are difficult to catch with your camera.

Palatki Heritage Site

This superb hike away from the crowds is well worth the effort. As it is unshaded all the way, start this 4 hour round-trip hike very early in the morning during summer months.

After so much natural beauty, this circuit through the Red Rock-Secret Mountain Wilderness wouldn't be complete without a visit to the Palatki Heritage Site not far from here.

Continue southwest on FR 152C for about 2.8 miles past the Bear Mountain trailhead, turn right on FR 525 and right again on FR 795 leading in 2 miles to the Palatki Red Cliffs Heritage site. Palatki's location is exceptionally beautiful, nestled at the end of a vast amphitheater under spectacular red cliffs. From the car park, a short trail leads you past the small Visitor Center to just below the Sinaguan cliff dwellings. The ruins proper aren't particularly remarkable. The red hues of the masonry and overhanging cliffs are noteworthy and make for attractive shots in the right light. Another short trail leads to some alcoves harboring rock art consisting of pictographs representing animals and abstract scenes as well as a very photogenic shield-like painting. You are free to hike on your own and volunteer rangers are stationed at the end of both trails to provide interpretation.

Officially, Palatki must be seen by reservation, which you can make at the Sedona Cultural Park Information Center in town or by calling the site directly (*see Appendix*). The best light being in the early morning, try reserving the first viewing, which is at 9:30 AM. The next viewings are at 11:30 AM and 1:30 PM. They are not recommended for photography as the ruins are basked in direct sunlight from mid-morning on. If you have to choose between the two, try the 1:30 PM viewing and linger as long as you can until the site closes at 4:30 PM. Quotas permitting, it is sometimes possible to visit Palatki without a reservation. Count on 1½ to 2 hours to visit Palatki. If you visit Palatki until the 4:30 PM closing time in summer, you still have plenty of time left for Doe Mountain or Cathedral Rock (*see previous section*), which will be in good light by then.

To return to Sedona, take FR 525 south for about 6 miles from the junction with FR 795, then turn left on US 89A and drive 9.5 miles to the Y.

Aside from the above-described circuit, I recommend the easy Soldier's Pass Arches hike. It starts on the outskirts of town and offers interesting photographic opportunities in the scenic red rock environment. To access the trailhead, follow US 89A for 1.3 miles west of the Y, make a right on Soldier Pass Road for about 1.5 miles, then turn right on Rim Shadow Drive and follow the signs for trailhead #66's parking lot. Not far from the trailhead, you'll pass a huge sinkhole known as the Devil's Kitchen, whose highly geometric forms—of both the rock and the hole left in the cliff—are quite photogenic. A bit further, don't miss the partially water-filled depressions of the Seven Sacred Pools on your left, before arriving at the wilderness boundary sign where the jeep road ends at a cable fence. Cross over the fence and continue for about 200 yards inside the wash until a fork where you leave the main trail and bear right. Climb uphill for about 15 minutes, with scenic views, to reach the cliffs where the hidden cave-like arches are located. The most interesting of these arches is the one located at the beginning of the cliff, partially hidden behind trees. There, you'll find a smallish Indian ruin and, to the right, a choke stone that you can scale to enter a sort of elongated grotto, lit by an opening in the rock face. From the edge of the inside ledge, its symmetrical shape evokes some kind of temple. The light is best in mid- to late-morning and

Soldier Arch

allows you to create typical slot canyon images. Count on 2 or 3 hours for this 4 mile round-trip hike.

Alternatively, you can easily include in this hike a foray to the Brins Mesa Overlook (*previously described in this section*). To do so, simply continue on the ledge trail, passing by the other caves and following a narrow but good trail at the base of the red cliff. The trail then leaves the cliff, climbing through dense vegetation with a few minor obstacles before joining the Brins Mesa Trail. Turn right until you reach the rim shortly and turn left on the rim trail to the overlook. Conversely, you could incorporate a jaunt to the Soldier's Pass Arches while hiking the Brins Mesa Trail. Following the regular trail via the Soldier's Pass switchbacks, down the canyon and up to the arches would be a very long way. Take the cutoff trail to the south at 34°54'16" 111°47'11" and you can reach the arches rather quickly. The trail is a bit harder to follow going down than if you were coming up from the arches.

AROUND SEDONA

Sycamore Canyon

Just west of the Red Rock-Secret Mountain Wilderness lies the rugged and less visited 56,000 acres of the Sycamore Canyon Wilderness area. Somewhat comparable in size and beauty to Oak Creek Canyon which it parallels, Sycamore Canyon winds for more than 20 miles along Sycamore Creek, from its north shore in the wooded area south of Williams until its deserty mouth in the Verde Valley. This scenic canyon consists of red sandstone, white limestone and brown lava, forming a colorful palette of sheer cliffs, buttes and pinnacles harboring many different habitats and bordering a desert riparian area with much wildlife. There are no roads to intersect this remote canyon and the principal access to the north and west is through a network of rough roads leading to the trailheads through the Kaibab National Forest. As you've guessed by now, you can only explore this wild region and experience its solitude by hiking and backpacking.

The southern access is a lot easier and, coming from Sedona, offers a glimpse into Sycamore Canyon by taking the Parsons Trail (#144). This easy 7.5-mile round-trip walk is popular and you will likely not be alone. From the trailhead, you descend rapidly to the creek with a perennial stream. You follow it most of the time on its eastern shore on a mostly flat trail with a few easy crossings (unless you visit just after snowmelt has begun, your feet should stay dry). Despite the presence of cairns, the path is not easy to follow in places because flash floods have washed out parts of the trail. About halfway through the walk, after crossing the creek and right after a bend toward the west, look for a large pool at the foot of a cliff, which makes a great swimming hole on the way back on a hot summer day. Turn back when you reach the muddy pool of Parsons Spring—a source from which the water reappears after an underground voyage from upstream. This pleasant walk can be done in summer because the trail is often shady as it meanders through a rich variety of riparian trees. Its diverse vegetation, colorful sandstone walls, flat ledges above the clear water, colorful boulders at some of the crossings, offer many interesting shots. The canyon is quite open and well lit and the light can be harsh around midday.

Getting there: From Sedona, take US 89A west to Cottonwood. Turn right on Main Street North and follow it for 4 miles toward Clarkdale, then turn right on Tuzigoot Road toward the national monument. Just after crossing the Verde River Bridge, turn left on a paved road which soon becomes a graded dirt road (FR 131 when you enter Coconino National Forest), which you follow north for 10.5 miles to the trailhead. This road is sometimes rough but generally passable by passenger car in dry weather.

Time required: Count on about 4 hours for the hike alone, at a leisurely pace.

Tuzigoot

Tuzigoot consists of a cluster of about 80 dwellings straddling the top of a small hill, 120 feet above the beautiful Verde Valley. It is estimated that about 200 people of the Salado group of Sinaguan culture inhabited it, farming the fertile land below. Tuzigoot's fortress-like shape is quite unlike any other Sinaguan ruins in southern Arizona. The exhibits at the Visitor Center provide a glimpse into Sinagua daily life. The topmost dwellings have been nicely reconstructed, complete with a ceiling. The panoramic view from the top, as well as the approach from the Verde Valley, make this site quite interesting from a photographic standpoint.

Tuzigoot

The old mining town of Jerome can be seen in the distance, straddling the mountainside. If you are a birder and carry a long telephoto, you can photograph Jerome from the top of Tuzigoot. Jerome is more attractive for its superlative setting than for its buildings. Like many former mining towns, it has its collection of antique and craft shops, galleries and small cafes and it's packed on weekends. Still, when traveling between Flagstaff and Phoenix, it is well worth the detour.

Photo advice: The best views are from the left side of the ruins trail looking up toward the top dwelling. There is also a good view from the end of the trail below. An interesting medium telephoto shot can be had from the end of the dirt road marked "day use only", a couple of hundred yards before the monument.

Getting there: From Sedona, take US 89A to Cottonwood. Turn right on Main Street North and follow it for 4 miles toward Clarkdale. Turn right on Tuzigoot Rd. From there, it's 1.2 miles to the monument's entrance. If you come from I-17, use US 260 from Camp Verde to reach Cottonwood.

Time required: About an hour.

The Granite Dells

Granite Dells (photo by Philippe Schuler)

Not far from Prescott—whose downtown area has kept some of the Victorian charm it acquired during its short stint as Arizona's capital—is an interesting geologic phenomenon called the Granite Dells. The Dells are hills consisting of large continuous granite boulders with beautiful shapes. You can photograph them anytime along two miles of US 89A; but, they are at their best when reflected in the waters of pretty Watson Lake, especially if you are blessed with a nice sky.

Photo advice: From Watson Lake Park, the Granite Dells have better light and color from mid-afternoon on. Park at the top near the ramada for a good view overlooking the lake and the rocks. For closer shots of the rocks reflected in the water, you'll need to cautiously work your way around the lake by boulder hopping, as there is no real trail. You are better off parking at the main car park before the boat launch area.

Due to the proximity to Prescott, avoid summer and weekends or you'll end up with plenty of canoeists, fishermen, hikers and rock climbers.

Getting there: From Prescott, head north following US 89N for about 4 miles and turn right at the Watson Lake Park sign.

Time required: 1 hour or more if you want to walk on the rocks.

Montezuma Castle & Well

Montezuma Castle Nat'l Monument is a great photographic location that you don't want to miss. The castle is a spectacular multi-storied limestone dwelling, built high into a cliff recess. It has a nice ocher color under the right light, contrasting with the white cliff, the deep blue sky and the sycamores lining Beaver Creek below. Like several of its counterparts in the Southwest (Aztec Ruins Nat'l Monument comes to mind), it was misidentified by Anglo settlers as being of Aztec origin. It was, in fact, occupied by the Sinagua between the 12th and 14th centuries, well before the time of the great chieftain after which it was named.

Photo advice: Montezuma Castle is best photographed in mid-to-late afternoon for great color, with minimum shadows. Visitors are not permitted in the fragile dwellings and all ladders have been removed. As a result, you'll be taking all your pictures from the path following Beaver Creek using a medium telephoto. Depending upon the time of your visit, walk along the path to locate the most suitable angle.

Getting there: It is a short 5-minute hop from I-17, 30 miles south of Sedona. It even has its own freeway exit (289).

Time required: Less than an hour.

Montezuma Castle

Montezuma Well is located 11 miles northeast of the Castle. It is part of the same National Monument. Montezuma Well combines the attraction of a natural curiosity with a historical interest. The well is a limestone sinkhole formed eons ago by the collapse of a huge underground cavern. In the process, it has created a pretty lake continuously fed by springs. The lake was used by the Sinagua and the Hohokam, which have left behind a few pit houses and other dwellings. An excellent paved trail dotted with a few viewpoints follows the south rim of the well and a short spur trail leads to the bottom.

Photo advice: The well is best lit in the morning and the moss that grows on the lake adds color and interest to the scene. A 24mm or wider lens is needed to capture the entire well.

Getting there: From Montezuma Castle, go back to I-17 north, take exit 293 and follow the signs leading east for almost 5 miles. You can also come directly from the V-Bar-V Ranch on a good gravel road, as explained in the next section.

Time required: Less than an hour.

V-Bar-V Ranch

The V-Bar-V Ranch Petroglyph site is the largest and best known petroglyph site in the Verde Valley. It is located about 30 minutes from Sedona and is very close to I-17. It's well worth a visit if you're in the area on a day it's open. At the time of this writing, visiting hours are limited to 9:30 AM to 4:30 PM (the entrance gate closing at 3:30 PM), Friday through Monday only, so it is not exactly easy to visit for most people.

From the large car park, walk down to the small but interesting Visitor Center. From here, a 0.5-mile trail leads through pleasant tallgrass to the panel.

V-Bar-V Ranch petroglyphs

The panel is very nice and unusual, with a bit of green moss on the right side.

Photo advice: The panel is well exposed and can be photographed at any time. On sunny days, however, it can get partially obscured by branches and foliage from a nearby tree in mid-afternoon.

Getting there: From exit 298 on I-17, drive 2.5 miles southeast on Forest Road 618, turning right soon after passing the one-lane bridge and continuing for 0.3 mile to the large parking area. The Ranch is well signed from the freeway exit on. If you come from Montezuma Well, you can save time by using a connecting road bypassing the freeway. Turn right on the good gravel road just before exiting the monument and follow it for 3.2 miles until it joins FR 618 0.5 mile southeast of I-17.

Nearby location: If you are interested in Indian ruins, consider a visit to Agua Fria National Monument, about 45 minutes southwest of V-Bar-V Ranch via I-17. The recently-designated monument is still relatively unknown. It is bound to get increased visitation in years to come, if only because of its status as a national monument. It is known to contain at least 450 late-Sinaguan sites and there are likely many more. The sites consist of clusters of stone masonry pueblos containing large numbers of rooms. There are also vast amounts of rock art throughout the totally undeveloped monument. Agua Fria is located just off I-17 and can be accessed from either Bloody Basin Road (exit 259) or Badger Springs (exit 256). ✿

Siphon Draw on the Flatiron Trail

Chapter 8

THE SUPERSTITION MOUNTAINS

The mighty Superstitions

THE SUPERSTITION MOUNTAINS

The Superstitions represent the "classic" Arizona mountains. They rise 3,000 feet above the desert floor, rugged, with fantastic jagged peaks, saguaros and ocotillos, and the name to go with it. Definitely the stuff of "western movies". There is a vast photographic potential awaiting you to evoke the mystical atmosphere of gold miners and outlaws. But all that stark beauty is tamed into a more gentle landscape when the mountain is carpeted with wildflowers in March and April. There is also great bird life present in all seasons.

You can visit the Superstitions with relatively little effort, due to their proximity to Phoenix and the fact that the range is quite compact. There is a vast network of trails, but I'll concentrate on easy ways to photograph the Superstitions from the two main trailheads: the Lost Dutchman State Park and Peralta Canyon.

Lost Dutchman

The Lost Dutchman State Park is the hub for a network of excellent trails covering the western flank of the mountains. Whether you spend just a couple of hours or a few days, you'll be rewarded with spectacular views and a true outdoor photography studio. Just be sure to be there at the right time: Lost Dutchman is a late afternoon to sunset location.

If you only have a few hours, I suggest that you walk the trails directly facing the main bulk of the Superstitions' west flank. All the trails close to the car parks offer an awesome view of the stark mountain, rising from the lush landscape like a phantom ship. In springtime, you'll have an abundance of wildflowers, with ocotillos and cacti in bloom.

If you have half a day, the Siphon Draw Trail #53 is a very rewarding hike with great photographic potential. The trail climbs gently at first, then reaches the Siphon at 1.6 miles. The Siphon is a very steep, bare slickrock gully running for about 500 feet at a 45° angle. Despite the steepness, you can climb without hands assistance by ascending it sideways. You'll need good soles for traction, especially on the descent. Needless to say, it should not be attempted during or after a rain. From Siphon Draw, you have a awe-inspiring view of the Flatiron's prow, majestically perched 1,300 feet above you.

If you have a full day, and with an early departure, you can ascend to the top of the Flatiron. Don't underestimate the ascent, however. It really isn't a trail—although it isn't hard to follow. You're basically hiking up a very steep gully with loose scree. This is a potentially dangerous hike, requiring no fear of heights. Use extreme caution and avoid hiking alone. Past the draw, the ascent resumes in the form of a route with occasional boulders to cross, until you hit the bottom of the main gully leading to the top. From here on, it's a straight-on climb inside the gully, gaining 1,400 feet in less than a mile. The panoramic view from the top is incredible, but it will not yield any great photography. The good stuff is really at the bottom, especially when the wildflowers are out and the cacti are in bloom. Be sure to be back at the trailhead about 1½ hours before sunset and have the park's brochure handy for reference.

A short distance before reaching the Siphon Draw trailhead as you come down the Flatiron, take the unmarked trail to your right cutting north to the Prospector's View Trail #57 at the base of the Flatiron. From the Prospector's View Trail, a short 0.5-mile jaunt brings you to the Green Boulder. This trail offers excellent views of the Praying Hands formation on the north side of the mountain. Retrace your steps on trail #57—thus passing trail #56—and bear north (right) on the signed Jacob's Crosscut #58 for 0.8 mile. This part of the trail offers excellent views of the splendid mountain, with plenty of chollas, saguaros, ocotillos and wildflowers in the foreground.

The Flatiron

Superstition Sunset

Finish your hike by taking the Treasure Loop Trail #56 northwest (left). This part has the densest vegetation and offers superb views of the mountain during the golden hour. This is where you'll end up doing most of your photography until after sunset. A short 20-minute walk will bring you back to your car at the Siphon Draw trailhead. Most backpackers start or finish their traverse of the Superstition Mountains at the First Water trailhead, further to the northeast. It has a network of longer trails, which can be done as dayhikes with an early start.

Photo advice: Views from the Lost Dutchman are awesome and easily photographed in late afternoon without too much walking. The south side is great in the morning and for hiking. There are great views everywhere and the rich Sonoran environment is well complemented by the uniquely rugged peaks. You can use a whole range of lenses there. Summer is too hot for hiking and is not well-suited to photography because of the haze.

Getting there: The Lost Dutchman State Park is located five miles northeast of Apache Junction off AZ 88, east of Phoenix and north of US 60.

Time required: If you are pressed for time, a couple of hours are sufficient to photograph the Superstitions from the lower Lost Dutchman trails or from the vicinity of the First Water trailhead. This is a place where you'll want to return over and over again.

Peralta Canyon

This southern approach to the Superstitions is best in the morning and offers more alternatives for hiking deep inside the mountains without too much effort. The most popular and crowded approach is by way of the Peralta Canyon Trail #102. It is a moderately strenuous walk inside a beautiful canyon with a gradual ascent of 1,500 feet. It brings you in 2.3 miles to the Fremont Saddle, from where you have an open view on Weavers Needle. For a closer and much better view of the Needle, follow the easy 1-mile round-trip path to the right of the

Saddle to a great viewpoint called Weavers Outlook Ridge. You'll be facing the Weavers Needle directly in front of you with nothing in between.

When returning from the Weavers Outlook Ridge, after about 0.2 mile you'll notice a faint trail heading southeast. This is the Cave Trail #233, a rough cross-country trail with a limited amount of cairns which should only be taken in the downhill direction to return to the Peralta trailhead via the Bluff Spring Trail. Although more of a route than an actual trail, it is featured on the 7.5' topo map. The 1.7-mile long Cave Trail provides an alternate return route to adventurous parties knowing what they're doing. This trail passes by the Geronimo Caves, which can also be spotted on the ridge line to the east of the Peralta Trail.

An interesting alternative to see the Weavers Needle from a different angle is a combination of the Bluff Spring and Terrapin trails up to the Bluff Saddle. Adventurous hiking parties can also leave the Bluff Spring Trail northwest near the pools at mile 2 and follow the faint Upper Barks Canyon Trail to connect with the Cave Trail for a an exhilarating cross-country loop. This is a very rough trail requiring scrambling and routefinding skills. The excellent Weavers Needle topo map found on the Superstitions Search & Rescue web site (*http://superstition-sar.org/*) has colored overlays to help locate and follow these routes.

All these trails are enormously popular due to their proximity to the greater Phoenix area. To avoid the crowds, you should be on the trail before dawn. You are then almost guaranteed to have little or no traffic. I have hiked both the Peralta and the Bluff Spring trails on several occasions at the height of the season. By leaving the trailhead 20 minutes before sunrise, I encountered the first group of hikers when I was already well into my descent. Starting early will also make your hike much more enjoyable as the heat is usually very manageable during the first couple of hours after sunrise. You'll be hiking by yourself in the cool morning in an exquisite environment, catching sunrise as you reach the higher elevations for a truly exhilarating experience.

Getting there: Drive almost 8 miles southeast of Apache Junction on US 60. The Peralta trailhead is 7.5 miles up the dirt road. The car park where you pay your fee provides access to both Peralta Canyon and Bluff Spring.

Time required: 2½ to 3½ hours for a quick in and out trip to the Peralta or Bluff Spring saddles. Half a day for the Barks Canyon/Cave Trail cross-country loop.

Weavers Needle

AROUND THE SUPERSTITION MOUNTAINS

The Apache Trail

The 44-mile long Apache Trail, officially AZ 88, starts at Apache Junction and winds through rugged mountains and canyons on the north side of the Superstitions until it reaches Roosevelt Lake. The first half of the road, coming from Apache Junction, is paved. The eastern section of the road is still unpaved and very narrow in places. It is suitable to passenger cars in dry weather. Large RVs don't belong on this road. Your first stop will be at Canyon Lake, a spectacular viewpoint overlooking the blue waters of the lake. It looks incongruous in this desert landscape. A couple of miles further, you'll pass the famous little settlement of Tortilla Flat. You leave the asphalt shortly after that and encounter a couple of worthwhile viewpoints providing sweeping vistas. The descent just before Fish Creek is very narrow and has a 10% grade. Be extremely cautious, especially in blind curves. Fish Creek is popular with hikers and rock climbers and the canyon is a good place for photography. The second part of the drive follows Apache Lake and the views are less open. A stop at the Apache Lake Marina is worthwhile to break up the trip. The road becomes quite dusty toward the end, before opening up on the vast expanse of Roosevelt Lake and rejoining the asphalt. The lake—the largest in Arizona—is bordered on its north shore by superb mountain scenery. There is an outstanding campground in the direction of Globe, just past Tonto Nat'l Monument.

Rugged peaks

Being so close to Phoenix, the road is often crowded, especially on week-ends. You are likely to encounter dozens of pick-up trucks pulling motorboats. Still, it's a wonderful drive.

Getting there: Drive 25 miles east of Phoenix on US 60. The Apache Trail begins at Apache Junction heading northeast as AZ 88 (Idaho Road).

To return to Phoenix from the Roosevelt Dam, continue southeast for 30 miles on AZ 88. The views along the lake are expansive and very scenic. At Miami/Globe, take US 60 toward Superior. The last ten miles before reaching Superior are in a particularly scenic canyon.

Time Required: Expect to take at least 2 hours to drive the Apache Trail with a couple of briefs stops to stretch your legs and take photos.

Nearby location: Just past Superior, you can stop at the Boyce Thompson Arboretum (8 AM to 5 PM). The arboretum preserves a great variety of desert plants from all over the world in a beautiful 300-acre park.

Tonto National Monument

Tonto is a must see, not only for the Salado cliff dwellings it preserves, but also for its spectacular setting. It is high on a cliff with an outstanding view of Roosevelt Lake and the mountains bordering it to the north. I strongly recommend a visit to this little-known monument. As a photographer or just a casual visitor, you won't be disappointed.

A short and easy 0.5-mile paved trail, with 350 feet of elevation gain, brings you to the Lower Cliff Dwelling. The trail provides a close up view of typical Sonoran flora. There are plenty of gorgeous saguaros, ocotillos and chollas that can be easily photographed from above or below. Birds of prey patrol the deep blue sky far above the trail. The ruins of the two-story dwelling have been reconstructed. The rooms are not particularly outstanding, but you can enter and photograph them. It is the construction of the dwelling inside a natural alcove that makes this place very special, and so is its towering location, high on the hillside.

The Upper Cliff Dwelling can only be accessed on a ranger-led tour during the months of November through April. It is a strenuous 3 to 4-hour walk. The upper dwelling has incurred very little reconstruction and you are not allowed in. Although the dwelling is twice as large, it lacks the superb location and angle of the Lower Cliff Dwelling.

Photo advice: Tonto is best photographed in the early morning when there is good sidelight from a couple of vantage points on the trail below. It is completely in the shade by mid-afternoon. The monument opens at 8 AM throughout the year, which rules out the possibility of a nice warm light during summer months. Try visiting in March or April when the wildflowers are out.

Getting there: 4 miles east of the Roosevelt Dam or 30 miles northwest of Miami/ Globe on AZ 88 (the Apache Trail).

Tonto's Lower Cliff Dwelling

Time required: About an hour. This visit should be combined with the Apache Trail drive (*see previous section*).

Casa Grande National Monument

At first glance, Casa Grande may not seem like a place you'd want to photograph, especially in view of the large man-made structure erected above the "Great House" to protect it from the elements. However, you'll be in for a surprise when you get there. The fortress-like building is truly impressive with its four foot thick mud walls and the large open area around the Great House bestows the compound with a sense of majesty. Casa Grande immediately commands respect. Also, I find the roof structure artistically matched with the building. Although there is no great ball court, such as the one at Wupatki Pueblo, the Mesoamerican impact is in evidence through the vast plaza, which reminds us strongly of the great Aztec structures of Mexico. Excellent modern exhibits explain how the Hohokam harnessed the waters of the Gila River through extensive irrigation channels to create rich farmland and became the most advanced civilization in Pre-Columbian North America.

Hohokam ruins and the Great House at Casa Grande

Photo advice: Casa Grande is best photographed in the early morning light. The side light is more interesting on the western plaza than on the deserty eastern side. Nevertheless, late afternoon is also quite good. There is a group of tall walls on the southwestern side of the plaza that provide excellent perspective. A normal lens is perfectly suited to the shot. There is also an interesting symmetrical shot of the main structure with its four great pillars. Shoot it upward with a wide-angle lens.

Getting there: Between Phoenix and Tucson on I-10, take the Coolidge exit, drive north on AZ 87 for almost 20 miles, following the numerous signs to the monument. Do not make the mistake of driving to the town of Casa Grande, which is actually many miles away from the national monument.

Time required: About an hour. ❀

Kofa Ocotillo in Bloom

Chapter 9

SOUTHWEST ARIZONA

Life inside an Organ Pipe

SOUTHWEST ARIZONA

The Kofa Mountains

The Kofa Mountains form a spectacular, barren ridge with many jagged peaks, stretching over 50 miles from north to south in the southwestern corner of Arizona and in close proximity to the California border. They can be seen and accessed along US 95 between the snowbird meccas of Quartzsite and Yuma. The Mountains are located inside the huge 665,400-acre Kofa National Wildlife Refuge, which protects many native plants and several hundred bighorn sheep.

Palm Canyon is by far the most visited landmark in the refuge, due to its easy accessibility by passenger car and the attraction of its native Washingtonian palm trees. A very good gravel road, suitable for passenger cars, leaves from US 95 about 19 miles south of Quartzsite. It leads in 7 miles to a large carpark at the mouth of Palm Canyon. Several interpretive panels mark the entrance to the wilderness area at mile 3.2. Soon after that, you'll begin seeing great vistas of the Kofa Mountains. This is typical Sonoran desert landscape, with saguaros, cholla cactus and ocotillos along the road, offering great photo opportunities during the evening golden hour. A medium to long telephoto works best here.

From the carpark, an easy 1-mile round-trip trail leads to a viewpoint from where a cluster of about 40 palm trees can be observed. Visitors hoping to see a Washingtonian Palm oasis similar to those found in California's Joshua Tree Nat'l Park might be disappointed. The 40+ palm trees are tucked high in a narrow ravine, looking small and rather unspectacular. A 200mm telephoto is necessary to isolate them. Be sure to start looking for the sign to the left after 0.4 mile on the trail. It is easily missed. The viewpoint is just a few yards to the left of the sign. If you miss the viewpoint, what could pass for the main trail continues up-canyon for quite a while. It becomes progressively rougher and requires some scrambling over large boulders. After 0.7 mile, you'll reach a high spot providing a nice view of the canyon below, with the barren La Posa Plain in the distance and an even more impressive view of Signal Peak towering well above you to the right. A small arch can be seen on the canyon wall to the left. Climbing beyond this point requires almost constant Class 3 scrambling—and pants getting scratched during the descent—over large boulders and limestone slabs with lots of small pebbles on which your soles love to slide. The higher part of the trail is not recommended for the lone hiker.

Arguably more interesting from a pure scenic standpoint is the Kofa Queen Canyon road, which starts to the left of the interpretive signs at the wilderness entrance on Palm Canyon road. It leads in 4.6 miles to a nice view of the scenic low mountains before entering Kofa Queen Canyon where a high-clearance or preferably 4WD vehicle is necessary to reach the unmarked trailhead to Ten Ewe Mountain and, further up, the Kofa Queen Mine.

After returning to US 95, drive 8.5 miles south toward Yuma. Time permitting, take the signed King Road at mile marker 76, leading to the King of Arizona mine district from which the refuge gets its name. The track is normally well-maintained, alternating between gravel and sandy passages. A high-clearance vehicle is a must for safety given the 50-mile round-trip distance. From the mine area, it is possible to continue deep into the refuge and exit to the north or south with a 4WD vehicle.

Back on US 95, continue south toward Yuma for 21.5 miles until you see the sign announcing the Castle Dome Road at mile marker 55. Don't be fooled by the excellent paved road leading in less than 2 miles to a military facility to the right. The remaining 7.5 miles to the Castle Dome Mining district are on a gravel road. Although it is well maintained, it isn't much fun in a passenger car. A small museum and reconstructed ghost town provide some interesting history on

Kofa Mountains Sunset

the area's mining activity in the late 19th century. This area, which is at the southern edge of the refuge, is dominated by the impressive mass of Castle Dome, a few miles to the northeast. With a 4WD vehicle, you can continue over McPherson Pass and join the previous road leading to the King of Arizona mining district, about 27 miles to the northeast.

For a more in-depth trip into the heart of the Kofa Mountains, drive 5 miles south of Quartzsite on US 95 and turn left on the good Pipeline Road for about 26.5 miles. Turn right on a good gravel road, suitable for high-clearance vehicles, ascending toward Red Rock Pass between the Kofa Mountains to the west and the Little Horn Mountains to the east. After the pass, the track traverses rugged remote country allowing many opportunities for camping and photography and providing views of the east side of the mountains. Time permitting, with your SUV you can continue south to exit the refuge. If you are interested in further explorations inside the Kofa Mountains, get a copy of *Backcountry Adventures Arizona* by Peter Massey and Jeanne Wilson (*see Appendix*).

Alamo Lake

Alamo Lake State Park is a little known destination in Arizona's State Park system. Its photographic potential is excellent during the wildflowe season and it has managed to stay largely out of the limelight. The area surrounding the lake is an interesting mix of Mojave and Sonoran ecosystems, with plenty of saguaros, chollas, ocotillos and lots of wildlife. In a good year, spring rains can bring an abundance of wildflowers and a rainbow of colors, making for good photo opportunities. Except on week-ends, your only competition will be fishermen.

There is good camping right there in the park.

Getting there: The park is located 33 miles north of Wenden and US 60 on a paved road. If you are coming from Phoenix or Kingman, it is also connected to US 93 via a graded dirt road beginning 21 miles northwest of Wickenburg.

Time required: About 1½ to 2 hours, not including the driving time.

Jumping Cholla & Wildflowers (photo by Ron Flickinger)

Painted Rock

The small Painted Rock State Park preserves an interesting array of petroglyphs featured on a couple of small mounds rising no more than 15 feet high in an otherwise flat landscape. The most striking aspect of Painted Rock is the remarkable density of the petroglyphs, which appear as if they've been pecked on every single stone or boulder, regardless of size. On top of the largest mound, a tall rock reminiscent of a Celtic "menhir" is adorned with some geometrical shapes. Note that almost all the rock art is facing south and southeast. This park is a must for people traveling on I-8.

Getting there: The park is located 11 miles north of Exit 102 on I-8, about 13 miles west of Gila Bend. The road is paved and there are signs guiding you to the park.

Time required: About 2 hours, including driving time from I-8.

Painted Rocks

Organ Pipe Cactus National Monument

This remarkable National Monument has a lot going for it. It preserves a large area of dense Sonoran ecosystem—including the rare Organ Pipe Cactus. It's not crowded. It's a gateway to wonderful scenery in Mexico, and it has great camping and good accommodation in nearby Lukeville and Ajo.

The majority of visitors to Organ Pipe Cactus fall into one of two groups: snowbirds in large recreational vehicles and people from Phoenix on a weekend outing. Then there are those passing through, with boats in tow, on their way to Puerto Penásco in Mexico, also known as Rocky Point.

Once you get past the main road you have a rich desert ecosystem practically to yourself. A loop drive and a couple of short roads provide excellent access to the backcountry with ample opportunity for some great photography. All roads are unpaved, but well graded, and are no problem for cars. They are not recommended for recreational vehicles.

There is one caveat. In recent years, the Park has found itself in the middle of the contentious immigration issue due to its geographical location. This complex situation involves illegal immigrants, vigilantes trying to prevent the former from entering the country, drugs runners, and the U.S. Border Patrol. Violent inci-

Sonoran Afternoon on the Ajo Loop

dents have occasionally occurred inside the Monument, placing visitors at risk and forcing the Park Service to close some of the roads until further notice.

As of this writing, the beautiful Puerto Blanco Drive can no longer be driven as a loop, deep inside the most remote section of the Monument. However, the first 5 miles of North Puerto Blanco Drive remain open. The track has been resurfaced and is open in both directions, providing access to the Red Tanks trailhead. This is the starting point for the 16-mile round-trip hike or backpack to the beautiful Senita Basin, an outstanding area of dense Sonoran desert. Here the Sonoran throws just about everything it has at you. There are organ pipes, saguaros, chollas, senitas, ocotillos, even a rare elephant tree—normally found much farther south. If you are not discouraged by the distance, this is probably the best area of the park for hiking and photography. Further up on North Puerto Blanco Drive, a new picnic area has been built at the turn-around point by Pinkley Peak. Regrettably, South Puerto Blanco Drive remains closed as of this writing and there is currently no access to the lush Quitobaquito Oasis area. Hopefully, it will reopen at some point in the future.

The other route, the Ajo Mountain loop, is 21 miles long and follows the foothills of the Ajo Mountains. It is a great drive, especially in late afternoon, with a large number of Organ Pipe Cacti. However, it receives quite a bit of traffic due to the closure of the Puerto Blanco Drive.

If you are still looking for more photo ops after this, hike the 2.5-mile Palo Verde Loop Trail connecting the camping area to the Visitor Center or the short 1.2 mile Desert View Trail.

Don't be put off by the closures. There is still plenty to explore and enjoy in Organ Pipe Cactus Nat'l Monument.

Photo advice: The most outstanding landmarks on the Ajo Mountain loop are Birdseye Point at mile 6.3, Estes Canyon at mile 11 and especially marker #18,

Ocotillo & Senita

which provides a great late-afternoon view of Diaz Spire and the Ajo Mountains basked in a reddish glow with a saguaro forest in the foreground. This is probably the best evening location in the park. Needless to say, sunsets are remarkable and the cacti make great silhouettes.

Getting there: About 135 miles south of Phoenix via US 85 or the same distance west of Tucson via US 86.

Time required: At least 1½ hours for the Ajo Mountain loop. You should stay the night at the campground to fully enjoy both sunrise and sunset.

Nearby locations: There are several interesting areas adjacent to Organ Pipe Cactus Nat'l Monument that merit a special mention. West of Ajo, Cabeza Prieta Nat'l Wildlife Refuge is a personal favorite for outstanding solitude, although it is now becoming well known. The U.S. Air Force occasionally uses the refuge as a gunnery range and it is subject

Ajo Mountain Dusk

The Ajo church on the Plaza

to closure from time to time. North of Cabeza Prieta, part of the Barry Goldwater Air Force Range has now been incorporated into the recently-designated Sonoran Desert Nat'l Monument, which sets aside vast tracts of Sonoran desert.

In Ajo, on US 85, you shouldn't miss the lovely Spanish colonial-style Plaza and its beautiful church, as well as the giant Cornelia open-pit mine. Although it has been closed for many years, the mine can still be observed from a viewing point located right in town. The Tohono O'Odham reservation is nearby.

I highly recommend the drive to Puerto Peñasco (aka Rocky Point), assuming you have your own vehicle, as you are not allowed to take rentals into Mexico. Armed with your Mexican auto insurance, cross the border at Lukeville, just outside Organ Pipe Cactus NM and drive through a remarkable area of huge Saguaro and Cardon cacti that dwarf those you've just seen north of the border. Puerto Peñasco, located on the Sea of Cortez, is less than 2 hours from the border and has a lot to offer. It's easy to spend a couple of days there, enjoying the relaxed pace and great seafood.

About 10 miles before Puerto Peñasco, you can turn right to venture into the unspoiled wilds of Reserva de la Biosfera del Piñacate y Gran Desierto de Altar, home of spectacular calderas and the largest dune field in North America. Given the current border situation, it may not be advisable to visit this area unless your party consists of several people traveling in at least a couple of cars.

Picacho Peak

For eleven months of the year, Picacho Peak State Park is just a pleasant hiking destination for residents of greater Phoenix and Tucson. For one month each year—at least in a year that saw plenty moisture—it becomes a fantastic nature lovers' and photographers' playground when the wildflowers are out in force. Incredibly dense carpeting of richly colored Mexican poppies, beautiful saguaro specimens rising far up on the steep bajada, shining delicately in the sidelight. I have been fortunate enough to stop at Picacho Peak at the height of the wildflower season in one of these good years and I highly recommend that you plan

Opposite page: Saguaro & Poppies

your visit accordingly. Peak time varies from year to year, with mid-March is usually a safe bet. You can follow the bloom's progress almost in real time on the web for many Southwest locations (*see www.desertusa.com/wildflo/wildupdates. html*). Unfortunately, there is a price to pay. The State Park is located just 45 minutes from downtown Tucson. It is mobbed during wildflower season, to the point where finding parking space can be a challenge. This shouldn't deter you from going. There are superb shots waiting.

Cactus Garden

Two trails leave from the main car park area: The 1.4-mile round-trip Calloway Trail follows the base of the bajada to an overlook and the 4-mile round-trip Hunter Trail climbs to the top of the peak—a seemingly impossible feat when seen from Tucson. Actually, it is not so bad, but occasionally you need to use steel cables on some very steep slopes.

Photo advice: You won't have to go far to find a good angle. Just walk up one of the trails. A mild warming filter works well to bring up the orange in the poppies. It gives pleasant warmth to the saguaros. This is both super wide-angle and telephoto territory. You'll want the wide-angle to create great depth-of-field and bring up the poppies as close as possible to the lens. Telephoto shots compressing the perspective on the slope create fantastic color palettes. This is an excellent place for macro-photography. The best time to catch the wildflowers well lit and fully open is around mid-morning.

Getting there: About 40 miles northwest of Tucson, just off I-10 (Exit 219).

Time required: One hour is sufficient for photography near the entrance station. More time is required if you come for wildflowers. It takes 3 hours round-trip to hike to the top (1,400 feet elevation gain) and to linger a bit.

Nearby location: Ironwood Forest National Monument (just south of Picacho Peak) and Sonoran Desert National Monument (west of Casa Grande township) are two recently-created National Monuments dedicated to preserving ancient Hohokam ruins, rock art, and artifacts as well as a variety of plants and animal species (such as bighorn sheep). These parks have no specific landmarks. They offer remarkable opportunities for solitude in the Sonoran environment. ✿

Reaching for the Sky

Chapter 10

SOUTHEAST ARIZONA

Roadsign Saguaro

SOUTHEAST ARIZONA

Saguaro National Park – Tucson Mountain District

Saguaro National Park has the distinction of being the closest national park to a major center. Tucson, Arizona is a growing city which separates the park into two distinct districts: Tucson Mountain is on the west side of town and Rincon Mountain is on the east side. Together, they preserve a vast tract of the spectacular Sonoran desert ecosystem.

"Saguaro West", which you can access at no charge, is the most developed of the two districts and it gets the most visitors.

Coming from Tucson over Gates Pass and just before the park boundary is the superb Arizona-Sonora Desert Museum. It is best seen on week days to avoid crowds. Continuing west on Kinney Road for about 0.2 mile, just before passing McCain Loop Rd, you'll see a pullout on the left. This is a good place to stop and walk around for good pictures of the dense Sonoran flora. Your next stop should be at the Red Hill Visitor Center (particularly rich in maps and publications of all sorts), before going on to the Bajada Loop Drive, the most popular attraction of the park. This 6-mile graded dirt road will take you through a remarkable concentration of Saguaro cacti. The road is a bit dusty if it hasn't rained for a while and it's best to get out of the car as much as possible. Your first stop on the Bajada Loop should be at the Valley View Trail. The 0.8-mile round-trip hike takes you through a saguaro forest to a sweeping panorama embracing the area known as the Basin and Range Province. It is named for the Tucson Mountains jutting up abruptly from the valley floor. To the south, you can easily identify incisor-shaped Baboquivari, sacred mountain of the Tohono O'Odham tribe. Turning around, you see Picacho Peak and the Silverbell Mountains and a bit further

Signal Hill petroglyph

you can distinguish the white domes of Kitt Peak observatory. Your next stop will be at the Signal Hill picnic area, where you can take a break, watch the birds and listen to the silence. This is without a doubt an area highly conductive to relaxation. Once refreshed, climb up the short trail to see some interesting Hohokam petroglyphs. At the very top, do what tens of thousands of other folks do. Photograph the interesting circle petroglyph with strands of saguaros and the mountains in the background. Be sure to check your depth-of-field.

After finishing this auto tour, you may want to stretch your legs and enjoy a closer view of the Sonoran Desert. The nicest hike in the Western District is the popular King Canyon Trail. This trail usually has excellent bloom and wild-flowers during springtime. Although the trailhead's car-park is unmarked, it is fairly obvious, just a hundred yards to the west of the Arizona-Sonora Desert Museum. From here a short 0.9 mile on an old Jeep road brings you to an intersection leading to the Mam-A-Gah picnic shelter to the left. Continue straight ahead on the King Canyon Trail and you'll lose more than half of the crowd. From then on, the trail becomes more interesting with plenty of typical Sonoran vegetation.

Ready for a fight (photo by Philippe Schuler)

About 1.3 miles from the picnic area, you'll reach the junction of the Sweetwater and Norris trails. You can either retrace your steps from here as there is plenty to photograph on the King Canyon Trail; or, if you're looking for a more challenging

hike, you can do a loop using the Norris and the Sendero Esperanza trails to return to the Mam-A-Gah picnic spot. The entire loop from the picnic spot, including the short side trip to Wasson Peak, is about 6 miles on a good trail. The section leading to Wasson and Amole Peak gains 600 feet in a short 0.5 mile. To return to your car from Mam-A-Gah, hike inside the sandy wash instead of the Jeep trail. There are a few easily bypassed dryfalls and it is more interesting than hiking on the Jeep trail.

Gates Pass at sunset

Photo advice: The Bajada Loop Drive is wonderful in late afternoon or early evening when the warm sun lights up the ocher mountains and provides wonderful texture to the cacti. Perhaps the most striking view of sweeping saguaro forests in the park area is from Gates Pass. Pull off at the vista point, mount a long telephoto and shoot strands of Saguaros with side lighting or against the light. You can also photograph Chollas with a wide angle lens. Gates Pass is best at sunset.

Getting there: From Tucson, leave I-10 at exit 257, take Speedway Blvd then Gates Pass Road, which is really spectacular and the way I recommend. From I-19 (Exit 99), take Ajo Way (US 86) and Kinney Rd, passing Old Tucson on the way. It's also possible to come from the north, leaving I-10 at exit 246 or 248.

Saguaro National Park – Rincon Mountain District

The Rincon Mountain district of Saguaro Nat'l Park, east of Tucson, preserves a large tract of the Rincon Mountains and offers many possibilities to explore and seek solitude on foot or horseback. There is one striking characteristic to this sector: It is very rugged and feels very isolated—much more so than its western counterpart. Yet, you are very close to the city and, at least on the loop road, you almost never lose sight of housing tracts. "Saguaro East" is my favorite sector of the park and I strongly recommend it to photographers, who will find few crowds and a more intimate kind of landscape. If you can devote at least half a day to this inspirational area, you'll come out with beautiful images of the Sonoran desert flora and avian fauna. All you have to do is drive very slowly along the paved 8-mile Cactus Forest Drive and stop at the first sight that catches your imagination. There are numerous pullouts so it's never a problem to stop at a whim. You can walk anywhere you want. In fact, you are constantly enticed into walking farther and farther as your eyes rest on interesting compositions or some abstract details. If you're visiting with a partner or family, this is one place where you'll find real use for those little portable radios that have been languishing in the car. Do not miss cruising both side roads. Mica View leads to a very riparian area, where you can lose yourself—figuratively—for hours. Javelina is another superb example of dense Sonoran deserts with an amazing variety of vegetation. At Javelina, do not miss the 1-mile Freeman Homestead Loop Trail. Follow it counter-clockwise. Halfway through the walk, the trail follows a little wash and bends slightly toward the parking lot. Look to your left and you'll see a monumental cactus with numerous branches.

Photo advice: For more intimate photography of the desert, I recommend saving your film and creative juices for the Rincon district. Be there in springtime when the wildflowers are out in force and the ocotillos are blooming. You'll want to spend the night in Tucson and come back early the next morning for more photographs. Even better, be there during or after a rain. Unless it's a downpour, don a raincoat and walk around the desert for an unforgettable experience of amazing light and fantastically rich colors. In the field, always be very cautious around chollas (aka Teddy Bear cactus). They are actually intelligent creatures whose mission in life consists in jumping on you and planting their little barbs deep inside your skin. Once they've done so, it will take days to extract those nasty little aliens from your sensitive human skin.

Cactus garden

Getting there: From downtown Tucson via East Broadway Blvd and the Old Spanish Trail. From I-10 (Exit 275) via Houghton Road and the Old Spanish Trail. Count on a good 45 minutes from downtown.

Nearby locations: On the northeastern outskirts of Tucson, Sabino Canyon Recreation Area offers a very similar experience to "Saguaro East" in a more concentrated setting.

Kartchner Caverns State Park is on AZ 90, 8 miles south of I-10 near Benson. You need to reserve weeks in advance, as there is a quota of 50 persons a day and it's almost always full. A few first-come first-serve tickets are available every day; but, people stand in line at 6 in the morning to get them. No photography is allowed.

The Spanish Missions

Saguaro & Mission San Xavier del Bac

Although out of this book's primary goal of document-ing natural landmarks, the Spanish Missions of Southern Arizona integrate very well into the landscape and photo-graph so nicely that it would be sad not to mention them here.

There are two very beautiful and popular Spanish Missions in Southern Arizona: San Xavier del Bac and San José de Tumacácori. Both are defi-nitely worth stopping by, even for a brief visit.

Mission San Xavier del Bac is gorgeous inside and out, with its colorful murals and wonderfully ornate facade. The white structure is easily outlined against the deep blue sky for a classic photograph, if you can avoid people in front of the church. The Mission is still undergoing restoration at the time of this writing and the facade is now partially cov-ered with scaffoldings, pre-venting the classic shot of the adorned entrance. Work on the Mission is expected to be finished in 2008. The Mission is located close to Exit 92 on I-19, 6 miles south of I-10, and is well indicated.

Tumacácori Nat'l Historical Park preserves the oldest mis-sion in Arizona. It is a much

Tumacácori

simpler architecture than San Xavier del Bac and the beautiful structure seduces with its simple lines and unadorned decoration. Avoid week-ends as it is a prime location for weddings and receptions. The Mission is located 45 miles south of Tucson on I-19, Exit 29.

Nearby location: The lovely little town of Patagonia, south of Sonoita and 20 miles northeast of Nogales on AZ 82, is absolutely charming although most buildings appear shut down on its large Main Street. It is a major center for birding, with many preserves in the surrounding area.

Chiricahua National Monument

For most people, the word Chiricahua evokes Cochise and Geronimo. Few people have actually seen the region which the famous Apache chieftains used as their stronghold to launch raids against Anglo settlers, U.S. cavalry and Mexican farmers. Even fewer know where Chiricahua Nat'l Monument is located. This small park receives very little visitation because of its location outside of the classic tourist routes. However, it preserves a remarkable and truly unique landscape and I strongly encourage you to visit it, especially if you're coming from Tucson and are on your way to the Gila Wilderness or the White Sands in New Mexico (*see Volume 3 – Colorado & New Mexico*).

The Apaches first called this section of the Chiricahua Mountains "Land of the Standing-up Rocks". Later on, white settlers called it "Wonderland of Rocks", due

On the Echo Trail

to the awesome display of thousands of huge pinnacles, spires, columns, stone towers and balanced rocks that populate the park. Interestingly, these spectacular rock formations are quite reminiscent of Bryce Canyon in their shape and size, although they lack the glorious colors of Utah's sandstone, as the stone is of volcanic origin (rhyolite) and is mostly gray or green (due to a lichen layer partially covering it). On top of its remarkable geological features—the result of constant punishing erosion—Chiricahua NM offers a surprising variety of vegetation comprising cacti, plants native to neighboring Mexico and forests at higher elevation. It has a lot of wildlife, including javelina, ocelots and mountain lions; but, you're more likely to encounter raccoons.

The best time to visit the park is in spring, when many birds, including some rare species, frequent the region. Winters can be brutal in the Chiricahuas, which reach 9,000 feet in the monument. Snowfalls require occasional closures. Summer brings frequent afternoon thunderstorms that require exercising caution on the trails.

An 8-mile long winding scenic drive, called Bonita Canyon Drive, climbs to the eastern border of the monument at Massai Point. On the way, you pass some beautiful formations, the most interesting being the Organ Pipe. It's a cliff eroded into a multitude of impressive stone pillars. This gives you a pretty good idea of what awaits you on the monument's extensive trail system.

Looking down from Massai Point

About 0.5 mile before Massai Point, you'll find the trailhead for the Echo Canyon Loop at the beginning of a side road. It is a very rewarding 3.5-mile round-trip trail that you should not miss. The trail is relatively easy and can be hiked leisurely in about two hours. Going counterclockwise, Echo Canyon Trail winds its way down through many photogenic stone formations before reaching the lovely wooded area of Echo Park. As you hike down, you'll be hard-pressed not to draw comparisons with the Navajo/Queen's Garden loop in Bryce Canyon. Although the environment and color are very different, both trails have many aspects in common. After intersecting the Rhyolite Trail, the trail makes a sharp turn to the east and follows a high path above the canyon, offering splendid open views on the hoodoos and stone columns across the canyon. A telephoto will work best to capture these views. Return to your car via the Ed Riggs Trail, which goes up gently to the north in the forest.

At the end of the scenic drive, the short Massai Point Trail offers spectacular panoramic views of the park and its rocks, the Sulphur Springs valley and surrounding mountains. There is a very nice balanced rock near the trail, close to the observation point. Take the short trail climbing to the orientation table for great views. Looking east, you'll see the Head of Cochise, a small mountain forming a surprisingly suggestive profile of a reclining Native American.

For a more in-depth view of the park and to capture more interesting rocks and panoramas that the monument has to offer, combine the Echo Canyon Loop and Heart of Rocks Loop. The entire loop is about 8.5 miles long. However, it is more strenuous than the mileage would lead you to think. You'll be constantly walking up and down and you'll be on the trail for a minimum of five to six hours. It guarantees your heart and legs a complete workout. If you choose to do this loop, do it clockwise, finishing with Echo Canyon in the afternoon. Start via the Mushroom Rock and Big Balanced Rock trails. Along the way, take the short 1-mile round-trip spur—incorrectly labeled as "0.5-mile roundtrip" on the sign—leading to Inspiration Point. This is a great spot to photograph the vast expanse of the monument. At the end of the Big Balanced Rock Trail, you'll reach the aptly-named Heart of Rocks Loop, which passes by some of the weirdest rocks in the park. They are Duck on a Rock, Kissing Rocks, Punch and Judy, Pinnacle Balanced Rock and many other unnamed, but equally as suggestive, formations. Continue on the Sarah Deming Trail to reach the Rhyolite Trail leading up-canyon to rejoin the Echo Canyon Loop which leads to your car.

Photo advice: Most of the rock formations are on the west flank of the Chiricahuas and are in shadow for a good part of the morning. You'll do most of your photography from mid-afternoon to early-evening, shooting north and south from open areas on the trails as well as from the viewpoints. You'll find it challenging to bring out Chiricahua's beauty on film. The spires are so tightly packed that they can appear without much depth. At close range, they generate a lot of shadows on each other, which makes them hard to photograph from the trails. Some of the best photos I've seen include groups of people dwarfed by the formations. Green trees come to the rescue, helping the eye get a feel for the great height of the spires. You'll need good side light and a low angle to bring out depth; but, this also carries a negative effect: The high contrast, which works so well on red sandstone, is not kind to the Chiricahua formations due to their pale color. A warming filter will add some punch to the rocks and enhance the green lichen.

Overall, you'll find it easier to photograph from the Massai and Inspiration viewpoints. Shoot slightly downward to capture the vast expanse of the formations with a wide-angle lens or extract small patches with a medium telephoto. In any case, you should finish the day at Massai Point at least a half hour before sunset.

Getting there: From I-10, get off at Willcox and follow AZ 186 for 32 miles though gorgeous grassland scenery before turning east to reach the park in an additional 3 miles.

Time required: Half a day, or a full day if you hike the Heart of Rocks Loop.

Balanced Rock

Cochise Head (photo by Philippe Schuler)

Nearby locations: In dry weather and with a high clearance vehicle, you can take Pinery Canyon Road. It is a narrow and winding dirt road, beginning at the park entrance station and taking you eastward across the Chiricahua Mountains to Cave Creek Canyon near El Portal. The drive takes about 1¼ hour. This deep and pristine canyon displays some interesting cliffs and is a great sanctuary for bird life. It's a good camping spot if you are on your way to White Sands.

Tombstone, the most famous Wild West town in Arizona, is well worth visiting, especially its graveyard located north of town. Tombstone is 24 miles south of Benson on AZ 80.

The old mining town of Bisbee is 23 miles south of Tombstone and 25 miles west of Douglas. Bisbee has tremendous character. If you can, spend the night in one of the lovely turn of the century B&Bs. ✿

Petrified Trees

Chapter 11

AROUND INTERSTATE 40

Sunset Crater aerial (photo by Thomas Wiewandt)

AROUND INTERSTATE 40

Sunset Crater

Just north of Flagstaff and I-40, I highly recommend the 36-mile detour from US 89 through Sunset Crater and nearby Wupatki National Monuments, provided the light is right when you're there.

You get your first good view of Sunset Crater right after you enter the park. A large pullout with plenty of parking space provides an open view toward the crater to the east and the San Francisco peaks to the west. The adjoining meadow can be a delight from mid-spring to late summer, when wildflowers and tallgrass make a great foreground for distant shots of the crater. In the late afternoon sun, the darker shape of the cinder cone creates a remarkable hue. You can get interesting images from this spot with anything from a wide-angle to a telephoto.

The road traverses lava beds between the Visitor Center and the Lava Flow Nature Trail. Although there are shorter alternatives, the 1-mile loop trail is well worth taking in its entirety. All along the trail, there are numerous opportunities to photograph the crater, as well as flowers and pine trees on a stark background of lava and cinder. You can also hike the short Lenox Trail for a closer, more level view of Sunset Crater, and to experience climbing a cinder cone. The drive to O'Leary Peak is now closed, requiring a strenuous 7-mile round-trip hike to gain a distant view of the Sunset Crater caldera from the top of the lava dome.

Photo advice: A medium wide-angle will work great to photograph the cinder cone and the lava flow in the foreground. Some of the best views of the crater can be obtained from the very beginning of the Lava Flow trail. The view from Observation Point is good, but not very open. You'd do better by getting closer to the cone.

Sunset Crater from the Nature Trail

Getting there: From I-40 just east of Flagstaff, take Exit 201 to US 89. Follow it north for 13 miles and turn right at the Sunset Crater sign. Continuing past Sunset Crater will bring you to Wupatki NM before eventually rejoining US 89.

Wupatki

In Wupatki National Monument, the remains of several dwellings built with very colorful stone dot the landscape. Excellent interpretive trails make the visit a worthy experience, doing a great job of preserving and providing a glimpse into the Sinagua culture. The Sinagua way of life (lit. *without water*), which consisted of a vast farming community spread east and south of the San Antonio peaks, was at its prime in the 1100s. The Sinagua grew crops in this harsh environment, with very little water and arable land. It is likely that they lived in constant fear of Sunset Crater, which was active at the time. The Sinagua finally gave it up around 1250 after Sunset Crater exploded one last time. They relocated to the east, and became part of the Hopi, Zuni and Pueblo Indians.

Located at the end of a short side road, Wukoki Pueblo is a spectacular structure, built on top of a promontory and overlooking a wash. There are far fewer visitors here than at Wupatki Pueblo. As a result, it is easier to photograph without human presence. There are some really good close-up shots of the ruins from the inside of the structure, using a wide-angle lens. I find that the most interesting views are from the wash behind the building.

There are quite a few structures still standing at the Wupatki Pueblo complex and the surroundings are very nice. Due to the close proximity of the Visitor Center, however, you'll find a lot of people on the trail around the ruins. This makes photography difficult, unless you're willing to be patient and wait until

Wukoki Pueblo

people move out of your field of vision. So take your time, move around and look for interesting angles. Walk down to the community room and the ball court, where you'll find far fewer people as well as interesting compositions.

A couple of miles beyond Wupatki Pueblo, stop at the Doney Mountain parking area. Walk a few minutes toward the small butte to your left, until you reach a viewpoint with a great panoramic view of the area.

Wupatki sunrise

Lomaki is the least visited group of ruins in the monument. While not particularly spectacular, it makes for a pleasant visit due to the lack of crowds. From a rocky outcrop, to the right of the structure as you come down the trail, there is an excellent view of the main standing wall towering above the wash.

Nearby, the Box Canyon dwellings have little left of their original walls. There are good open views toward the San Francisco Peaks.

From the car park along the road, it's a short walk to the top of the Citadel Pueblo and it's well worth it. If you happen to have good light and an interesting sky at the time of your visit, you'll be able to photograph an impressive wall with great color in late afternoon. The views to the west and the San Francisco Peaks are truly spectacular.

Time required: Allow half a day for the Sunset Crater/Wupatki loop, to stop at most of the exhibits, walk on the trails and take pictures without feeling rushed. If you can't spare at least 3 hours of your time, don't even bother.

Walnut Canyon

Walnut Canyon is a sad example of the massive pillaging of ancient pueblo dwellings that took place at the end of the 19th century. The purpose of the monument is now simply to preserve what's left of this extended Sinagua settlement. The site, occupied between 1125 and 1250, is now very bare. There isn't a single shard of pottery to be seen and not one wall fully standing on any of its structures. Still, there is plenty of beauty to be found in this lovely canyon.

Walnut Canyon

After a short walk on the Rim Trail, don't miss the Island Trail which encircles the mesa and is very pleasant. In this densely wooded area, views of the canyon are pretty, with dwellings peppered on just about every limestone cliff. You'll get a great workout going down and back up the 240 stairs to the museum. The trail closes at 5 PM in summer and 4 PM the rest of the year. It can occasionally be closed by snow in winter. For fewer crowds and more dwellings, sign-up for the ranger-guided ledge walk, usually scheduled Wednesday and Sunday at 10 AM.

Photo advice: The wider the angle is, the better to photograph dwellings on the Island Trail. A 28mm is barely adequate. A medium to long telephoto (135mm to 200mm) works best on the Rim Trail.

Getting there: Just 9 miles east of Flagstaff on I-40 (Exit 204), then 3 miles on the park road to the Visitor Center.

Time required: About 2 hours to visit the museum and walk both trails, stopping at every ruin or viewpoint.

Grand Falls

The Grand Falls of the Little Colorado River are a remarkable site... under the right circumstances. Unfortunately, the spectacle of the raging muddy falls only occurs for a few days during the year, either during spring snowmelt (March and April) or after a period of intense monsoon rainstorms (usually from mid July to mid September). The rest of the time, the Little Colorado River is reduced to a trickle of water. Nevertheless, it is surprising that this site is not better known, as it is a spectacular geological phenomenon in its own right. It is an amazing sight when at its best. The falls were created when a flow of lava altered the normal course of the Little Colorado, following an eruption from nearby Rodan Mountain. The river formed a new bed on top of the plateau before cascading 185 feet—higher than Niagara Falls—over the sheer cliffs to resume its natural path inside the gorge. The whole area is strewn with cinder cones.

Although Grand Falls is a Navajo Tribal Park, there isn't a single sign announcing its presence and you will have a hard time finding it without these directions. The only sign of the park is the presence of four small shelters, conveniently built along the rim, which allow you to view and photograph the falls comfortably during rainstorms.

Grand Falls (photo by Isabel Synnatschke)

If you are travelling through the Flagstaff area during the monsoon, chances are you will encounter a few days of heavy rains. This would be the perfect time to go to Grand Falls. There is one caveat. The rains that make the falls what they are can also create havoc on the dirt road leading to them. There is a possibility of getting mired in the mud, unless you have the right vehicle with adequate tires.

As of this writing, you are not required to obtain a backcountry permit from Navajo Parks & Recreation (*see Appendix*) to visit Grand Falls. However, this could change in the future. You should verify this in person by calling the Cameron Visitor Center (*see Appendix*) prior to your trip. The area is day use only.

Getting there: from I-40, take exit 207 to Cosnino or exit 211 to Winona, of Route 66 fame, then turn onto Navajo Road 15 and follow it for 13 miles toward Leupp. You then have two choices. First, you can turn left on Road 70 and follow it for 8 miles to the intersection with Navajo Road 6910. Then drive another mile and turn left on a rough unmarked road leading in another 0.5 mile to the Grand Falls overlook. If you should miss the rough road, which is easy to do, you'll soon come to the Little Colorado crossing, from where you can see the shelters to your left and get your bearings. Some sections of Road 70 are very sandy and rocky. A better alternative is to leave Road 70 to your left and continue about 7 miles to Road 6910, located a couple of miles within the Navajo Reservation. Take the latter until you reach the intersection with Road 70 about 1.5 miles before Grand Falls overlook. There is a "Grand Falls Bible Church" sign that makes road 6910 easy to find. This road is much better maintained, as it is used by the school bus taking kids to school in Leupp.

The Little Painted Desert

If you are passing through on I-40 and have a little bit of time or if you leave it on your way to the three mesas of the Hopi Reservation, try devoting an hour or so in late afternoon to this little-known Navajo Tribal Park. The small park contains superb formations of Chinle badlands, remnants of an ancient sea bed carved by wind and rain. The badlands are just as spectacular as those in the northern part of Petrified Forest Nat'l Park, perhaps even more varied in color during the golden hour. One big advantage is that they are much closer and easier to photograph. Also, unlike Petrified Forest, you can stay as long as you want in the evening to photograph the badlands and watch the sunset over the San Francisco Peaks. You can photograph the Little Painted Desert from the overlook; or, you can walk on the dirt road following the rim which is usually closed to driving. There is no official hiking trail down into the badlands, but it's relatively easy to get down there and walk around to your heart's content.

Photo advice: The Little Painted Desert is an excellent late afternoon location. The badlands are facing west and are in shadow until mid-morning. By that time the light is too intense and the delicate hues are lost.

Getting there: From I-40, take Exit 257 and drive 13 miles north of Winslow on AZ 87.

Time required: 1 hour for some nice late-PM shots.

Nearby locations: Homolovi State Park, north of the intersection of I-40 and AZ 87, preserves some interesting ruins and has an excellent campground.

Going west toward Flagstaff on I-40 is Meteor Crater at Exit 233. It's a mildly interesting attraction, best suited for aerial photography. A super wide-angle is a must.

Little Painted Desert

Coal Mine Canyon (Honooji)

This little-known gem lies 16 miles southeast of Tuba City on AZ 264, close to the edge of the Hopi reservation. Consisting mostly of whitish Mancos shale and yellow and pink sandstone, with a thin stripe of black coal near the top, Coal Mine Canyon is a striking jumble of hoodoos and pastel-colored badlands. It's a Bryce of a different color and could be called a proving ground for forces of erosion.

There are good views from the rim. An unofficial path goes down into the canyon from the northeast corner of the picnic area. It's extremely steep and slippery at first and doesn't yield particularly great views from the bottom. Access to the canyon is closed as of this writing.

You can also explore Ha Ho No Geh canyon—meaning "too many washes"—which is a bit farther. Not knowing whether the access dirt road was on private land, I asked a Navajo family who confirmed that it was on public land. This road deteriorates badly as it approaches the canyon rim. It leads to spectacular vistas on both sides. It would be impassable after a rain because of the steep grade. I couldn't find an easy way to descend into the canyon from this area. There is plenty to photograph from the rim.

Coal Mine Canyon

Photo advice: Early to mid-morning and late afternoon are the best times to photograph the canyon; otherwise, the subdued pastel colors of the spires tend to be washed out. If you photograph during the day, overexpose by half a stop to prevent the white shale from turning grayish.

Getting there: This is the hard part. There are absolutely no signs. To reach Coal Mine Canyon, drive 16 miles from Tuba City on AZ 264 and take a dirt road to the left, close to mile marker 337, leading toward a windmill. Drive a little over 0.5 mile, crossing the flat and arid Moenkopi plateau, and go around the windmill. You'll soon come to the edge of the canyon and the picnic area, northeast of the windmill. The turnoff for Ha Ho No Geh canyon is also on the left, 2 miles further on AZ 264. The most interesting part is located between 2 and 3 miles from the turnoff.

Time required: About 1 hour per canyon.

The Hopi Mesas

It would be sad to write about the Southwest and not say a word about the interesting Hopi villages located on First, Second and Third Mesa along AZ 264. However, the Hopi tribe strongly prohibits any sketching, videotaping or photography on its land and I can't give any advice in that respect. Instead, I suggest that you leave the camera in the bag and just enjoy Hopiland and its wonderful culture. The three mesas form the southern end of Black Mesa. They are awesome promontories, jutting out of the plateau and towering 600 feet over the Painted Desert below.

A number of Hopi villages are perched on top of the three mesas. Some are truly outstanding and warrant a visit. Some areas are off-limits. On Third Mesa, you should stop and look around Old Oraibi. Although it doesn't have the spectacular setting of some other villages, it has a couple of interesting galleries where you can see the famous Kachina dolls and beautifully crafted jewelry. You can wander around Old Oraibi on your own and look around all you want; but, please no photos. Old Oraibi is said to have been settled around 1150 AD and claims to be the oldest continually-occupied community in the United States—a claim that is challenged by Shungopavi on Second Mesa. Although Shungopavi was moved to the mesa top in the late 17th century, it has a particular aura as the most traditional of all the villages, keeper of Hopi traditions. The community is very active in basket making and weaving and holds many dancing ceremonies that are open to the public. Shungopavi's location at the tip of Second Mesa is striking. Second Mesa is to Hopiland what Cape Royal is to the North Rim of Grand Canyon. Standing at the tip of the promontory and looking down at the immensity of the Painted Desert is a humbling experience.

Eight miles farther east, as the crow flies—but about twelve miles by car—is First Mesa and the extraordinary village of Walpi, the crown jewel of Hopiland. With a location equally as commanding as Shungopavi, Walpi adds a remarkable architectural style to the setting with its multi-floored dwellings, partially reconstructed in the traditional Hopi way. Walpi is a great sunset location. Although you won't be able to take photographs, you should still make it a point to stop and visit. Walpi is off-limits without a guide. Walking tours depart very frequently as soon as there is a small group. Inquire at the Hopi Cultural Center on AZ 264 near Second Mesa or at the First Mesa Consolidated Villages Tourist Office on the mesa top. By all means sign up for this extraordinary walk (*see On the Go Resources in Appendix*).

If this brief description of the Hopi villages enticed you into going, get yourself a copy of Robert Casey's *Journey to the High Southwest*. This book has excellent background information on Hopi culture and very detailed descriptions of the various villages.

Getting there: You'll find the Hopi Mesas along AZ 264 about 60 miles southeast of Tuba City, or about 60 miles north of I-40 via AZ 87.

Petrified Forest National Park

Petrified Forest Nat'l Park preserves the largest concentration of petrified wood in North America, perhaps in the world. What sets it apart from other petrified wood sites is its scenic surroundings of badlands, which provide an otherworldly feeling to the experience. The petrified logs and badlands you come across in the park are remnants of an ancient forest interspersed with marshy lands, once located in the tropics at the approximate latitude of current Panama. Millions of years of continental drift have moved the landmass upward to its current location, bringing us this extraordinary landscape.

I generally prefer entering the park from the south, making my way up and finishing either at Blue Mesa or at the Painted Desert for sunset. If you do so, your first stop is at Giant Logs, just behind the Rainbow Forest Museum. There are some truly spectacular logs here. It's probably the best location in the park for colorful close-ups of petrified wood. The paved trail and crowds make it very difficult to photograph the logs, however.

One of my favorite walks is nearby Long Logs because it is much less crowded and it has a nice background of badlands that look downright prehistoric and provide an excellent backdrop for your compositions. The unpaved trail takes you right to the base of these badlands and large pieces of petrified wood are strewn along the way. It's an excellent location for early and late photography. Don't miss the short detour to partially reconstructed Agate House. It yields a nice picture by framing the structure tightly and packing in a lot of texture and color on the petrified rock. If you are at the south entrance of the park at opening time, I recommend you start at Long Logs and visit Giant Logs later.

Crystal Forest is very flat and people are constantly visible on the trail. It is not conductive to good wide-angle photography, so concentrate on close-ups of the logs instead.

The Long Logs Trail

Jasper Forest is a good morning location, but by then you'll be eager to go to Blue Mesa, the crown jewel of the park. The Blue Mesa Trail winds through a spectacular landscape of eroded and colorful badlands. This one-mile loop trail is superlative. As it goes deep down into the badlands, there are large areas in the shade in early morning and evening. Generally speaking, the best time to photograph Blue Mesa is in late afternoon—and if you are lucky enough, after a summer storm. That's when you'll get the best-possible color on the logs and the formations. There is a spectacular shot of chunks of petrified tree trunks cascading down a ravine on the west side of the trail. This photographs better in early to mid-morning. You can also wait until the slices are entirely in shadow in late afternoon.

The Teepees are perfectly suited to the panoramic format and you can get a great shot in mid to late afternoon right from the pull-out with a normal lens to a very short telephoto.

The trail leading to the base of Newspaper Rock is now permanently closed and the two panels must be viewed from a platform, requiring at least a 400mm. The NPS has installed a couple of telescopes to view the rock art. The Puerco Blanco ruins are not particularly rewarding in terms of photography, except for some interesting petroglyphs. Time constraints will probably chase you toward the north entrance to catch good late afternoon light on the Painted Desert.

Puerco Blanco petroglyph

The first three viewpoints in the Painted Desert section offer close views of the badlands to the northwest. In my opinion, they offer more interesting compositions than the other viewpoints with their wide-expanse vistas of the characteristic red-colored badlands. They are all exclusively late afternoon photography. Furthermore, Chinle Point offers the most sweeping vista of the Painted Desert to the north, but the view is quite distant. The last three viewpoints offer good views to the northeast at both sunrise and sunset with a short telephoto.

A vast tract of the Painted Desert inside the park is designated as the Black Forest Wilderness Area. The wilderness gets its name from the dark color of its petrified wood, which is quite different from the petrified wood to the south.

Of the thousands of visitors passing through the park, only a tiny fraction ever visit this wilderness, which is only accessible on foot or with pack animals from the car park at Kachina Point. Day trips to the area do not require a permit and you are free to wander anywhere you want in search of interesting clusters of petrified wood to see and photograph. Overnight or longer trips do require a permit. This permit is free and is the best way to photograph the Painted Desert at sunrise or sunset. Most day hikers who venture in the Painted Desert do so in search of Onyx Bridge, an interesting petrified trunk spanning the course of a shallow wash. A few years back, the bridge broke apart at one edge. The section spanning the wash is still intact as of this writing; but, the Park Service expects it to collapse in the near future. For now, it has been reinforced with petrified wood on one side.

Onyx Bridge

It is said that many visitors do not find the bridge. I myself did not find it on my first visit there. The main reason, I suspect, is that the spot marked as Onyx Bridge on the 7.5' USGS map is either incorrect or there once was a bridge here and it has collapsed. Regardless, the real Onyx Bridge is still there and is located at 35°06'31" 109°47'32", about 0.2 mile from the incorrect spot. Locating the bridge is not too difficult thanks to a very precise little map that you may request at the Visitor Center.

This map will assist you in finding the bridge once you are in the general vicinity. It is essential that you also rely on the 7.5' USGS map to get there, as the area is vast and everything tends to look the same. The trail down from Kachina Point disappears shortly after you hit the bottom of the plateau and after a few cairns you are entirely on your own. Count on about 2 to 2½ hours round-trip just to see Onyx Bridge. The bridge itself is more of a curiosity than anything else; but, there are petroglyphs along the way and the immediate surroundings are well worth exploring. To the north of it is a flat plateau with an enormous amount of black petrified wood. To the northwest, there are three very interesting badlands hills and to the west and southwest there is a good concentration of nicely colored petrified trunks.

To see more of the Black Forest, you can follow Lithodendron Wash and explore some of its side canyons. There is petrified wood just about everywhere to the north and west side of the wash. I have found a good concentration of wood and collapsed bridges about 3.8 miles north of the car park. For an over-nighter, Rangers recommend the area to the southwest of the Painted Desert, which they call the Little Devil's Garden. This area of the Park has hoodoos and a greater variety of colorful badlands than what is visible from the viewpoints.

Be sure to take plenty of water when you explore the Black Forest Wilderness. There is an endless quantity of beautiful petrified wood to see and photograph and you will most likely be tempted to go farther than you originally thought.

Photo advice: Photographing in the early morning is a pleasant experience, with no crowds around; but, the light isn't as good on the Painted Desert. In all circumstances, you should begin your visit at the south entrance and finish at the Painted Desert.

Photographing in the park during the golden hour is made very difficult by the fact that it is only open during daytime. In the evening, it requires that you be quick and mobile. It isn't kind to the view camera photographer. Even with 35mm, you will feel rushed and careless with your last minute compositions.

In winter, the park opens at 8 AM and closes at 5 PM. The shorter the days the better, in order to get good morning light and sunset on the Painted Desert. The fact that Arizona doesn't observe Daylight Savings Time somewhat alleviates the problem. If you travel in early spring, try to time your visit to coincide with the switch to the 6 PM closing time, which usually occurs on the second Sunday of March. This maximizes your chances of good light. Summer hours are 7 AM to 7 PM. Closing time means that the gates close at the entrance stations and cars are no longer allowed to enter. The official rule is that you should be in your vehicle and driving out at closing time. You have one hour after closing time to make your way to the other end of the park without stopping. In practice, the rangers are tolerant of photographers trying to capture the last rays of the sun from the Painted Desert viewpoints, as these are only a couple of minutes away from the north exit. Although you are unlikely to be ticketed, you should cooperate and be on your way immediately and with a smile. The southern stops close earlier to cars so rangers won't have to chase you on the trail.

Blue Mesa Sunset

Blue Mesa Badlands

A late winter storm or summer thunder showers will go a long way to add drama to this surreal, somewhat flat landscape, as well as to bring out color in the petrified logs.

If you are unhappy with the crowds in the park and want to photograph more badlands without having to worry about opening and closing times, check out the Little Painted Desert County Park (*see section above*). The views are spectacular and the badlands extremely colorful.

Getting there: The park is located about 4 hours northeast of Phoenix, 1 1/2 hours east of Flagstaff and approximately 1 hour from Window Rock or Gallup. The north entrance is right on I-40 (Exit 311), allowing direct access to the Painted Desert. Holbrook has a number of good and amazingly cheap motels and is only 18 miles from the south entrance on US 180. If you come from Phoenix you'll be hard pressed to choose between two superlative roads, either through Payson and Heber or Globe and Showlow. Both are outstanding in their own way.

Time required: The average visitor spends two hours in the park. I recommend that you spend at least an afternoon and the early part of the next morning photographing the park. It will require that you spend the night in Holbrook or at one of the campgrounds located just outside the south entrance. If you don't have that much time, concentrate on late afternoon and early evening, when the light is best. Add a full day if you want to visit the Black Forest Wilderness.

Nearby locations: If you are spending the night in Holbrook and are not returning to Petrified Forest the next morning, consider visiting the Old West Museum, located next to the Chamber of Commerce inside the Historic Navajo County Courthouse at the northeast corner of East Arizona Street and Navajo Boulevard. This free museum—staffed by volunteers eager to help—has interesting displays depicting the life of the local inhabitants over the past two centuries. You'll also visit the former jail.

Driving east on I-40 past Holbrook and near Joseph City is Rock Art Ranch, a private property containing a large number of petroglyphs in Chevelon Canyon. They arrange visits for groups only by prior reservation (*see Appendix*). ✿

Spider Rock

Chapter 12

CANYON DE CHELLY

Spider Rock under a fresh dusting of snow (photo by Alain Briot)

CANYON DE CHELLY

Introduction

This superb National Monument—pronounced "Canyon de Shay"—really warrants the detour to this remote area of the Navajo Reservation. If you decide to go, it's probably because your eyes have been irresistibly drawn to a superb picture of Spider Rock shot from the rim more than 1000 feet above the floor or to the famous scene of the White House nestled beneath a striated, gilded wall of desert varnish. They're classics! I have my own story about it. About thirty years ago I dreamed of one day visiting Canyon de Chelly after seeing it in the film "McKenna's Gold" in a movie theater in New Delhi, India.

Canyon de Chelly is actually two canyons. They are de Chelly itself, which is the south fork and Canyon del Muerto (Spanish for "Canyon of the Dead"), the north fork. Each canyon is bordered by a rim drive with a number of overlooks. Most people find the south fork more interesting when seen and photographed from the rim, due for a large part to its famous Spider Rock overlook.

Despite the fact that the monument is under NPS jurisdiction, about 40 Navajo families still graze their sheep and livestock at the bottom of the canyons and inhabit them part of the year. Therefore, entering the canyons on your own is not allowed and requires that you join an organized tour or hire a private accredited guide. There is one exception: It is possible to walk down into the canyon on the trail leading to the White House ruins, located on the south fork. However, you can't go any further.

Photo advice: All the south fork locations are best photographed from the rim in mid- to late-afternoon. Except for Mummy Cave, the north fork locations (Canyon del Muerto) are better in the morning. All the ruins and rock art make for exceptional shots from the canyon floor. Be aware that it's much easier to take photographs with a private guide than when accompanied by a large group of people. Taking into consideration that you can see most south fork locations quite well from the rim, that you can hike down to White House, and that the most impressive rock art is located inside the north fork, a private trip concentrating on Canyon del Muerto is more rewarding.

Time required: Plan on spending at least an afternoon there. A day and a half to two days would be better for taking a guided tour inside the canyon and because so many of the locations call for the afternoon sun. You can't be everywhere at the same time. You should definitely hike down into the canyon to White House Ruins—a 2 to 3 hour project. Although this can be done at any time of the day, the ruins photograph best in late afternoon. Note that there are only three (expensive) motels close by—which must be reserved in advance most of the time—and one rather basic campground (free) near the monument's entrance.

Getting there: Canyon de Chelly is located just east of Chinle on US 191. Although there are many roads lead-
ing to Canyon de Chelly, none are as interesting as the two roads coming from the east over the Chuska Mountains. NM 134 over Narbona Pass (formerly Washington Pass) and Crystal is spectacular. N 13, aka Red Valley Road, over Lukachukai Pass is now paved, but it is rarely maintained in winter. Inquire about road conditions at the Chapter House or by asking locals before venturing on this road. There is a nice picnic spot in the ponderosas at the crest, with a view of Shiprock (*see Volume 3*).

Antelope House ruins

Canyon de Chelly (South Rim Road)

The south rim road offers several open views from the rim and you'll catch your first glimpse into the canyon at the Tsegi Overlook. At Tsegi, the canyon is still shallow and you can clearly see the arms beginning to rise toward the east. Junction Overlook lets you see the confluence of the south and north forks and has some minor ruins visible right before the junction.

One of the highlights of any photographic trip to Canyon de Chelly is the classic view of the White House ruins. The White House Overlook provides a lovely view into the canyon, with the ruins tucked in under a massive cliff streaked with desert varnish. During springtime and autumn, when the cottonwoods are in bloom or turning, it is absolutely gorgeous. From the rim, a 200mm will work best to capture this scene perfectly in late afternoon.

The trail leading to White House zigzags from the overlook for about a mile along the flank of the canyon. It is not difficult. After a descent of about 400 feet, you find yourself in the canyon where a short walk brings you to the footbridge over the river and on to the ruins. During summer the river is very shallow, while it is often frozen in winter. The hike to the ruins is superb and it would be a shame to miss it, especially in view of the fact that it is the only one allowed inside the canyon. The best time to photograph White House is mid to late afternoon, when the canyon is basked in a warm light and the cliff above the ruins reveals striking detail. Early in the morning, the light is simply too crude for good results and the curve of the canyon to the east of the ruins may block the sun.

Desert Varnish

The Sliding House Overlook offers a good view of its namesake ruins as well as an open view into the canyon on both sides. Soon, you'll want to be on your way to the Spider Rock Overlook to catch the view of the monumental Spider Rock that rises 832 feet into the sky like a gigantic antenna to the heavens. You'll need a wide-angle lens to fit the entire spire and its surroundings in your image, although there are also excellent compositions with a normal lens and telephoto. Photographers will want to be there in late afternoon to capture the best light on the spire. Don't come too late, however, or the bottom will be in deep shadow. The view is striking enough to spend an hour at the viewpoint, playing with the light using various focal lengths.

Canyon del Muerto (North Rim Road)

The north fork of the river follows Canyon del Muerto and doesn't leave the same memorable impression than its southern counterpart, seen from the rim. To fully appreciate Canyon del Muerto, you will need to take a guided tour into the canyon or drive your own 4WD with an accredited Navajo guide.

If you do not have the time or inclination to do so, you can, nonetheless, take the rim road until Antelope House or Mummy Cave Overlook. The first stop along the road is at the Ledge Ruin Overlook and is a bit of a letdown. Things get much better at Antelope House Overlook. Not much remains of Antelope House, and seen from above, it's a bit disappointing. You'll be hard-pressed to notice, let alone photograph, the paintings after which it is named. However, the view of Navajo Fortress is stunning: A 21 to 24mm is necessary to catch the entire rock and the two canyon arms around it. Photographically, you'll have better luck concentrating on the Mummy Cave Ruin—a striking structure perched high on a promontory mid-way down the cliff. This is a great afternoon shot, which you'll catch from the Mummy Cave Overlook with a long telephoto. Massacre Cave deserves a stop and a thought for the people whom Spanish soldiers exterminated so ruthlessly.

Mummy House ruins

The Inner Canyon

A regular guided tour of the canyon is a rewarding experience. Half-day and full-day tours are available and stop at the main sites in both canyons. The most popular tours, which leave from the Thunderbird Lodge, are given in large 4WD trucks—some dating back from the Korean war—with open-air seats rigged to a high platform in the back. Bring sunscreen and a hat as you'll be baking in the sun, notwithstanding breathing in a fair amount of dust on windy days. The tours are very informative and well worth the cost. The half-day tour usually takes you as far as Antelope House Ruins in Canyon del Muerto and White House Ruins in Canyon de Chelly. The full-day tours go as far as Mummy Cave—where they usually stop for lunch—and to the base of Spider Rock. This may vary depending on weather and track condition. There are also shorter tours going only to the White House ruins.

A privately guided tour with an accredited Navajo guide in your own 4WD vehicle is an excellent alternative, especially if you are interested in Ancient

Narbona Expedition panel

Puebloan ruins and rock art. This solution offers more flexibility with the itinerary and timing. It allows you to focus on sites that are of particular interest to you or that are not visited by group tours. For a party of three, the cost of a private guide in your own SUV for a full-day tour is lower than the group tour (but the latter includes lunch). Guides are assigned on a first come-first serve basis at the Visitor Center. If you do not have a 4WD vehicle or don't feel comfortable driving in the sand, some guides are licensed to take you in their own vehicle for an additional fee. Visiting the canyon with a private accredited guide does not grant you any additional privileges. It does, however, facilitate obtaining permission from landowners and the Park Service to enter private property and observe rock art at close range. Such arrangements should be made at the Visitor Center before you leave by calling the landowners on the phone. Permission may or may not be granted and sometimes a donation may be required. If you are lucky enough to meet the landowners while in the canyon, you may also ask permission on the spot. All the guides are or were residents of the canyons at one time and most have some kind of family connection with one another. However, it is important to understand that the Navajos are very private and have great respect for each other's private property. They are therefore somewhat reluctant to ask permission on behalf of visitors due to their respect for the privacy of other families.

If you are lucky enough to get permission to enter private land, this is still no panacea. Park regulations stipulate that you may not go past cultivated land and climb on to the rock art panels and ruins. Bring a pair of binoculars to spot the distant ruins and rock art panels and a long telephoto zoom lens, at least 300mm and preferably 400mm, to photograph them.

With your guide, you enter the canyon just opposite the road leading to the campground and Thunderbird Lodge. The first couple of miles inside the canyon are in the very broad Chinle Wash whose condition varies greatly, ranging from extremely dry, with very deep sand, to flooded after heavy rains. The Park Superintendant and head guides jointly decide when it is safe to allow visitors inside the canyon.

Opposite page: The White House Ruins

Riders panel at Blue Bull

Canyon del Muerto begins at Junction Rock, which the Navajos call Dog Rock. You've most likely seen this junction from the overlook on the south rim road. Canyon del Muerto tends to see less traffic than Canyon de Chelly.

The main landmarks in Canyon del Muerto are the Ledge Ruins, Antelope House Ruins, The Navajo Fortress, Ceremonial Cave, the Standing Cow and Blue Bull sites, and, of course, Mummy Cave. The Standing Cow site has large white paintings depicting Spanish riders from the Narbona punitive expedition. Unfortunately, the panel is on a high ledge and impossible to photograph without prior permission from both the National Park Service and the Navajo landowners. Even in this case, a 300mm telephoto is necessary. The Blue Bull site has arguably the finest Navajo paintings in Canyon del Muerto—especially very nice horses and riders—and is easy to visit and photograph.

Back at Junction Rock, you'll turn southeast into Canyon de Chelly, where the wash is less pronounced and the 4WD road generally better. The main destinations are the ubiquitous White House Ruins (*see South Rim Road section*), Cave Ruins, Sliding Rock Ruins, the Window and Spider Rock. The latter is less spectacular seen from its base than from the rim overlook. The steep trail to the Window brings you to a spectacular arch with a great view of the canyon inside its span. This scene is best seen and photographed from a nearby alcove reached via moki steps and some scrambling on a short but steep slickrock slope. This requires a modicum of agility and caution when going up and down. A 24 to 28mm is necessary to capture the scene.

The Window

AROUND CANYON DE CHELLY

Hope Arch

Hope Arch is a little beauty of an arch, with a 65-foot span, located a few miles to the northwest of Chinle. To get there, reset your odometer at the Canyon de Chelly turnoff on US 191 and drive north for 2.3 miles, turning left on the dirt road and taking the right road at the Y. Continue on this road for almost 6 miles until you reach the power line. Be sure not to stray off the main track and onto private property. The road is very washboardy for the most part. It becomes wide and well graded toward

Heart of Stone

the end as it merges with a wider graded dirt road coming from Chinle (but harder to find in town). Leave the main road and take the track to the right following the power line. The arch comes into view to the northwest of the power line. You have the option to park here and walk 1 mile round-trip to the arch or you can locate a small dirt track leading closer to its base.

The arch photographs well and has great color at sunrise from the east side, where it forms the shape of a heart. A mid- to late-afternoon shot is also possible from the west side. When you're done photographing the arch, you can walk or drive to the tall, ubiquitous pinnacle rising to the southwest of the arch, with a butte looking like a fort in the background.

Return to Chinle using the wider graded dirt road skirting the rim of Ventana Mesa, keeping to the right at the bottom of the descent.

The Sentinel & The Fort

The Lukachukai Mountains

Sandstone Castle

The Lukachukai Mountains are a small range, to the northwest of the larger Chuska Mountains which separate the San Juan basin to the east from the Black Mesa basin to the west. It is a great area for photography with its colorful rocks all around. It requires that you respect the privacy of Navajo families living in the area and refrain from intruding on private land without permission. Basically, all land located on the sides of dirt road is private land, even if it isn't fenced.

Coming from Canyon de Chelly via Many Farms on US 191, you'll pass an area of badlands from which emerges a gigantic butte similar to those in Monument Valley. This is Round Rock. Continuing north on US 191 past the junction with N 12, look for some interesting spires on the northwestern side of Round Rock Butte.

A deep foray into the mountains can be done from the little community of Round Rock, by taking the good dirt road leaving to the east from the trading post on US 191, at the junction with N 12. After fording Lukachukai Creek, the road (IR 172) leads toward the spectacular Los Gigantes Buttes, consisting mostly of deep red Wingate sandstone. You reach good views of the buttes after about 7.5 miles. The highly photogenic buttes can easily be photographed from IR 172 or from a side road heading west just before reaching them. It's a good sunset location. Farther along IR 172, the road deteriorates as it serves small farms. There are great vistas of tall Wingate sandstone cliffs to the right and Los Gigantes looking back, as well as small sand dunes making good

The Dancing Rocks (photo by Alain Briot)

foregrounds. You can stop and photograph as much as you like from the road; but, you shouldn't walk in the area without first obtaining permission from the land owners and you must be willing to brave the dogs guarding their flocks of sheep. You can continue on that road for about 5 miles past the Los Gigantes Buttes, passing many alcoves and windows on the left side, until you reach private property.

Back on US 191, drive north toward the Rock Point Chapter House for more good views of this mini-Monument Valley. After about 12 miles, look to your right for two intriguing formations called the Dancing Rocks. Another excellent view of these formations can be had by driving a short distance on N 8009 at a sign marking the Circle Dee Ranch. You can park your car and walk to the top of a small hill to look back toward the Dancing Rocks.

Window Rock (Tseghahoodzani)

Window Rock, known to the Navajo as Tseghahoodzani (Rock pierced by a hole) is a most engaging Navajo town, set at the foot of spectacular cliffs. It is a great place to visit and pay homage to the Navajo Nation, which has its capital here.

A visit to the wonderful Navajo Museum is a must to further your understanding of Dineh society. One major benefit of a visit to the Museum is that you'll find very knowledgeable people willing to answer candid questions about every aspect of Navajo life on the "Big Rez". Government, chapters, clans, marriage, family life, religious practice, property ownership, and other topics of interest that are normally a bit awkward to ask ordinary citizens.

I always find the view of the great arch of Window Rock peaceful and inspiring in late afternoon, when things get quiet and the arch is basked in warm light. A large slab of Entrada sandstone broke off from the arch in 1997; but, this didn't leave a scar affecting its beauty. The arch is located just behind the grounds of the Navajo Nation's administration compound and is easily seen from the main Window Rock crossing. There are excellent views of the arch from the rotunda with a 35mm to 85mm depending on how much surroundings you want to include in your image.

The Great Arch at Window Rock

There are some spectacular sandstone formations located to the north of the arch, east of N 12. You can get close by driving past the high school parking lot and walking to the base of the cliff. Excellent shots of the southern cliffs can be had easily by parking near the main intersection of town on the road to Gallup and walking toward the cliffs.

Getting there: Window Rock is located 30 minutes northwest of Gallup on the excellent 4-lane AZ 264 and about 1 hour southeast of Canyon de Chelly via US 191 and AZ 264.

Time required: About 2 hours, including a visit to the Museum.

Nearby location: Hubbel Trading Post National Historic Site is located 30 miles west of Gallup on AZ 264, on a side road just past Ganado. It makes a good stop when coming from the west on AZ 264, on the way from the Hopi mesas to Canyon de Chelly. Hubbel is the oldest continuously operating trading post on the Navajo Nation. Despite the modern amenities and the presence of park rangers, it succeeds at conveying an old days atmosphere with its authentic counter tops, its sundry goods displayed like in the old days, a variety of Navajo crafts, including artists-at-work weaving carpets, and a nice little museum. Count on about 1 hour for the visit. ✿

Monument Valley from Hunt's Mesa

Chapter 13

MONUMENT VALLEY

Valley view from Artist Point

MONUMENT VALLEY

Introduction

Monument Valley—or Tse' Bii' Ndzisgaii as the Navajos call it—is the symbol par excellence of the American Southwest. Used hundreds of times as a backdrop for films and video clips, and seen in innumerable TV and magazines ads, Monument Valley has become a kind of "transitory object" of humanity's collective psyche. Its subliminal imagery invokes a powerful associative reflex. The world intuitively knows that such a landscape only exists in the American West. A simple image, a profile on the horizon, is enough to make us dream of great spaces, individual freedom, infinite possibilities, and escape from the daily grind of our lives. Even its audacious name "Monument Valley"—who would think of calling a piece of the planet such a name—somehow conjures up a mystical world of gigantic proportions. In any case, whether it's dreams or products, Monument Valley delivers.

A visit to Monument Valley shouldn't disappoint you. You'll get your money's worth for the dream that made you come here in the first place. Arriving for the first time at Monument Valley, everything is here just as you envisioned it: The hundreds of miles to get there, the long rectilinear ribbon of road glimmering in the heat waves miles ahead and the fantastic monoliths profiled on the horizon. But it's no longer just a vision... You are now living the dream.

Having said this, I feel a responsibility to inform my readers of a few recent negative aspects. Many of us who have come to Monument Valley for several decades feel somewhat disenfranchised by the steady flux of restrictions and increased commercial exploitation. As much as I respect the stewardship of the land by the Navajo Nation, I am dismayed by the exploitation of this marvelous natural site, which is definitely world heritage material. I'm taking as an example the increasing presence of sales booths at several viewpoints on the Scenic Drive. They sell jewelry and questionable trinkets—sometimes with a radio playing in the background. I'm also saddened by the posting at viewpoints of young children in traditional garb, to extract a few dollars from visitors. Mostly, I deeply resent the restrictions on free visitation and the concerted effort to push people to see the site from "cattle carts". With the exception of summer, the limited hours of the Scenic Drive are not adequate to enjoy the best light for viewing and photography. This has gone on for years and I think it is contrary to the spirit of the place—a grand icon of human spirit and freedom, if there is one. In other words, the dream is slowly being broken.

But enough complaining, let's start our visit of wonderful Monument Valley.

The Scenic Drive

Our visit of the Monument Valley Navajo Tribal Park begins at the Visitor Center where your gaze embraces a scene of extraordinary beauty over the valley and the landmark buttes of West Mitten, East Mitten and Merrick. Protected by a hard top layer, the soft de Chelly sandstone buttes look like they've been cut with a sharp knife, down to the friable Organ Shale forming the base. This geologic combination gives the buttes their characteristic stair-step effect.

To get the most out of Monument Valley, and bring back quality photos, you have to spend a bit of time and descend by car into the valley. A 17-mile self-drive circuit will lead you into the middle of the monuments, passing by some extremely photogenic spots along the way. The Scenic Drive is a bit rough on the descent. It becomes much easier later on despite a few sandy patches here and there. Except after a rain, it presents no challenge to passenger cars or even campers. Don't hesitate.

If you do the Scenic Drive circuit on your own, you may feel that you are missing out since signs at each crossing remind you that driving off the self-guided

Totem Pole & Yei-Bi-Chei (photo by Charles Wood)

tour road is not allowed. At each stop, you'll see signs reminding you that walking around is prohibited. This is very discouraging since you'll really want to get closer to the formations (in particular to the Totem Pole, which is quite far from the viewpoint). The self-guided Scenic Drive opens at 7 AM in summer—May to September—(8 AM in the other months). It closes at 8:30 PM in summer (4:30 PM during the other months). In some months, you'll be forced to enter after sunrise and get out before sunset.

One of the most complete ways to visit the valley is to make two forays inside the park. The first in late afternoon with a guided group tour and the second early in the morning in your own vehicle on the self-drive circuit.

Visits with your own vehicle, accompanied by a private Navajo guide, are no longer authorized as of this writing. If you want to see more than what the self-drive has to offer, your only option is to join a group tour. Despite the severe limitations this imposes on photographers, it still offers several benefits. It allows you to penetrate further inside the valley, go around Thunderbird Mesa—the mesa just south of Rain God Mesa—visit the Totem Pole and Dunes area, and see several geologic features. Some guided tours offer to take you behind Mitten and Merrick buttes, allowing you to vary the angles and lighting effects. Others offer you a visit to a hogan—the traditional Navajo home built of wood and topped with clay—where you can meet Navajos in traditional costume working at their weaving looms. With guided tours, the only way to stop whenever and wherever you want is if there are enough of you to form your own group.

One dismaying consequence of the new restrictive policy is that you can no longer visit the valley before and after the official opening and closing time of the scenic drive. This policy also applies to group tours. This greatly reduces the possibilities of photographing under good light.

Early the next morning, familiar now with the circuit road and the layout of the place, you can take your time to return and photograph the valley in your own vehicle, albeit staying on the very limited drivable circuit.

Photo advice: There is plenty to photograph in Monument Valley. Happily, the beginning of the morning and the second part of the afternoon are both interesting. However, the end of the afternoon is always preferred since colors are very warm and pleasant. A blue sky with thick white clouds will let you get good results most of the day. If the sky is cloudless, you'll get really good photos only at sunrise and sunset. In Monument Valley, perspectives are varied and you'll be constantly changing focal lengths. A zoom lens will prove extremely useful.

From the Visitor Center, a very wide angle lens (28mm minimum, 24mm preferred) is necessary to photograph the three buttes. A short telephoto can isolate each butte and, at sunset, eliminate the shadow zone produced by the vast mesa on which you are standing. Between the Visitor Center and the gate to the scenic drive, you'll notice two round boulders with vertical striations. They make an excellent foreground for a photo of the Mittens. This photo has long become cliché, but it is truly a lovely perspective. Don't feel bashful and add it to your collection—you won't be the only one doing so anyway. The ideal time to photograph from the Visitor Center is in the evening as the setting sun embraces the buttes, especially with a stormy sky and a few sun rays on the buttes. You can also get great back-lit shots of the buttes profiled against a blue and red-charged sky by coming back just before dawn.

On the scenic drive, the loop made by the road around the Rain God Mesa will let you adapt to the lighting conditions. You can photograph just as well in the morning as in the second part of the afternoon. After leaving the Visitor Center, the road descends in switchbacks to the valley below. It's possible to get some lovely shots of the buttes from a wide opening located at one of the bends in the road, or from the dunes situated at the bottom of the descent.

A bit further, John Ford's Point offers an excellent view of the Three Sisters group. You can capture it with a short telephoto lens, preferably in the morning since you would be shooting against the light in the afternoon. In the afternoon, shoot the wonderful classic view of Merrick Butte and the Mittens.

In the morning, you can get a very nice photo of the Hub with a long tele-photo lens that will compress the area between the Navajo hogans situated in front of the Hub with Wetherill Mesa in the background.

The scenic turnoffs of Totem Pole and Sand Springs lead to two remarkable, albeit distant, views of the Totem Pole and Yei-bi-chei. A 135 to 200mm lens is necessary to photograph them, preferably in the warm light of afternoon. The Sand Springs viewpoint offers the best angle to photograph the Totem.

If you are with a guided tour, you will be driven close to the Totem and

Red Skies Tonight...approaching from Mexican Hat

Yei-bi-chei, so they can be photographed with the dunes in the foreground. This is otherwise impossible from the scenic turnoffs of Totem Pole and Sand Springs where the dunes are almost invisible. If possible, ask your guide to drop you off at the bottom of the dunes and climb on. You'll get the best ripple effect on the pink keystone sand in the early morning and the Totem Pole will have a nice side light from the left. The dunes are lovely in late afternoon. However, to photograph the Totem Pole, you'll have the sun right behind you and this will completely flatten any detail in the sand. Instead, climb a bit on the dunes and point your lens toward one of the Mittens for great ripple effect on the sand and beautiful light on the butte.

Further ahead, be sure not to miss Artist's Point for a fantastic panorama of the valley using either a wide-angle or a telephoto lens. It's particularly spectacular in early to mid-morning. Between Artist's Point and North Window, you have a very nice perspective over the Three Sisters. It is very different from what you saw at John Ford's Point earlier. The stop at North Windows offers a superb view of the Mittens that you can frame in the "window" that opens in front of you.

When you visit the Tribal Park, please remember that it is forbidden to photograph the resident Navajos without their permission.

Getting there: Coming from Page or Tuba City via US 160, take US 163 in Kayenta for about 24 miles. From Moab or Blanding on US 191, turn onto US 163 right after Bluff and continue for 41 miles, passing by Mexican Hat. The latter road becomes absolutely awesome as you approach Monument Valley, offering great sunrise or early morning shots on a good day. Leaving US 163, a 4-mile long paved road takes you to the Visitor Center, where concessionaires take turns offering organized tours of the park.

Time required: Allow 1-1/2 to 2 hours to tour the scenic drive on you own, plus a 1/2 hour at the Visitor Center to take in the awesome panorama; more if you want to enjoy sunset. Plan on the afternoon as well as the next morning to add a tour and to shoot under different light. For this you can spend the night at the Mitten View Campground (next to the Visitor Center), in a motel in Kayenta or Mexican Hat, or at the historic but expensive Goulding's Trading Post, just a short distance from the park and with a distant view of it. Mexican Hat has affordable lodging, cheaper than in Kayenta, and you'll benefit from the spectacular approach from the east at sunrise. If you're there during spring or summer, bear in mind that the Navajo Nation follows Mountain Daylight Savings Time, which is not the case for the rest of Arizona.

Tear Drop Arch

This little jewel is somewhat ignored by the guided tours due to its location outside the Tribal Park. Access is from the dirt road continuing to the west behind Goulding's Trading post. However, you have to cross private land to get there and you must do so with a Navajo guide. There are pockets of deep sand on the track so 4WD is required. You might as well use your guide's own vehicle.

Photo advice: Plan on being there about 45 minutes before sunset and be sure you have a short zoom lens. A 70 to 100mm focal length will allow you to bring up the buttes through the arch. Shorter focal lengths will work well to frame the arch but will make the buttes appear very distant. To shoot the actual Monument Valley skyline in the background, you'll need a high spot and your guide will need to provide some kind of ladder. You should make these arrangements beforehand.

Close to sunset, the distant buttes will appear glowing red. Meter on the sky through the arch or spot meter on the buttes and let the framing arch go black. Take a few more shots, and open up to get more detail from the arch. You'll be able to choose later what's most pleasing to you. Better yet, if you shoot with a tripod and cable release (as you should), take one shot exposing

Tear Drop Arch sunset

for the rock frame and one shot exposing for the distant butte. Later, you can merge both images in a graphic application using a mask, to produce a perfectly well exposed image throughout.

Time required: Altogether, count on about 1½ hours from Goulding's.

Mystery Valley

Want to see Monument Valley away from the crowds? Have an interest in arches, cliff dwellings and pictographs? Then Mystery Valley is for you. However, it is located inside the Tribal Park and there is no self-guided drive, just very rough roads that require 4WD and an accredited Navajo guide. Simply select a guided tour at the Visitor Center, at Goulding's or in Kayenta and go for it. If you choose to go on a private tour—a much nicer alternative for photography—I suggest that you go for at least 4 hours in order to go deep into the valley. Although less spectacular than the views from the Valley Drive, there are superb vistas from a variety of vantage points and some of the Ancient Puebloan dwellings are very well preserved.

Some outfitters also offer combination tours of Mystery Valley and a hike to the top of Wetherill Mesa in one day.

Hunt's Mesa

No visit of Monument Valley is complete without contemplating the view from its most spectacular vantage point: Hunt's Mesa. The Mesa towers 1200 feet over the valley floor and has many good vantage points where you can place your tripod and capture awesome views of the valley. Considering the complex logistics and cost of going to Hunt's Mesa, it is best to spend the night there, camping under the stars. Plan on being there in late afternoon for the best light. An early afternoon departure is best. The next morning, be sure to get up well before sunrise to catch glorious hues in the eastern sky. Overall afternoon and sunset is better than sunrise from Hunt's Mesa, unless you're blessed with some partial morning fog lingering between the monoliths. Go during the autumn season. Summers are great for big monsoon clouds; but, camping on the mesa is hazardous because of potential thunderstorms. Autumn has the best angle of the sun to light up the mesa and the probability of having good weather is high.

Photo advice: For an afternoon and evening shoot, ask your guide to take you to the ridge where the B-52 crashed. This is by far the best view in late afternoon. The view from the tip of the ridge is awesome, offering great depth and no foreground clutter. Sun's Eye, Thunderbird Mesa, Rain God Mesa and the rest of the Valley all seem to be in perfect alignment in your viewfinder. A wide-angle lens works best from this spot. For a morning shoot, drive to the easternmost viewpoint and walk to the end of the promontory. Wide-angle and short telephoto lenses work well from this spot. Again, the foreground is uncluttered and you'll catch some well-lit monoliths just after sunrise. The main camping spot on Hunt's Mesa, located close to the end of the foot trail, is well protected from

Hunt's Mesa sunset

the wind. It is not a very good location for photography.

Even with a wide angle, you'll be hard-pressed to capture the incredible panorama of Hunt's Mesa. A 6x17 cm panoramic camera will do wonders here. If you're not amongst the lucky few who own one, consider taking several images covering a very wide angle—using the same manual exposure—and patching them later in your digital darkroom.

Getting there: There are two ways to go. You may walk up or charter a 4WD. In both cases, you'll need to be accompanied by a Navajo guide. If you walk up, you'll be coming from the Valley. If you go by 4WD, you'll be coming up from Kayenta. The hike up takes about 2 hours. It is not particularly difficult. There is a tricky passage near the top involving the use of a ladder and requiring that you do not have any fear of heights. There is one disadvantage to hiking up. It limits the photographic equipment you can take, given that you'll already be carrying your tent, sleeping bag/pad, food and water. Meals can be pre-arranged with your outfitter, but they charge quite a bit more money for this service. If you don't mind roughing it a bit on a diet of gorp, jerky and granola for breakfast, you'll do just as well and will save yourself some money. The better—albeit more expensive—way to get to the mesa is by 4WD. You simply charter a Jeep or Suburban with a driver/guide for the day or for a 24-hour period. The road is very sandy in the middle section and becomes very rough near the top. This kind of trip usually includes all the equipment and food. You can take all your photo equipment on the mesa and concentrate on your photography. This is the way to go if you are serious about photographing Monument Valley. For a list of outfitters, see *On the Go Resources* in *Appendix*.

AROUND MONUMENT VALLEY

Agathla Peak

The awesome sight of "El Capitan"

Just southwest of the Monument Valley Tribal Park, on US 163 about 8 miles from Kayenta, you'll encounter a gigantic conical monolith on the east side of the highway. This is Agathla Peak (which can be translated as "Much Wool"), better known as El Capitan. In geological terms, Agathla Peak is a diatreme, or volcanic plug, created by a powerful gaseous explosion. The mass of El Capitan makes a sensational photograph. Capture it with a telephoto lens from about a mile away on either side of US 163, depending on the time of day and angle of the sun.

On the opposite side of the road is Owl Rock, a mildly interesting rock outcrop, dwarfed by the proximity of its giant neighbor. Resist the urge to "document", you'll be disappointed. Instead, spend the time scouting different angles for Agathla Peak.

Church Rock

Church Rock

About 8 miles East of Kayenta on US 160 is a very interesting perspective shot encompassing Church Rock in the foreground, the edge of the Comb Ridge in the middle and Agathla Peak in the background. Drive slowly until you reach the optimum point, on top of a ridge, where you can line up the monoliths while filling up the frame. A medium telephoto works best for this shot. You can also photograph Church Rock by itself. It's one of the most fractured volcanic plugs you'll ever see. I find it highly reminiscent of the weird architectural work of Antonio Gaudi—although I doubt surveyors had Gaudi's seminal work "The Sagrada Familia" in mind when they named it.

About 6.5 miles further to the right of US 160 is an interesting group of sandstone spires called Baby Rocks. Myriads of small pinnacles reach for the sky in a tightly packed formation. It's almost guaranteed to pull you out of your car for a few snapshots. I have yet to see a decent photo taken there.

Navajo National Monument — Betatakin

Navajo National Monument protects some outstanding Ancestral Puebloan ruins, tucked under overhanging sandstone cliffs in a beautiful setting of pastel-colored canyons. The two main pueblos, Betatakin and Keet Seel, are exceptionally well preserved. I will examine them separately, beginning with the more readily accessible Betatakin.

You have two alternatives to see and photograph Betatakin, which means "ledge house". You can either observe it from afar, from a scenic viewpoint close to the Visitor Center; or you can see it at close range on a semi-arduous ranger-led tour.

From the Visitor Center, the 1-mile round-trip Sandal Trail affords a spectacular, though distant, view of the alcove under which the Betatakin "town"—as archaeologists call it—is located. Any time of the year is fine to photograph the ruins from this overlook. In winter, the rangers try hard to keep the Sandal Trail open at all times. Still, it may remain closed for extended periods of time when the snow level is too high.

From the Sandal Trail, you can also take the steep 0.8-mile round-trip Aspen Forest Overlook Trail leading to a nice overlook from which you're looking down at a surviving ancient forest nested at the bottom of the canyon. The ruins are not visible from this overlook.

To get a better feel for Betatakin, you'll need to take a ranger-led walk leaving every morning from the Visitor Center year-round. The guided walks depart at 9 AM and 11 AM from Memorial Day to Labor Day and at 10 AM the rest of the year. Call the Visitor Center to confirm as it may change from year to year. There are 25 permits per day available on a first come, first serve basis. Be there

Betatakin, seen from the Sandal Trail

early, as crowds are rather unpredictable. One day the quota may be full and the next day you may only have a few companions. Occasionally, there may not be enough Rangers on hand to lead both tours. Camping in the park makes it easier to secure a spot. Watch for cold nights (you are after all at 7500 feet). If you prefer moteling, the nearby Anasazi Inn is only about 15 miles and 25 minutes away under dry conditions.

The 5-mile round-trip hike is quite exposed and strenuous. Bring your sunscreen and plenty of water. Rock fall from the roof of the alcove almost killed some tourists in 1999. This forced the NPS to put most of the town off limits, but you can still come fairly close to the dwellings. The hike is delightful and the mostly Navajo guides are a good source of information on Dineh culture. Betatakin offers a remarkable introduction to visiting unaltered Ancient Puebloan dwellings in the Southwest.

Photo advice: A 50 to 70mm lens is perfect to capture the entire sweep of the ruins and the arch from the Sandal Trail viewpoint. A 100mm lens will let you frame the alcove nicely and a 300mm would be necessary to bring some of the dwellings closer. The ruins lie at the bottom of a deep canyon and you'll have to wait until mid-morning to have any sun. The alcove is actually never completely lit. In the early morning, it is entirely in the shade, and this will yield a decent shot if you have a tripod and can eliminate any direct light in the frame. A 3-stop graduated neutral density filter will be necessary to keep the shadow in check on the right side of your frame. There is good light radiating from the left in mid-afternoon. Don't wait too long because the main ruins with the best relief are located to the left in the bend of the arch and they'll be in shadow later in the day. At the town proper, a wide-angle lens will take care of most compositions.

Getting there: About 19 miles southwest of Kayenta on US 160, at Black Mesa take the 9 mile long AZ 564 leading to the Navajo National Monument. About half way, there is a pull out offering a nice view of Tsegi Canyon.

Time required: 1-1/2 to 2 hours, including the short walks to the Betatakin viewpoint on the Sandal Trail and the Aspen Forest Overlook. Going to Betatakin on the ranger-led tour takes about 4 to 5 hours.

Navajo National Monument — Keet Seel

The National Park Service is under tremendous pressure from diverse interest groups to restrict access to Keet Seel. The Hopi resent the fact that their ancestors' dwellings are paraded to the public. The Navajo are wary of visitors getting lost on their land or scaring their cattle. Archaeologists fear the effects of foot traffic—notwithstanding the disappearance of artifacts. The Park Service lawyers live in fear of multi-million dollar lawsuits when a slab of slickrock eventually comes loose from the alcove and flattens a group of visitors. All these fears and grievances have their own merit. All in all, the Park Service has a most sensible policy: A restricted window of opportunity, a small quota of permits and a thorough pre-hike orientation.

Twenty permits are available each day to dayhikers and overnight campers for the 17-mile round-trip self-guided hike to Keet Seel, from Memorial Day to Labor Day. Outside of this period, dayhikers can also hike to the ruins twice a week, accompanied by a Park Ranger if one is available (check with the Visitor Center, *see Appendix*). In all cases, you'll receive an extremely thorough orientation at the Visitor Center. During the regular season, you hike on your own and upon reaching Keet Seel, you sign in with a backcountry Ranger who leads an interpretive tour of the dwellings. The Ranger usually limits groups to five persons and you may have to wait for your turn. The town is reached via a tall wooden ladder anchored to the cliff face at a steep angle.

So is it all worth it? The answer is a resounding yes: Keet Seel, which means "remains of square houses", is a truly awesome experience. There is a palpable sense of presence and history that no other archaeological site of the Southwest can match, and that includes Betatakin. Walking inside the almost intact pueblo is a humbling experience. It is so well preserved that you feel its inhabitants have just wandered out and will reappear round the bend any minute. Even some of the original roofs are still in place. It is a great privilege to visit Keet Seel and the memories you will bring back will be with you forever.

Photo advice: There is one important detail you should know before you sign up for Keet Seel: No tripods are allowed in the town itself. You'll have to work handheld, which drastically limits what camera format you can take. Cameras or lenses equipped with gyro-stabilizers will be a plus and so will a very wide angle lens. You have plenty of time to take pictures. Even if the quota of twenty visitors is full, you can count on about 1 hour inside the town.

Getting there: The first step is to obtain a permit, which is required for both day hiking and overnight backpacking, with a limit of twenty hikers per day (organized groups are limited to ten hikers per day). Permits are available free of charge by calling or writing to the Visitor Center (see Appendix) several months prior to your visit. Call to confirm seven days before arrival or your reservation may be canceled. If you do not have a reservation, you may call up to six days prior to the day you wish to hike and even the same day if you arrive before 8:00 AM. Permits from cancellations are given on a first-come, first-served basis.

Although not particularly challenging, except for the long ascent at the end of the return trip (shared with Betatakin), the hike to Keet

Walking through Keet Seel

Seel is no walk in the park. What makes the hike difficult is a combination of its length—17 miles round-trip—heat, elevation and lack of a clean source of water. The water in the river is too heavily polluted by cattle to be thoroughly filtered and the old spring by the ruins has been permanently closed because of pollution and the presence of traces of uranium. This means that you'll need to carry your own water. You'll need lots of it. The path is well marked, through an open canyon, with numerous ankle-deep river crossings. If the water is high, you may need to get your feet wet at the first two crossings. Cattle range freely in the canyon as you are actually crossing private land owned by Navajo families. Only a small area surrounding the ruins proper is actually under the stewardship of the NPS.

Eggshell Arch (photo by Ron Flickinger)

All these factors combined present a real challenge to the photographer. If you decide to make it a day hike, you must be in excellent physical condition and have prior experience with long trips at elevation. You can get away with a gallon of water, by stashing some of it along the trail for your return trip. You can also do this trip as an overnighter. A primitive, but shaded and very pleasant campground is located near the ruins. The NPS recommends at least two gallons per person for an overnighter. On a hot day, you'll definitely drink that and maybe more. That's 16lbs of water in your backpack, just for starters. Next, you'll need a tent with a fly because of the strong possibility of thunderstorms. Your other basic camping conveniences, food and photographic equipment, all contribute to a high pain factor.

Nearby locations: There are several places of interest to photographers in the Tsegi Canyon and Shonto area. The Inscription House cliff dwellings, which form a detached section of the Navajo Nat'l Monument, are sacred to the Hopi and are off-limits to visitors. Other sites, such as the amazing Eggshell Arch, are located on private land or pass through property leased for grazing. Complaints of trespassing, disturbing livestock, and leaving gates open have prompted the Navajo Parks & Recreation Department to declare them off-limits. As of early 2006, neither the local chapter houses nor the Department and Visitor Centers will issue backcountry permits for these areas. Eggshell Arch is only mentioned here for future reference in the hypothetical case this decision would be reversed. ✿

Inner Sanctum

Chapter 14

ANTELOPE CANYON

The Eagle's Eye

ANTELOPE CANYON

Introduction

Antelope Canyon has become so well known to the public and the media, that it is hard to imagine that until the end of the 1980's few people had heard of this extraordinary slot canyon and only a few stray professional photographers had ventured into it.

I was fortunate enough to visit the canyon in the eighties, driving to its entrance in my own vehicle and spending a few hours of sheer astonishment all by myself in this humbling sanctuary. Today, things have changed drastically and visitation is highly regulated, in order to accommodate the demand from an ever-increasing flow of visitors—including a large contingent from foreign countries. What used to be private property, accessible only by prior arrangement with the owners, has become the Antelope Canyon Navajo Tribal Park, with well-organized tours. Needless to say, you will not be alone. Regrettably, the fee has increased steadily almost every year. At the rate it's going, it may at some point become almost as onerous to visit both sections of Antelope Canyon as to visit all the National Parks in the U.S. with an "America the Beautiful" pass.

Despite the aggressive exploitation, the popularity of this small slot canyon—a must-see for any photographer doing the big trek through the Southwest—is amply justified by the incredible mineral sculptures of swirling Navajo sandstone. Their colors are sublimated (at the right time) by one of the most extraordinary light you can imagine. Antelope Canyon will almost effortlessly give you photographic results you'll be proud of.

Antelope Canyon consists of two distinct sections, although they are not very distant from each other. They are Upper Antelope Canyon (the most well-known section, drawing the vast majority of visitors) and Lower Antelope canyon (which closed for about a year until 1998 after a dramatic flash flood).

Photographers with little time available and a limited budget might wonder whether it is redundant to visit both sections. Well, I strongly encourage you to visit both sections, as they each have a very distinct personality.

In spite of its short ±200 yards length, Upper Antelope Canyon is exceptionally beautiful. Its intricate convolutions, as well as the rays of lights that strike its walls around mid-day, rejoice photographers and non-photographers alike.

Lower Antelope Canyon is both quite a bit longer and more rugged. The slot itself is slanted. You enter from the top and go down quite a bit, using several ladders. It has a higher fun factor, reinforced by the fact that it is less heavily frequented. On the other hand the light is less spectacular—while still extremely interesting if you know how to tame it.

Even if you have little time, you can easily visit both canyons during the same day. Begin with Lower Antelope Canyon in the morning and follow immediately afterwards with Upper Antelope Canyon, preferably before noon.

The following sections provide specific information pertaining to each part of the canyon.

Getting there: To reach Antelope Canyon, leave Page southeast via Coppermine Road to AZ 98 in the direction of Kaibeto, aiming towards the power plant. The entrance to Upper Antelope Canyon is about 2 miles from the junction with AZ 98, just past mile marker 299. It is on the right side of the road, well marked, and you can't miss it. The road leading to Lower Antelope Canyon is located almost opposite the entrance to the Upper canyon and is well marked too.

Upper Antelope Canyon (Tse Bighanilini')

Upper Antelope Canyon is at once both simple and difficult to photograph. Many compositions and shooting angles are quite obvious, and it's often the way you tame the exposure that makes the difference. To obtain the best results, you really need a tripod. If you don't have one, you can rent one in town. A cable release is also recommended. If you don't have one, the self-timer on your camera will work to prevent blurred pictures due to camera shake. This increases the risk of someone crossing in front of your lens at the decisive moment.

Generally speaking, the best time is from mid-morning to a little bit past noon. The superb light beams that have become the trademark of Upper Antelope Canyon occur from April to October only, with the best months being mid-May through mid-July when the sun is at its zenith. This is a blessing for photographers, who rarely have such interesting possibilities during the middle of the day. On the other hand, the concentration of photographers at that time of the day during the high season is unparalleled anywhere else. Dust can be a major problem—although it does enhance the light beams. The beams start happening around 11:30 AM and tend to move fast. They pop up at different spots inside the canyon at different times. Your guide will point out where and when. The exposure differential between the light beams and the dark canyon is huge, something in the order of 10 f/stops. Many people wonder whether my "Beam Me Up" photograph on the next page is a photo-montage; but, this kind of image is in fact easy to create once you understand that anything inside the beam of light will be wildly overexposed.

Even though light beams do not occur out of season, there is still plenty to photograph. The light is softer and there is a wider color palette. The walls of the canyon are around 130 feet high and the sinuous nature of the narrow passage makes it difficult for the light to penetrate. Whatever light comes it can produce nice pictures. Don't be put off by the absence of sunshine, just take longer exposures. You'll be pleasantly surprised with the results. Also, consult the general photo advice for slot canyons in the *Photo Advice chapter* and try to protect your equipment from the omnipresent dust.

Getting there: Upper Antelope Canyon is open year round—subject to weather—and can be visited with group tours or independently depending on the season. As of this writing, the four accredited tour operators based in Page all have keys to the gate and offer tours year round. As the fee station is not staffed during the winter months, a guided tour will be your only option to visit the upper canyon at that time. Tour operators charge a flat fee ($28 for the basic tour). Generally, they stay with the group inside the canyon. So-called "photography tours" are more expensive (about $45). They stay an additional hour inside the canyon and a guide provides valuable advice to photographers. Be sure to thoroughly investigate each tour operator's offering, as they each have different schedules that may or may not be convenient to you. I recommend that you book your reservation through the Powell Museum, which provides a chart with departure times and complete information on each tour operator, both in town and through their web site (*see On the Go Resources in Appendix*).

From April to October, it is possible to visit Upper Antelope Canyon independently—and a bit more economically—between 8 AM and 5 PM MST by just driving to the park's entrance station and paying the Tribal Park fee ($21 as of this writing, but it may have increased again by the time you read this). The price includes the usual $6 Navajo backcountry permit fee, 4WD transportation to and from the entrance to the upper canyon and almost 1 hour inside. There is an additional charge of $5 for one extra hour. The $6 backcountry permit fee is deductible from the Lower Antelope Canyon fee. At the gate, you may also purchase a permit for Water Holes Canyon (*see next chapter*).

Time required: At least 1 hour round-trip to get there from Page, including waiting and transit time by 4WD vehicle to the canyon's entrance, plus 1 hour minimum inside the canyon. A 2-hour limit is imposed on photography tours.

Opposite page: Beam Me Up!

Lower Antelope Canyon (Hasdeztwazi)

The Young family has done a tremendous job installing a series of metal ladders to facilitate your descent into the canyon. They have also installed a series of strategically placed emergency nylon ladders that can be dropped from above in case of flash flood emergency. Because it is such a narrow canyon, you may find pockets of mud at any time during the year, although it is a rare occurrence in summer. If you want to explore the canyon when mud is present, bring a pair of sandals or, better yet, a pair of boots that you do not care too much about, as they will be a mess when you come out of the canyon.

The importance of respecting the dangerous forces of nature was tragically illustrated in August of 1997, when the lives of 11 tourists were lost in Lower Antelope Canyon. They died because they failed to heed the warnings of their guide when a violent storm struck about 8 miles to the southeast. It was not raining on the canyon. For all slot canyons or narrows mentioned in this series of guidebooks, always follow warnings from rangers or other responsible parties. Flash floods are frequent and it doesn't necessarily have to be raining in the canyon. You should never risk going into a canyon if a storm is threatening close by, which is to say anywhere within a 10-mile radius.

Photographing Lower Antelope Canyon is great fun. It is also somewhat of a challenge if you want to bring back photos of a high caliber. There are far fewer light spots here than in Upper Antelope canyon. There are no obvious light beams, so you'll need to be more creative and look for interesting angles and compositions. In particular, you'll need to pre-visualize combinations of rock texture and reflected light. You'll get the best results by following the recommendations from the *Photo Advice chapter*.

The best time to photograph Lower Antelope and obtain a rich palette of colors is from very early in the morning until about 11 AM. Light becomes somewhat less interesting after that.

Getting there: Lower Antelope Canyon can only be visited independently. It may not be open at all times during winter months, depending on staffing availability. It is usually open from 8 AM to 5 PM. If you want to arrange an early visit of Lower Antelope for best light, you'll need to call Ken Young the day before (*see On the Go Resources in Appendix*). As of this writing, the fee at Lower Antelope Canyon is $18.50 for 2 hours, plus $5 per hour thereafter, despite the fact that no transportation is involved. It is partly justified by the infrastructure enhancements. As it includes the $6 Navajo backcountry permit fee, you can deduct $6 from the Upper Antelope fee of $21 if you visit the latter on the same day.

Time required: If you are serious about your photography, you may very well end up spending the full 4 hours allowed inside the canyon. Take water in summer and warm clothes in winter. It can get unbearably hot and stifling during the summer months and very cold in winter, especially if there are mud holes in the slot.

Opposite page: Surreal Rock

Peach Canyon (photo by Ron Flickinger)

Nearby locations: If you want to photograph another slot canyon in the Antelope style and without any crowds, Overland Canyon Tours in Page (*see the On the Go Resources in Appendix*) offers accredited tours of the upper section of Peach Wash, which they call Canyon X. This tour requires more time—the tour lasts 5 to 6 hours, including the 32-mile round-trip out of Page—as well as some mild scrambling. It costs $150 as of this writing.

There are other nice slot canyons in the surrounding area. At the time of this writing, Upper Kaibeto, Navajo Canyon, Choal Canyon, Peach Wash (except the Canyon X tour), and Butterfly Canyon can no longer be visited. Complaints of trespassing on private land, disturbing livestock, leaving gates open and requests for rescues have prompted the Navajo Parks & Recreation Department to declare them off-limits. As of early 2006, neither the local chapter houses nor the Department and Visitor Centers will issue back-country permits for these areas. They are only mentioned here for reference, in case they should reopen to the public at some point. ✿

Moonrise over Gunsight Butte

Chapter 15

AROUND PAGE

Dominguez Butte & Crossing of the Fathers

AROUND PAGE

Created from scratch in 1957 to shelter the thousands of workers who built Glen Canyon Dam, Page has turned itself into a significant tourism center, essentially by virtue of being the main access point to Lake Powell with its vast recreational potential centered around boating. To photographers, it is an ideally located hub, right in the heart of the Colorado Plateau. It makes a perfect base to tap into a boundless trove of photographic treasures, some of which are described in this, the previous, and the next two chapters.

As to Lake Powell, it continues to generate controversy half a century later. Some see in it a major ecological catastrophe, having slowly submerged under its waters thousands of miles of canyons, arguably amongst the most beautiful in the West. One prime example is the exquisite Cathedral in the Desert. Others prefer to see in it the apex of man's embellishment of nature through the harmonious pairing of red rock and water along thousands of miles of spectacular shoreline (longer than the entire West Coast of the United States).

The debate is still raging today. It has been exacerbated by several years of dry weather which have drastically lowered the lake's level, and revealed many previously engulfed side canyons. Proponents and adversaries argue vehemently about the possibility of draining the lake or at least keeping it at a permanently low level. Highly visible organizations, such as Friends of Lake Powell, on one side, the Sierra Club and the Glen Canyon Institute on the other, are still lobbying the public and its elected officials.

The purpose of this guide is not to participate in this debate, which goes far beyond esthetic and photographic considerations. Regardless of our individual sensibilities, it is unlikely that we will see again the full beauty of the original Glen Canyon during the next decade. So, let's set aside the debate and concentrate on photographing the natural beauty that the Page area, including Lake Powell, offers us today.

Horseshoe Bend

A few miles to the southwest of Page, the Colorado River forms one of its most spectacular bends, providing a breathtaking view that you don't have any excuse for missing, as it's so close to Page. Seen from the rim, the steepness is really impressive. Always exercise caution, as there are no guardrails.

Photo advice: The bend is very wide and requires a 24mm or preferably a 21mm lens. A 28mm lens just won't do if you want to include both sides of the river. If you don't have an ultra wide-angle lens, take several shots to assemble them later in your digital darkroom. Try to include a little bit of rock in the foreground in order to convey more accurately the depth of the canyon, using a small aperture for good depth-of-field.

You'll get great results early in the day when the sun hits the Vermilion Cliffs on the horizon. A graduated neutral density filter is a must to avoid having the sky and the plateau look washed out since the canyon will still be in shadows. At the end of the day, the view is equally splendid if you have a nice sunset.

Climbing on the small sandstone mound to the right, the view towards Lake Powell is lovely. During the frequent summer thunderstorms, the sky is often a deep gray, even though the sun bathes Tower Butte in a blaze of light. A 100 to 150mm lens gives the best results.

Getting there: Leaving Page from North Lake Powell Blvd, set your odometer to zero as you reach the intersection with US 89 and follow the latter to the south for 4.2 miles. From the intersection with US 98, this distance is about one mile. The access road veers off to the right towards a car park located a couple of hundred yards away. Park and follow the old 4x4 track to the bend, about half a mile further on.

Horseshoe Bend (photo by Isabel Synnatschke)

Time required: 1½ hour, from Page, including the 1-mile round-trip walk to the edge of the canyon and about ½ an hour at the viewpoint.

Nearby location: Another very nice view, albeit less impressive, can be had from the overlook located on the small road parallel to US 89 between the NPS Headquarters and the intersection with North Lake Powell Blvd. Look in the direction opposite to the dam to see the Colorado River snaking in the canyon. This is a good morning view.

Water Holes Slot Canyon

You're still excited by your visit to Antelope Canyon (*see previous chapter*) and you've photographed it to your heart's content. But you're also fuming at the crowds and dreaming of a little stretch of slot canyon all to yourself! Well, here is the deal. For a fee of $5 as of this writing, you can purchase a Navajo backcountry permit to visit nearby Water Holes Canyon. You can do so at the gate of the Antelope Canyon tribal park.

Even though Water Holes Canyon doesn't have the unique form, color and light of Antelope Canyon, it nevertheless has some nice formations as well as some narrows reminiscent of the slot canyons of the Grand Staircase-Escalante such as Peek-a-Boo (*see Volume 1 Chapter 7*). As its name implies, you may encounter water holes, murky pools and soft mud that can make your progress difficult, if not impossible, in places. However, if it hasn't rained for a while, the canyon may be entirely dry and easy to visit. Needless to say, you should not venture into Water Holes Canyon if there is a chance of rain in the area.

The canyon is bisected by the bridge on US 89 and each section is worth exploring. Its eastern side, upstream, is easier to visit with a section of interesting narrows; but, it is not very deep. The western side, downstream, has more obstacles. Only the beginning part, which has several sections of narrows, doesn't require canyoneering equipment and expertise.

Coming from Page, after parking near the gate on the left side of US 89 just before the bridge, enter and head east towards the power line. In about 250 yards, you'll come to a depression on the right that will allow you to descend on a slickrock slope into the dry bed of the canyon. Note the place where you came down so you can find it easily when you come back.

Walk in the dry bed to your left to explore the upstream part of the canyon. At this point, the canyon is still fairly wide. About 0.5 mile further along you'll enter into lovely narrows where you'll catch sight of the first water pockets. The narrows eventually turn into a slot canyon with beautiful walls and lighting effects. When you reach an impassable vertical rock face, retrace your steps.

Return to the spot where you entered the dry bed of the canyon. Continue about 200 yards downstream toward the bridge and you'll find a superb steep wall about 150 feet tall with a narrow passage. Almost under the bridge, you'll come to a 15-foot drop-off. From here on, the lower part of the canyon is currently off-limits and the following description will be of help solely if it reopens. Just past the drop-off, you'll see the carcass of a car vertically encased in the canyon. If you are agile, you can descend this drop-off relatively easily with some caution and with the help of the car. Don't attempt it if you're not confident in you climbing ability. Soon, you'll come to some interesting narrows before the canyon broadens again. In a turn, you'll see to your right a steep side gully with a cairned path. Using caution, you can use this later to climb back to the rim and return to your car without tackling the drop-off with the stuck car. Do not attempt to take this path from the top as you may not find it and the descent would be dangerous if you attempted it at the wrong spot. Continuing down-canyon, you'll encounter other narrows alternating with broader sections, as well as two drop-offs where ladders have been installed. Retrace your steps from here as the lower section is only for experienced canyoneers equipped with ropes.

As you retrace your steps back to your car along the rim, notice the nice fins and striations on the small sandstone outcrops.

Photo advice: This canyon receives more light than Antelope Canyon as it is shallower. However, a tripod is still necessary to take good shots of the rock texture with sufficient depth-of-field. An ISO of 400 to 800 will let you take

Water Holes (photo by Philippe Schuler)

acceptable photos hand-held. Remember to avoid contrasting areas or direct sunlight on the walls. Instead, concentrate on reflected light. Mid-morning and mid-afternoon light is best. Water Holes Canyon is a particularly good spot to get photos of yourself or your friends in the nooks and crannies of the canyon or in one of the water pockets with water up to your thighs.

Getting there: Water Holes Canyon is located about 6 miles south of Page on US 89. Its presence is first announced by a sign a few hundred feet before the entrance and by a second one just before the bridge spanning the Water Holes Canyon gorge. There is a pull-out on the left side of the road. Don't park directly in front of the gate or on the right side of the highway. There have been reports of vehicles being ticketed for not displaying their backcountry permit.

Time required: From the carpark, at least 1 hour to visit the upstream part of the canyon. This visit can be easily combined with nearby Horseshoe Bend (*see previous section*).

Marble Canyon and Lee's Ferry

Crossing US 89A at Navajo Bridge, Marble Canyon offers an excellent opportunity to stop, observe and photograph the Colorado at close range. You'll be about 470 feet above the river, which at this point flows slowly between two precipitous walls.

Arriving at the twin Navajo Bridges—built respectively in 1929 and 1995—you'll find it hard to resist taking the classic wide-angle picture of the two bridges with their identical steel arches forming a perfect symmetry against the backdrop of the Vermilion Cliffs. My preference is to shoot from east to west rather than from the Navajo Bridge Interpretive Center.

The descent to the edge of the Colorado River at Lee's Ferry—site of an old ferry used in the last century by travelers to cross the Colorado—is particularly interesting. It's the only chance to get down to the edge of the Colorado River for miles around, thanks to shale deposits which slope gently to the river here. As the road descends from the bridge to Lee's Ferry, you'll pass the pull-out for the Cathedral Wash hike (*see next section*). A little bit later, you'll come to a couple of spectacular balanced rocks flanking the left side of the road.

Balanced rock near Lee's Ferry (photo by Philippe Schuler)

Today, Lee's Ferry is essentially the launching point for Grand Canyon rafting trips. It serves also as a marina for flat-bottom fishing boats. If you visit Horseshoe Bend (*see section above*), you're bound to observe one of these boats coming and going to and from Glen Canyon Dam. For backpackers, Lee's Ferry is the exit of the 4-day hike inside Paria Canyon (*see the Paria Canyon section in Chapter 5 of Photographing the Southwest Volume 1*).

The Vermilion Cliffs, which surround Marble Canyon and the whole Lee's Ferry area, take on beautiful red and orange hues from early evening till sunset.

Getting there: To go to Marble Canyon from Page, take US 89 south for 25 miles and turn right on US 89A for 14 miles until Navajo Bridge. Just after the bridge, turn right and you'll be at Lee's Ferry in about 5 miles on a good paved road. Marble Canyon is easy to include after a visit to the North Rim of the Grand Canyon, coming via Jacob Lake.

Cathedral Wash

Close to Lee's Ferry, Cathedral Wash is a short, moderate, and uncrowded 2.5-mile round-trip hike inside an unusual canyon leading to the Colorado River. The canyon has some interesting narrows and is quite fun to hike. Although less colorful than the area's slot canyons, it has, nonetheless, some very nice, soft pastel hues. What makes it stand out is its great variety of shapes, a multitude of benches and ledges staggered at different levels, dry falls, and pools of water or dry mud. All contribute to create a moderate challenge, as well as interesting photo opportunities. Progressing through the narrows is a big part of the fun, as you must find your own way on different ledges to get around obstacles. It is never really dangerous as long as you use caution and are not afraid of heights. As with any canyon of this type, don't hike it if there is a chance of rain.

From the pull-out, cross the Lee's Ferry road and enter the wash toward the east, close to the concrete drainpipe. After walking inside the wash for about fifteen minutes, you'll come to an impressive drop-off. You can bypass it by descending cautiously on its right side. Now, things become really interesting, as you enter a narrower, deeper, and highly eroded section. As you progress inside the canyon, you'll encounter a series of pour-offs that you'll bypass for the most part by following ledges on the left side. This sometimes requires a bit of scrambling. No particular climbing skills are required and any normally agile person should be able to do it.

Eventually, the canyon widens and you start hearing the rumble of the Colorado River, which you reach a few minutes later at a rocky beach offering a nice view of the powerful river. Take your time and enjoy the moment. It is a wonderfully relaxing and meditative place. You'll find it hard to detach your gaze from the river. In hot weather, you can skinny-dip close to the bank before returning the way you came.

Photo advice: The Cathedral Wash narrows are quite wide and receive a lot of light around midday. Do this hike preferably in mid-morning or mid-afternoon to avoid high contrast areas and get some nice reflected light.

Getting there: From US 89A at Marble Canyon, just past Navajo Bridge, take the road to Lee's Ferry for about 1.5 miles. Park on the left side of the road at the second pull-out you'll see. You'll know

Hikers in Cathedral Wash

you're at the right spot if you see an interpretive panel explaining the phenomenon of cliff erosion.

Time required: From the pull-out, count on about 2 hours round-trip with plenty of time for photographing along the way. Time permitting, do yourself a favor and allow a bit longer to linger by the Colorado River.

Alstrom Point & Nipple Bench

Many people are curious as where to shoot great pictures of Lake Powell. For those with little time or a passenger car, one easily accessible location for a great late afternoon view of the Wahweap Marina with the Kaiparowits Plateau in the background is the scenic overlook located about 2 miles north of the Glen Canyon Dam on US 89. The overlook sits on top of a little butte reached by a short gravel road to the right. There is a sign indicating its presence. This road closes at dusk.

If you have time and a high-clearance vehicle, head to Alstrom Point, located on Romana Mesa, on the north shore of Lake Powell. There, you'll find a fantastic panorama of Padre Bay, with Gunsight Butte in the foreground and Navajo Mountain, Dominguez Butte, the Crossing of the Fathers and Tower Butte in the background. This is a favorite of professional and serious photographers, especially during the golden hour. Note that the pictures illustrating this section

Alstrom Point, looking toward the Kaiparowits Plateau

Padre Bay Dusk

were mostly taken in the mid-eighties or late-ninetees when the lake's level was very high. You might be somewhat disappointed if it remains low. It will lack a substantial portion of the beautiful waters that contrast so well with Gunsight Butte's colorful sandstone.

On the way to Alstrom Point, you'll pass under Nipple Bench. The Nipple Bench area delights many photographers with its spectacular badlands, soft pastel hues and intricate rock formations. You'll find surprisingly large rust-colored boulders that broke off from the bench. Some are perched on pedestals, contrasting particularly well in late afternoon against the grey badlands. You'll enjoy spending some time exploring this area, walking from one discovery to another. From the switchbacks and the top of nearby Kelly Grade, you have a spectacular view of the Nipple Bench badlands, with Lake Powell in the distance. The Kelly Grade is a steep and narrow portion of Smoky Mountain Road, which ascends 1,500 feet to the Kaiparowits Plateau before traversing it to the town of Escalante, about 56 miles to the north (*see Chapter 6 in Photographing the Southwest - Volume 1*).

Photo advice: The golden hour is the time to go to Alstrom Point. Although shooting at sunrise could be rewarding, sunset is the better time to catch the wonderful warm hues and you'll still have lovely pink hues well after sunset.

Padre Bay Ablaze

Moreover, on your way for the sunset at Alstrom Point, you'll be on time for good late afternoon shots at Nipple Bench. If you can time your visit with a full moon, you'll be rewarded with a truly unique sensory experience.

A wide-angle lens is the norm for panoramic shots taken from all the Romana Mesa viewpoints. A short telephoto will prove useful to catch interesting or well lit details in the distance.

Getting there: Passenger cars can go as far as the Nipple Bench badlands. However, a high-clearance vehicle is essential to go to Alstrom Point or ascend the Kelly Grade. I strongly recommend that you do not leave without *Glen Canyon NRA's official map and guide* and the *Grand Staircase National Monument Visitor Information* brochure, which includes a useful map with the BLM road numbers. Both feature almost all the local roads. The *Photographer's Guide to Page, Arizona*, which you can get for free at the Glen Canyon Visitor Center is also very useful. It describes in detail how to get there, including GPS waypoints.

From Page, take US 89 toward Kanab. Turn right at Big Water, about 14.5 miles from the dam, then right again onto BLM Road 300, going northeast toward Nipple

Nipple Bench formations (photo by Philippe Schuler)

Bench and the lake. You'll need to ford Wahweap Creek as you exit Big Water; but, it is usually not a problem as the crossing is cemented. Continue for about 12 miles on BLM road 300, entering Glen Canyon NRA and leaving Warm Creek Bay road to your right at about two thirds of the way. When you reach a sign protected by a small slanted roof, leave BLM 330 to your left and make a right in the direction of Grand Bench on BLM road 300. Continue for about 1 mile until you reach the Grand Staircase-Escalante entrance sign. To your left, BLM 300 continues toward the cliffs and the steep Kelly Grade—not for the faint-of-heart. For Alstrom Point, follow the direction of Grand Bench to the right on BLM road 340 for 4.2 miles. There, follow the sign for Alstrom Point. The track leaves the main road, leading at a right angle toward the lake. As long as the road is dry, your high-clearance vehicle should have no trouble negotiating the deep ruts in the track. After almost 5 miles, you'll be above a circular cliff with an excellent view of the Kaiparowits Plateau and Gunsight Butte. The view is even better if you follow the cliff for a few hundred yards to the left. After that, the track deteriorates rapidly as you climb a small hill. You'll be shaking back and forth on rocky terrain. There is a less visible track to the right allowing you to circumvent the bad path more comfortably by climbing the small hill. Past that point the track remains rocky, but it is never difficult. After a bit more than a mile, you'll come to a promontory yielding a superb view of Padre Bay. Look down to the left of the track and you'll notice another promontory. This location has the best view of Gunsight Butte.

Time required: For Alstrom Point, count on 1 hour and 15 minutes each way to and from Page without stops. You can also easily spend one hour just photographing along Nipple Bench, and more time if you drive the Kelly Grade to the top. You'll want to stay 1 to 2 hours on Romana Mesa, depending on your available time. I usually go in late afternoon and stay until dark.

Wahweap Marina Panorama

Rainbow Bridge

With a span of 275 feet, Rainbow Bridge is the largest natural bridge in the world. Its huge, albeit graceful, rounded curve of Navajo sandstone reminds one of Corona Arch near Moab. However, this bridge was formed by the action of water flowing from the slopes of nearby Navajo Mountain. It is a geologic process completely different from that of an arch, which is eroded by wind and rain. Considered a sacred place by the western Indians, it was very difficult to get to until the formation of Lake Powell. Until the late nineties, you were almost able to reach it by boat from the various marinas on the lake. Due to the low lake level at the time of this writing, you now need to walk about 1.5 miles from the docking spot. Enjoy it while you can, because Rainbow Bridge is bound to collapse at some point in the future, due to the inexorable grinding exerted on its base by Lake Powell.

Photo advice: Rainbow Bridge is best photographed in late afternoon. Although the Park Service cannot prevent you from walking under the bridge, they do ask that you refrain from doing so. It is considered a sacred place by many Native Americans. The viewing area is about 200 feet from the bridge and a 28 to 35mm lens is appropriate.

Getting there: Unless you own or rent your own water craft, you'll have to join an organized boat trip from the Wahweap marina, located a few miles north of

Page and about 50 miles from Rainbow Bridge. The concessionaire organizes visits all year long. From May to September, it's also possible to get there from the Bullfrog Marina (*see Capitol Reef and Around Cedar Mesa chapters in Volume 1*). You can also get here on foot from inland, leaving from the Rainbow Lodge or Navajo Mountain Trading Post. This requires two long days round-trip as well as a backcountry and camping permit from Navajo Parks & Recreation.

Time required: At least 7 hours round-trip from the Wahweap Marina. Obtain information on departure times in town or at the Visitor Center near Glen Canyon Dam. In summer, with a morning departure, you'll still have enough time after the boat tour to drive to Alstrom Point for late afternoon and sunset shots.

Amazing Rainbow Bridge

Stud Horse Point

There is a small but very nice cluster of pedestal rocks at the southern tip of a long ridge named Stud Horse Point, close to the Utah state line. It is worth a visit if you have some extra time. It's close to Page, easy to reach and a neat sunrise or sunset location. Half a dozen hoodoos with large cap rocks stand tall inside a depression, close to a rim overlooking the valley to the north with Lake Powell in the distance. The rocks take on a nice glow at sunset and photograph well in groups, or individually, with a wide-angle lens or a short telephoto, using fill flash after sunset.

Balancing act

Getting there: From Page, take US 89 northwest for about 5.6 miles from the Glen Canyon Dam; turn left on an old paved road located between mileposts 555 and 556. When the pavement ends after almost 0.8 mile, turn left and follow the small power line for 1.5 miles. At the Y, leave the power line and take the left fork. Continue past the cattle guard, driving northwest next to the larger power line. Take the easily-missed sandy spur to the right at 36°58'20" 111°35'44" (this spur is not featured on the 7.5° USGS map). Follow it for 0.3 mile, go right at the next fork and you'll come to a cattle gate after another 0.2 mile. This gate is occasionally closed when cattle is present; in that case, be sure to close it behind you. Another 0.5 mile brings you to the car park, just above the pedestal rocks, at 36°59'22" 111°36'07".

Time required: Less than 2 hours round-trip from Page. ✿

Blue Sky & Surf

Chapter 16
COYOTE BUTTES NORTH

The Main Wave

COYOTE BUTTES NORTH

The Coyote Buttes Wilderness is a protected area—subject to a permit system which I'll explain later—located in the northeastern tip of the Arizona Strip and encompassing some of the Paria River drainage and the Cockscomb fault. Most of this area is now included inside the recently designated Vermilion Cliffs National Monument.

Coyote Buttes protects an area of simultaneously gnarled, polished and twisted rock, amongst the most extraordinary formations on the Colorado Plateau. This area is administratively separated in two sections: Coyote Buttes North and Coyote Buttes South. Coyote Buttes North, which I discuss in this chapter, encompasses the Wave—the most popular highlight of the area that every nature photographer dreams to shoot. But, Coyote Buttes North and its immediate vicinity have much more to offer than simply the Wave, as you will find out in this chapter. The more difficult accessible area of Coyote Buttes South will be discussed in the next chapter and is also well worth a visit.

Although the most widely used trailhead for the Coyote Buttes North is located in Utah, most of the Coyote Buttes Wilderness area, including the Wave, is in Arizona and, hence, covered in the present volume. Other prominent sites located in close proximity of Coyote Butte North are covered in detail in

Photographing the Southwest Volume 1 – Southern Utah. This is the case of Old Paria, The Rimrock Hoodoos, Paria Canyon (northern section up to the confluence with Buckskin Gulch), and Cobra Arch.

The Wave

Within Coyote Buttes North lies the crown jewel of the area: The Wave is a magical place where the colorful sandstone gives itself to mind-boggling psychedelic gyrations.

"Discovered" in some coffee-table books, videos and magazines in the early nineties and kept away from the limelight for a few years, this truly unique site has become a favorite subject for photographers from all over the world. It would be terribly sad if its growing popularity would reduce it to a cliché.

The Coyote Buttes Wilderness is jointly administered by the Kanab Field Office of the BLM and the Vermilion Cliffs Nat'l Monument (part of the Arizona Strip Field Office in St. George, UT). Concerns about widespread ecological damage to this pristine area led to the establishment of a quota system in 1997, restricting visitation to a total of twenty permits a day (see details below). This quota may or may not be revised at some point in the future after studies show what impact a steady flow of visitors has on the land. The permits are issued for daytime use only and overnight camping is forbidden within the Wilderness area. Camping is still possible on the west side of House Rock Valley Road, in particular at the Stateline Campground.

Many people find the low quota system objectionable. I have no moral or scientific authority to pass judgment, but I am quite happy with the present system. A limit of twenty bodies a day seems indeed quite low at first glance. There are, however, several factors weighing heavily for keeping it that way. The vast majority of visitors come to the Coyote Buttes North to see the phenomenal, but fairly small, site of the Wave. A concentration of visitors in this particular area could not only impact the fragile sandstone striations, but it could deter from the enjoyment of the place.

To plan your visit to the Wave, you need to reserve your permit online well in advance by visiting the BLM web site at *https://www.blm.gov/az/paria/obtainpermits. cfm?usearea=CB.* As of this writing, you can enter the lottery three months in advance to

Secret Passage

obtain a permit for some of the ten slots available online each day. For a $5 fee, you can apply for up to three entry dates for any given month. If you are planning a trip less than three months in advance, begin by checking the calendar on the permit page to see if some slots are still available. This is more likely to happen during the winter months.

If you couldn't reserve a date on the Internet and are vacationing in the area, there is still a glimmer of hope: you can try to obtain a walk-in permit. The total number of permits varies by group size, but there is a total of twenty slots per day, ten permits being issued online as previously described and the other ten being issued as walk-in permits. Travelling as a group—a maximum of six per group is allowed—further diminishes your chances of finding your date of choice. Be ready to make some major scheduling concessions.

You can obtain a walk-in permit at the Paria Ranger Station from mid-March to mid-November, seven days a week. The station is located on US 89, about 30 miles from Page and 43 miles from Kanab, near milepost 21. From mid-November to mid-March, permits can be obtained at the BLM Kanab Field Office (*see Resources in Appendix*), five days a week. In both cases, you need to be

Brittlebush & Sandstone

there at 9AM MST (or 9AM DST in summer), but the drawing is not first come, first served. If there are ten persons or less seeking permits, you will be issued one for the next day; however; if all ten permits were not issued the previous day, a same day permit may be available. Competition is fierce during the warmer months and it is not unusual to see fifty bodies vying for the highly-prized permits.

If you've been lucky enough to obtain a walk-in permit, you may not participate in the drawing for another two weeks. Permits cost $5 per person as of this writing.

Do not attempt to go to the Wave without a permit. Access is often patrolled by rangers. If you got caught, you'd have to pay a hefty fine and face possible prosecution for trespassing on Federal land.

Getting there: From the Paria Contact Station turnoff, head west on US 89 toward Kanab for about 4.8 miles (just past Milepost 26). You'll come to a hard-packed dirt road branching off to the left where the highway makes a wide curve to the right, immediately past the Cockscomb. This is House Rock Valley

Opposite page: Sandstone Reflection

Heart of the Wave (photo by Philippe Schuler)

Road (BLM 700). Be careful not to miss it. It is not clearly visible when coming from Page due to its angle and the fact that it is slightly downwards from the highway. This well-maintained track, usually passable to passenger cars, can sometimes be closed for a while after a particularly strong storm, especially in summer. Following this road, pass the Buckskin Trailhead at 4.4 miles and continue for another 4.2 miles to the Wire Pass car park. This is the main trailhead for the Wave and for Wire Pass, as the name implies (*see the Wire Pass section at the end of this chapter*). Count on a half hour from the Paria Contact Station to the car park.

When reserving your permit, you'll notice on the form that there is another trailhead further south on House Rock Valley Road. This trailhead allows you to reach the Wave from the southwest via The Notch. It is less scenic and much more difficult to reach the Wave that way. No written directions are provided by the BLM and it could be risky if you chose the wrong path. Just forget it.

From the Wire Pass trailhead, it is approximately 3 miles to the Wave. Count on about 1½ hours to reach the Wave the first time around. It will depend on your routefinding ability and how much time you spend taking pictures along the way. Until spring of 2005, the BLM provided precious little information on how to reach the Wave and about 20% of visitors with a permit failed to locate it. This has radically changed now that excellent information accompanies each permit, in the form of three pages of precise directions, including landmarks with GPS coordinates and several photos overlaid with a dotted path. An extract of the USGS map indicating the way and the above-mentioned landmarks is included. Thanks to this package, you should have no problem finding the Wave.

Still, it is one place where a compass or a GPS can be useful, especially if you come back to the trailhead after dark. There are less obvious landmarks to rely on during the return trip and this is exacerbated if you are in darkness. In summer, you'll need plenty of water and adequate sun protection, as there is no shade along the way. Watch for possible thunderstorms and be prepared for high winds. That place wasn't formed by an occasional zephyr!

To let you prepare your trip before receiving your permit and assist you in locating the landmarks I'm describing in this chapter, here is a short description of the way to the Wave. From the trailhead, walk for about 10 minutes alongside and in the dry wash in the direction of the Wire Pass narrows. At the sign indicating Coyote Buttes, take the old jeep trail climbing to the right. Once on the plateau, sign the trail register and continue on the sandy path down to a wash at the foot of a slanted sandstone ridge. Walk a little bit to the left where the slope isn't too steep until you cross an easily located saddle. Take your marks immediately after crossing the saddle (37°00'56" 112°00'32"). There is a natural tendency on the way back to cross the ridge too early, forcing you to go down a very steep slope. Turn right past the saddle and walk south on the slickrock on the other side of the ridge, staying quite high on the slope. You'll soon come to a couple of large conical rocks called the Twin Buttes. Circumnavigate them on either side. Past the Twin Buttes, Top Rock comes into view in the distance. Top Rock is the ridge below which the Wave is nested. It is easily identified by a long black crack running vertically in its flank. Once you've found Top Rock and its crack, you will have no problem reaching the Wave. Just walk cross-country in that general direction. Stay high as long as you can on the slickrock slope until you come to a large wash. Descend into it and climb the steep sand dune on the opposite side, near a small isolated tree. A couple of hundred yards past the top of the dune, you'll reach a shallow gully leading in to the main entrance to the Wave (36°59'46" 112°00'23").

At the Wave, avoid walking on the thin ribs and ledges of sandstone that make the Wave so special. You don't need heavy boots to walk to the Wave. Wear lightweight shoes that won't leave marks. Also, be careful where you place your tripod. It is a privilege to experience the Wave and it's up to you to preserve it for those who will follow.

Photo advice: First, let me say that although the main corridor of the Wave is the focal point of any trip, there is plenty of wonderful scenery around it, as you'll see in the next section. Be sure to bring lots of film or enough digital storage, because the Wave and its surroundings will strongly stimulate your creative juices. You're not going to have another chance the next day, unless you have reserved successive days on the internet.

The Wave itself is usually better photographed around mid-day when there are no shadows. The heart of the Wave will be partially plunged in shadows as the

Modeling at the Wave (photo by Philippe Schuler)

afternoon progresses, creating potential contrast problems. Things get easier in late afternoon when a larger area is in shadow. Always avoid combining brightly lit and shadow areas on your images. The small passageway on the west side of the Wave, with its amazing melted striations, only photographs well when it is entirely in shadow. There is also a myriad of details all around the Wave that can be photographed successfully throughout the day. Arriving early in the morning, you'll be just in time to shoot in the direction of the Teepees or the colorful rock formations located to the right of the main corridor leading to the Wave.

To photograph the Wave itself, do not hesitate trying many different compositions. Even though the site is small, varying the height and angle of the camera will yield very different results. Make liberal use of the different optics you've brought with you, even from the same spot. For instance, when photographing the Wave's corridor from above with your back turned to the big crack, you can either use a very wide angle lens to capture all the gentle curves or a medium telephoto to zoom-in on part of the striations and compress the perspective of the different waves. A mild warming filter or a polarizing filter will give you pleasant results. I recommend using an ND Grad filter to keep the sky in check when photographing the Wave's corridor from above. After heavy thunderstorms, a pool may be present at the heart of the Wave, providing an opportunity for shooting superb reflections as long as there is no wind.

Time required: At least 4 hours round-trip from the Wire Pass trailhead to allow enough time for photographing the main Wave. A full day to include all the side-trips described in the following sections of this chapter (loop around the Wave via Sand Cove, exploration of Top Rock and the North Teepees).

Nearby locations: If you are not on your first trip to the Wave, you may want to try two sidetrips on your way to or from the Wave to see some interesting formations. The first one will be of interest to arch hunters. It is a small, original arch with a double span. It isn't widely known—despite being featured on the USGS map—because it is partially hidden inside a gully. Coming from the Wire Pass trailhead, leave the trail at the sandy wash reached after following the sandy path from the trail register on the plateau, just before entering the permit area. Instead of heading left to ascend the saddle on the slanted ridge, veer right into the wash for about 150 yards and right again at the first gully you encounter. Follow it southwest for about 0.4 mile, passing some easily-crossed slickrock slopes. Then look for a small side-gully climbing to your left to find the hidden arch in about 50 yards (37°00'37" 112°00'59"). If you meet a jumble of boulders in the main gully, you went too far and missed the side-gully with the arch. This

Coyote Pond (photo by Ron Flickinger)

is an afternoon location, better done on your return from the Wave. It is less interesting than some of the other features described in the following section. Keep it for a subsequent visit. Note that this arch is located outside the permit area and could be visited while waiting for a permit.

Another detour allows you to discover interestingly eroded rocks, with weird interlacings of thin sandstone plates pointing toward the sky. About 250 yards past the Twin Buttes (*see previous Getting there*), look to your right for large slickrock buttes with striations reminiscent of those found at the Wave. Instead of continuing toward Top Rock's vertical crack, walk slightly to the right in a short wash lined with trees. After about 300 yards, you'll reach a steep slope of whitish sandstone, which can be easily climbed. The eroded formations looking like fine lace are on a plateau just above it. Do not touch and use extreme precautions when photographing, as they are extremely fragile. Return the same way as it is very steep on the other side. This is a morning location (the formations are exposed to the northeast), better visited on your way to the Wave.

Lace Rock

Sand Cove & Top Rock

Many visitors fail to see the surrounding area of the Wave and to exploit its tremendous photographic potential. Newcomers have a tendency to relinquish the desire to scout the area because one is so elated by the sight of the main Wave. Many people are unaware of the existence of other fascinating subjects of the Coyote Buttes North. In this section, I will first describe the most accessible features, following an easy loop around the Wave. Afterwards, we'll embark on a more demanding exploration of Top Rock.

If you don't want to explore much further than the Wave's close proximity, I recommend you do the following loop, which will take you through several surrounding features from the Wave to Sand Cove. This loop is about 1.5 miles round-trip and can be done in about 1½ hours. Of course, it can take much longer if you spend quality time concentrating on your photography. It is best done from mid to late afternoon.

Begin by walking back to the place where you first entered the Wave, as if you were returning to the trailhead. Instead of going down toward the sand dune descending into the wash, follow the striated wall to your right for about 100 yards toward the back of a small cluster of colorfully-striated buttes harboring some unusual yellow stripes. There, you'll find a passageway leading inside the very heart of this surprising little formation.

Return to the main corridor of the Wave and leave it by walking up toward the big crack on Top Rock. Turn left and walk about 150 yards on a gentle slope with nice ground patterns until you reach a saddle—I call it the Wave's North Saddle—offering a good view of the distant Teepees, to the southeast.

Retrace your steps above the Wave and below the crack. Continue on a small plateau with amazing "brain rocks" and colorful cross-bedding. This plateau may have large puddles of water after heavy rains, making it even more interesting photographically. Some of the brain rocks have extraordinary shapes and color. Walk on this plateau for about 250 yards and follow a 10-foot high slope of widely-spaced diagonal striations. Go around it on the left and you'll suddenly discover what I call the Second Wave. This Second Wave consists of two exceptionally photogenic swirls of polished and striated sandstone. With its paler colors, the amazing Second Wave can only be photographed successfully from late afternoon until sunset. You can scout this spot earlier in the afternoon and make it your last stop before returning to your car.

From the Second Wave, walk a short distance to the edge of the plateau. Looking down toward the southwest, locate a cluster of small red buttes close to the wash. Descend cautiously the 200 yards separating you from the buttes. Cross to the backside of the buttes and you'll see some photogenic red and white striations on the slickrock to your right. It is best photographed in late afternoon with a wide-angle lens.

Next, descend into the wash—called Sand Cove—and follow it toward the north until it turns into a narrow canyon. Along the way, look for some nicely eroded rocks to your left. Just before entering the canyon, look to your left for a flat patch of whitish slickrock. Leave the wash here and aim northwest following a depression between a dune and the slickrock. After about 350 yards, you will reach an area with lots of interesting small boulders strewn about slickrock striations, aptly named The Bone Yard by Michael Fatali in a superb photograph.

Retrace your steps to the wash and enter the narrow canyon, which harbors an interesting mixture of sand and slickrock. Follow it for about 300 yards until you come to a dry fall, about 12 feet deep. To return to the Wave, don't climb down the dry fall. Instead, leave the canyon by climbing the small dune to the right. Continue in that direction and ascend the gentle slope until you reach the characteristic forms and shapes of the buttes surrounding the main Wave. You can then re-enter the main Wave through the narrow passageway on its west side. It is also possible to return to your car without going back to the Wave. To do so, simply bypass the dry fall on the left side and continue through the narrows of the small canyon. You'll end up in the wash you crossed on the way in, close to the previously-mentioned isolated tree at the foot of the sand dune leading to the Wave.

Opposite page: Crest of the Wave

Promontory (photo by Ron Flickinger)

For the more adventurous readers who have good route-finding skills and plan on spending an entire day discovering and photographing the area, I recommend an in-depth exploration of the top and backside of Top Rock. There, you can see more brain rocks, formations with very unusual shapes, superb crossbedding, a hanging valley with green trees and some nice arches.

To get there coming from the Wave, climb the very steep slickrock slope to the east, beginning at the widely-spaced diagonal striations just before the Second Wave (*see above*). At this spot, the slope is less difficult to climb. Nevertheless, this climb is very steep and not for everybody. You'll need to scramble a little and use your hands to pull yourself up. Good hiking shoes with gripping soles are a must. Exercise extreme caution at all times and carefully consider the fact that if you decide to come down the same way, it will be more difficult.

Just before the last cliff under the summit, you reach a somewhat flat area where you can walk almost level. Take your marks at this precise point, to ensure that you'll follow exactly the same path going down when it's time to go back.

Hourglass Rock (photo by Philippe Schuler)

From here, walk to your left toward the northeast almost above the crack. You'll discover an exceptional view of the Wave below, with all the surrounding colored buttes. The view is truly encompassing and goes far beyond all the surrounding ridges and the wilderness area. A medium telephoto will allow you to isolate the buttes and colorful brainrocks from an unusual angle. Retrace your steps and walk level southward on a sort of ledge and you'll come to a small flat hanging valley of slickrock. Look for a very nice alcove to the left with a small sand dune in front and colorful chiseled walls. From here, continue almost 100 yards and look for a small alcove to the left. Climb on the right side of this alcove and continue eastward about 50 yards amongst the little grey buttes forming the eastern side of Top Rock, for an exceptionally photogenic hidden spot (36°59'28" 112°00'20"). There is a nice little arch and, in the background, an alcove sheltering a

Arch & Alcove

small round dune and a window through which you can see the North Teepees. This magical place is best lit from the middle of the afternoon on. Using a wide-angle lens, it can be photographed from a variety of angles—not only the most obvious one. Coming back to the small hanging valley, you can walk a bit to the south on the flat area and explore the western edge of Top Rock. Look for some interesting rocks overlooking Sand Cove. Then, heading east, you'll soon find a

colorful slickrock slope with a mild slant leading down to the east side of Top Rock. From here, you'll be able to explore the area's cross-bedding to your heart's content. While going down the slickrock slope, look on your right for a group of small colorful sandstone outcroppings with weird shapes and explore them. There are some nice surprises here.

Close by, you'll also find a rock in the shape of a huge hamburger (36°59'22" 112°00'07"). From the bottom of the slope, you can walk about 0.5 mile cross-country to the Teepees if you wish (*see next section*). Otherwise, you can return to the Wave by hiking north on the slickrock slope to cross the North Saddle (36°59'45" 112°00'14").

Gnome

The Teepees

The area known as The Teepees lies about 0.5 mile east of the permit area of Coyote Buttes North. Note that there are also other teepees in the Coyote Buttes South area (*see next chapter*). There are in fact two distinct groups of teepees in the Coyote Buttes North area, commonly known as the North and South Teepees. Both are easily observed in the distance, on your way to the Wave or from the eastern edge of Top Rock. The Teepees are majestic sandstone outcrops eroded down to a conical shape reminiscent of Native American teepees, hence the name. This area is particularly attractive for its views of the Teepee shapes. It has great potential for abstract shots. Inside the North Teepees, you'll find some sandstone swirls reminiscent of those around the Wave, although different in color and texture.

Photo advice: Coming from Top Rock—behind which the Wave is nestled—you'll be on the west side of the North Teepees. They are photographically more interesting than the South Teepees. You'll find photogenic pink striations with black incrustations at the base of one of the North Teepees to the left. Walk around the right side of that teepee and you'll come to a narrow passage leading up to the heart of North Teepees. There are some good shots from inside when the swirls are not covered by sand. You can easily climb west to an open 'window' for a panoramic shot encompassing the South Teepees and Top Rock with part of your teepee. The very south face of the North Teepees is impressive and photogenic. Even though the west face of the Teepees is better lit in the afternoon, I recommend that you reserve the afternoon light for the short loop around the Wave and Sand Cove described in the previous section. On the other hand, if the sky is cloud-covered, I encourage you to head to the North Teepees and point your camera to the ground and the nice sandstone sculptures and patterns.

Getting there: The Teepees are located on the east side of the Coyote Buttes North, outside the permit area. Going around the permit area calls for a difficult and fatiguing cross-country trudge requiring good route-finding ability and lots of ups and downs in deep sand. Your best bet for visiting the Teepees is to include them in the morning on the day of your visit to the Wave with your permit for the Coyote Buttes North. From the Wire Pass trailhead, follow the path to the Wave (*see Getting there in the Wave section*).

Animal & Teepees (photo by Philippe Schuler)

When you reach the isolated tree at the foot of the sand dune leading to the Wave, do not climb the sand dune. Circumnavigate to the left and continue on the sandy/slickrock slope until your reach the eastern flank of the Coyote Buttes North. From there, you can make a cross-country beeline to the North Teepees on very sandy ground. It's less than a mile, but it's hard work.

Obviously, you may want to visit the Wave first—I can't blame you for that—and do the North Teepees round-trip later in the day. In that case, leave the Wave the way you first entered it, follow the striated wall to your right and go around Top Rock until you reach its eastern flank. From here, you can hike cross-country to the North Teepees. If, after visiting the Wave, you want to explore the upper part of Top Rock along the way to the North Teepees, follow the route described in the second part of the previous section.

Coming back from the North Teepees toward Top Rock, look for a black hole near the top of the cliff. This spot is the window located in the alcove behind the little arch described in the previous section.

Time required: From the Wave, walking around the base of Top Rock, allocate at least 2 hours to the round-trip for a thorough exploration of the North Teepees.

Inside the Teepees

Wire Pass — Buckskin Gulch

As the name implies, the Wire Pass trailhead is not only used for Coyote Buttes North but also for the Wire Pass narrows.

As you visit Coyote Buttes North, it's easy to plan a trip inside Wire Pass and a short stretch of Buckskin Gulch. It will give you a quick, but spectacular insight into the narrows of the Paria River area. Many people consider Buckskin Gulch as having the most interesting narrows on the Colorado Plateau.

Do not venture into Wire Pass and Buckskin Gulch if bad weather is threatening. Once in the canyon, you won't be able to get out in case of flash floods. The enormous tree trunks lodged in the walls several feet above you testify to the force and height of the flash floods that can hit any time of the year, but particularly in summer.

The marked trail begins at the Wire Pass parking area—where you pay your fee—and follows the dry bed of the wash for about 1 mile before reaching the entrance to the first narrows. These narrows, a few dozen yards long, will give

Wire Pass (photo by Gene Mezereny)

you a little preview of what awaits you further on. Soon, you enter the true narrows of Wire Pass and move along between very dark walls, over a hundred feet high. Depending on how the last flash flood affected the canyon, you may have to scramble over choke stones as high as 8 feet at the first and second narrows. In some years, this may present a mild difficulty to some. You'll eventually reach the junction with Buckskin Gulch, 1.6 miles from the trailhead. Look for some faint petroglyphs at the base of the right wall just at the junction.

You can follow Buckskin Gulch downstream as long as you like or time permits. Returning to the junction, you can go a little ways upstream inside Buckskin Gulch instead of returning directly to the Wire Pass narrows. At this spot, Buckskin Gulch frequently contains water and mud-holes. It will give you a good idea of what the narrows look like further down Buckskin Gulch and deep inside Paria Canyon.

Photo advice: The narrows of Wire Pass are generally around 10 feet wide, with some narrower passages about 3 feet wide. They are very high and, therefore, quite dark, except around mid-day. A wide-angle lens will let you maintain the depth-of-field and show the canyon's dimensions despite the wide aperture you'll be forced to rely on. With a firm grip and in good light, it's perfectly possible to photograph with a hand-held camera using a high ISO. Refer to the advice on photographing narrows and slot canyons in the Photo Advice Chapter.

Getting there: The Wire Pass trailhead is about 8.5 miles from US 89 down House Rock Valley Road (*see Getting there of the Wave section*).

Time required: 1 hour round-trip to get to the Wire Pass trailhead from US 89. Up to 3 hours round-trip from the trailhead to really enjoy the narrows. You can precede your visit to the Wave with a short foray inside Wire Pass. Departing the trailhead no later than 9 AM, you can easily reach the Wave around midday, leaving you with ample time for a pleasant visit. Enjoy! ❀

Control Tower

Chapter 17

COYOTE BUTTES SOUTH

Coyote Buttes South Sunset

COYOTE BUTTES SOUTH

Introduction

In the first part of this chapter, I will discuss Coyote Buttes South proper. In the second part, I'll explore a nearby area known as the White Pocket. Its visit is still free at the time of this writing and can be combined with Coyote Buttes South with some overnight camping.

This extraordinary remote area is overshadowed by the more glamorous Coyote Buttes North, with its famous Wave. It is sad because many people miss seeing a truly remarkable place. On the other hand, this works to your advantage if you seek an exhilarating hiking and photographing experience in complete solitude in some of the most unique landscape on the planet.

Remoteness, difficulty of access, and the permit system are the main factors contributing to the sparse crowds. The Coyote Buttes North are not particularly remote and access is relatively easy. Many people combine a visit to the Wave and its surroundings with a short incursion into Wire Pass for a memorable dayhike. The vast majority of people are back at their motel in Page or Kanab that same evening. By comparison, Coyote Buttes South requires a much longer and difficult trip, in a 4WD vehicle. Preferably, photographers will need to spend one night camping on location for an in-depth visit.

The good news is that a permit is considerably easier to come by. There is a 10-permit per day online quota for Coyote Buttes South, but it is rarely full. In fact, there are days when nobody even applies. Permits can be reserved on the web at the same site as for Coyote Buttes North (*see previous chapter*). An additional ten slots are also available as walk-in permits from the Paria Ranger Station on US 89 or fron the BLM office in Kanab, depending on the season (see previous chapter). If you've been trying unsuccessfully to obtain a permit for Coyote Buttes North, consider a jaunt inside Coyote Buttes South. It requires quite a bit more preparation, but you'll find it well worth it.

In truth, another factor may contribute to the lower visitation of Coyote Buttes South. It is the lack of one instantly recognizable iconic feature such as the Wave. This should not deter you because, as a whole, you may find Coyote Buttes South even more spectacular than the northern section, except for the Wave itself. I say this without any hesitation. Coyote Buttes South is one of the jewels of the Southwest, with its many colorful and unusual rock formations, numerous teepees and great views.

You'll need to spend quite a bit of time hiking in Coyote Buttes South to explore the area thoroughly. To be there bright and early, it's a good idea to spend the previous night at the small, but pleasant, primitive Stateline BLM campground. It is located about 10 miles from US 89 on House Rock Valley Road. After visiting the Cottonwood area, you'll probably want an extra morning on location to revisit certain spots for additional photography under better light conditions. My advice is to take your permit for two con-secutive days and to camp at Cottonwood, just outside the wilderness area, where low impact backcountry camping is allowed. The best place to do so is near the corral at the Cottonwood Cove trailhead, close to the most spectacular area. This allows you to explore and photograph until sunset and to catch sunrise at the heart of the Buttes.

The Hydra

If camping is strongly advised, a 4WD vehicle in good mechanical condition—i.e. you can trust it not to let you down in the middle of nowhere—is absolutely mandatory. 4WD is necessary because of patches of deep sand along the way. Deep sand is hard enough to cross when the terrain is flat. When you have to climb a sandy hill, it can get extremely dif-ficult, especially when previous cars have made deep ruts. By drastically lowering tire inflation (by about one third), you can increase flotation and gain much better traction. High clearance adds an extra measure of security by allowing you to do so without lowering the chassis too much. The number one rule while driving in deep sand is: don't stop. Try to maintain a constant speed at high revs. If there are deep ruts, turn your wheels slightly from side to side to avoid getting buried too low. The best time to drive through deep sand is after a rain when the sand is packed and traction is better. Don't even think of going to Coyote Buttes South in a passenger car, even with lowered tire inflation. Once you bury the chassis in deep sand, you'll never get it out. Getting help to get yourself unstuck in this remote country could not only take a couple of days, but would also be very expensive. All these considerations are not trivial. I have been to the Coyote Buttes South on several occasions. In a dry year, conditions can be very bad. Even a 4WD vehicle is no guarantee that you won't run into trouble under difficult conditions. I have personally seen a 4WD SUV stuck in the sand on the first hill after Paw Hole. We had to air down its tires and use a shovel to get it going again. The shovel is your best line of defense if you get stuck, even a small folding shovel. A larger one would be considerably better. Deep sand is not your only enemy. You'll also find some rocky sections. If in doubt, have a partner scout the track in front to help you place your wheels to avoid damage. Be sure to reinflate your tires when you return to the pavement.

Coyote Buttes South is one of the locations in the Southwest where the use of a GPS unit is of considerable help. It will help you know where you are and how to find your way back quickly to your car after a day of exploration. You can also use it to locate nice formations and specific spots. As far as specific locations are concerned, I again encourage you to make your own adventure and find photogenic places for yourself. Thus, I provide few GPS waypoints. Just hike around the buttes, get familiar with the topography, climb up to get a bird's eye view, follow tracks and you will discover all the best places by yourself.

There are two main sectors in the Coyote Buttes South: Paw Hole, relatively easy to reach, and the awesome but more remote Cottonwood area.

Paw Hole

Paw Hole is only 2.5 miles from the House Rock Valley Road. With a 4WD vehicle, it is unlikely that you will get stuck along this section of the sandy track. It will provide a good benchmark to evaluate whether you want to risk it to the more difficult Cottonwood sector.

Park at the pullout and follow the marked trail toward the spectacular first group of Paw Hole Teepees. From the beginning of the trail, you have superb views of the red Teepees at sunset.

A short walk on this trail leads you through the heart of the lower Paw Hole Teepees. You can climb behind the lower teepees and find several good spots to photograph them at close range, looking south and eye-level with the teepees. Proceeding past the lower teepees in a northeasterly direction, you'll lose the trail. You will, however, come quite naturally to an open area with interesting formations where you can spend quite a bit of time photographing.

Retrace your steps to the south of the lower teepees and circumnavigate them to the left in a northerly direction. Follow the western edge of the escarpment along the boundary of the permit area. Continue in this direction for less than 1 mile from the trailhead. You'll come to a particularly nice area with colorful striations, reminiscent of what you can find near the Second Wave at the Coyote Buttes North (*see previous chapter*). This spot and its vicinity is best photographed from late afternoon till sunset.

Time required: Count on about 2 to 3 hours to explore the Paw Hole sector thoroughly, preferably in the early morning or late afternoon.

Getting there: Leaving US 89 about 35 miles from Page or 38 miles from Kanab, drive about 16 miles south on House Rock Valley Road, passing the Wire Pass trailhead and the Stateline Campground. Continue to an unmarked dirt road leading east to the Lone Tree Reservoir a few hundred yards further. With a 4WD vehicle, continue the sandy road for about 2.5 miles with 400 foot of elevation gain, until you reach the Paw Hole trailhead.

Paw Hole Teepees

If you've enjoyed the ruggedness and solitude of Paw Hole, you'll delight in the Cottonwood sector, which is even more photogenic and requires more time to explore. Before you embark, however, you must carefully evaluate the situation. If you are on your own (single vehicle, one individual) and you've sweat bullets to make it up to Paw Hole, things are going to get worse from here on and it would not be advisable to continue. If, on the other hand, there are several of you and you have the appropriate vehicle(s) and at least a shovel, you should be able to make it to Cottonwood.

Cottonwood

So you've managed to reach the Cottonwood Cove trailhead near the corral (36°57'18" 111°58'48"). Now it's only about 0.7 mile cross-country to reach the Cottonwood Teepees to the northwest. You'll likely notice some footprints, just follow them to the edge of the Cottonwood Teepees. You'll easily find a natural saddle to cross into the plateau forming the heart of the Cottonwood area. Past the saddle, I recommend making a wide loop in a roughly counterclockwise direction. Begin by bearing right and you'll soon come to the back of a long sandstone ridge with outstanding colorful crossbedding. To the west, you can see Cottonwood Cove in the distance. Follow the crossbedding and continue straight north until you arrive at a high ridge. Walk to the right and follow the striations of a small sandstone amphitheater to reach a saddle. From this excellent viewpoint, which yields an outstanding photograph at sunrise and sunset, you have a wonderful view of Cottonwood Spring in the foreground, as well as the South and North Teepees directly to the north and Top Rock to the northwest. You are close to the border between Coyote Buttes North and Coyote Buttes South. Suddenly you'll envision interesting possibilities. For instance, it's easy to imagine a cross-country jaunt from the North Teepees (*see previous chapter*) to the Cottonwood Teepees. Such a hike would be only about 2 miles one way on mostly sandy terrain. You could thus come directly from Wire Pass and backpack to Cottonwood Spring, camping just outside the wilderness area. This would make an excellent trip for a seasoned backpacker without a 4WD vehicle, except for the hottest months as there is no water along the way.

From the saddle, descend through some small teepees onto the sandy bench to the northwest. You'll soon come to an outstanding isolated formation that some call Weird Rock, Control Tower or Dali Rock (36°57'49" 111°59'22"). This formation is best photographed in late afternoon.

Walking in a northern direction for about 200 yards, you'll see amazing formations looking like melted rocks, as well as striations reminiscent of a mini-Wave. From here, walk southwest and try locating a small hidden amphitheater with deep red walls under the right light (36°57'52" 111°59'28"). It's a very interesting place; but, it's not easy to find because its entrance is below and hidden by a sand dune.

After exiting the amphitheater the way you came, descend into the flat plain to the west and walk southwest inside the broad sandy wash toward Cottonwood Cove. There is plenty to explore at the southern end of the Cove, such as great colorful teepees, brain rocks, a narrow canyon below tall formations, and some spectacular melted rocks.

Hike back up to the Cottonwood plateau by just winging your way up the least vertical sandstone slope you can find. Walk southeast toward another group of formations roughly at the same latitude as the corral. There, you'll find some remarkable brainrocks and hoodoos with incredible shapes (36°57'18" 111°59'15"). You'll find it hard to resist the temptation of naming them. From here it is only about 0.5 miles

Red Wall

to the corral, where you parked your car. You can photograph until it gets almost dark if you are camping.

Another good reason for spending the night near the corral is to return to the Cottonwood plateau before daybreak the next morning. My favorite sunrise spot is the previously mentioned saddle looking north toward Cottonwood Spring and the Coyote Buttes North. If you have time for a little more hiking and photography, you can walk northeast from your car toward the group of teepees located about 200 yards from the east side of the track. You'll find some interesting formations, somewhat different from what you've seen on the plateau.

These are just some brief examples of what you'll see during your exploration. You'll pass outstanding scenery and come across many beautiful and surprising formations. Take your

Cottonwood Teepees (photo by Tony Kuyper)

time exploring as many nooks and crannies as you can. Most of the time you'll discover something that will stimulate your creative juices.

Getting there: Coming from House Rock Valley road, there are two ways to get to the unmarked Cottonwood Cove trailhead. The shortest way, but not necessarily the easiest, is to go via Paw Hole (*see previous section*). From Paw Hole on, it is strictly 4WD territory. It is 3 miles to Poverty Flat, where you turn left to go north. There is one nasty ascent in deep sand shortly after Paw Hole, as well as some rocky steps. Things improve a little bit after that. What remains of the ranch at Poverty Flat deserves a quick stop to look around. Nothing here will keep you for very long.

Turning north just before Poverty Flat, drive about 2 miles on a very sandy and almost level track to reach the

Sandstone Lace

corral where I suggest you establish your base camp. This corral is featured on the USGS map. This spot is marked as Cottonwood Cove Access on the BLM map that comes with your permit. Shortly after the corral, you'll find some good camping spots along the road, just outside the wilderness boundary. The dirt road used to continue about 1.3 miles further to another trailhead. In recent years it has badly deteriorated, to the point where it is almost completely gone.

Knotted Rock

Even if the BLM regraded it, you'd still be facing a steep ascent in deep sand with almost 300 feet of elevation gain on the way back. Thus, stop at the sign before the descent.

The second alternative is longer and must be used when Lone Tree Reservoir is flooded after a rain. In that case, continue on House Rock Valley Road for about 4 miles past the Lone Tree Reservoir turnoff. Turn east on BLM 1017, which is a good dirt road heading toward Corral Valley. Coming from the south on House Rock Valley Road, this turnoff is about 10 miles from US 89A. Follow BLM 1017 eastward for 3 miles and turn north on BLM 1066. Follow it for about 6 miles, passing by Red Pocket corral, until you reach Poverty Flat from the south. This dirt road has patches of deep sand and rocky sections and is 4WD only. It is usually easier to drive than the difficult section between Paw Hole and Poverty Flat. For this reason, some people prefer this alternative, even though it is longer and bypasses Paw Hole. On the west side of Poverty Flat, find the road heading north and follow the directions given for the first alternative.

Time required: Almost 1 hour to drive directly from Lone Tree Reservoir to Cottonwood Cove Trailhead. Add ½ hour for the second alternative. It is about 6 hours of hiking for a full loop around the whole plateau including Cottonwood Cove, with a fair amount of exploration and stops for photography. This hike is entirely off-trail with some slow walking in deep sand. Be sure to bring plenty of water. You'll make the most of your visit by spreading it over an afternoon, until sunset, and the next morning, starting before sunrise. You can then use the rest of the second day to explore more great geological features in the White Pocket area (*see next section*).

Overleaf: Coyote Buttes South sunrise

THE WHITE POCKET

Introduction

If you have been to the Coyote Buttes area, you may have wondered about a tall, squarish mesa protruding like a big ship in the distance to the southeast—I did for many years. Perhaps you looked at your USGS map and discovered that this formation had the intriguing name of White Pocket. As of this writing, it has become one of the new frontiers of the Arizona Strip, sort of like the Wave was in the early nineties.

Before I begin, I need to say a few words about how I came to decide writing about the White Pocket in the first place. In a broader sense, this also applies to other seldom-seen locations described in the different volumes of *Photographing the Southwest*. Many people cringe at the idea of discussing little-known locations, arguing that a sudden influx of human presence risks marring the landscape. They think that these kind of areas should best be left secret so that a few who are in the know can enjoy it better—and sometimes make money from it.

Although I do understand and respect this widely-supported position regarding little-known sites in general, I have come to the conclusion (from experience) that "secret locations" always end-up being revealed by a kind of collective force that is greater than us individuals. That's just the nature of the beast.

There is no way of preventing the dissemination of knowledge when it comes to places of great aesthetic value and photographic potential. And where it took years before, it now only takes months, thanks to the internet. People see pictures and ask around. If they insist, they always find out where something is. If only one individual publishes pictures, a report or information on a forum, a blog or a web site, everyone is able to find it in a search engine.

As I write this, the White Pocket itself is no longer a "secret". It is already on the web and will be more and more so. In the summer of 2005, pictures of the White Pocket were published in a free advertiser-supported publication for visitors in Kanab, and an outfitter in town was offering commercial tours to the White Pocket. And that's only the tip of the iceberg. If you had done a search on the web at the time, you would have found several photos and some very precise information on how

Sandstone gone wild (photo by Tony Kuyper)

Sunset on the White Pocket

to get there. Once the information is on the web, more and more people add to it. By the time you read this, these words will probably be ancient history and any effort to keep this place a secret may seem futile in retrospect.

The subject of damage to the environment should, of course, be taken very seriously. I have found that the White Pocket is quite a bit less fragile than the Coyote Buttes South, for one. Also, the BLM currently allows cattle grazing at the White Pocket. Cows are happily trampling the place without any particular damage that I can see, except for some cow patties and not-so-obvious paths in the sandstone leading to the tanks. At some point, however, an impact study will probably need to be undertaken in order to evaluate the opportunity to expand the wilderness area and create a permit system similar to the one protecting the Coyote Buttes.

Another point is the difficulty of access. All the 4WD routes leading to the White Pocket are terribly sandy. Adverse conditions—usually the norm rather than the exception—could prove fatal for the ill-prepared would-be adventurer. This point should be taken very seriously. There is no doubt that some people will get out there ill-prepared and end up getting stuck... meaning more head-aches and budget woes for an already resources-strapped BLM!

So, I'd like to do my bit for visitor education. Be forewarned that it is extreme-ly risky to go to the White Pocket due to the very deep sand. If you get stuck, you'll need to pay serious money to be rescued. Pack enough food and water for a few days, several sturdy shovels, and a tow strap. If possible, take some strips of old carpet to put under your wheels if you get stuck. And by all means, never, ever, go alone.

At the White Pocket

The White Pocket is one of these rare places that you discover at the last moment when the road ends. After miles of sandy tracks, you'll come to one last small hill with a tree to the right. Stop here and park your car (36°57'16" 111°53'35"). Then walk up the small sandy saddle and the most amazing sight awaits you. There is no more sand, only a sea of colorful sandstone.

On the USGS map, the White Pocket appears a little bit over 4 miles east of the Cottonwood Teepees. The White Pocket itself is the big butte I mentioned at the beginning of this section. By extension, the nameless sandstone plateau located approximately 0.5 mile to the east is also called White Pocket. It is this specific location I'll discuss here. Ranchers, undoubtedly, named the area for the prevalent white color of the sandstone, as well as the natural pools that can be found here. Although the White Pocket isn't comparable to the vastness of the Coyote Buttes South, it packs a tremendous punch in a relatively small size, perhaps less than half a square mile. I can pretty much guarantee, however, that you'll gasp when you first set eyes upon it.

Before beginning your exploration, take a minute to get your bearings. Doing so, there will be little chance of getting lost. Straight ahead to the west, you can see the high profile of the actual White Pocket Butte. Follow the natural path slightly to the right and within a couple of minutes you'll come to a spectacular swirl of red sandstone, protruding from the ground like the round spine of a giant dinosaur. This is your first indication that this place is going to be different.

Twirls (photo by Steffen Synnatschke)

In the background are twin rocks with striking yellow and red layers.

Continue northwest on that same natural path and, after cresting a little rise, you'll reach a divide and discover the western side of the Pocket. Here the twisted sandstone mass stretches for a few hundred yards, before dropping abruptly to the sandy plain below. This part of the Pocket will be your main playground. You can spend hours slowly exploring this phenomenal landscape of swirls, brainrocks and remarkably well-defined crossbedding. The mostly grayish top layer, only a few inches thick in places, caps an underlayer of deep red sandstone. It pops up here and there, like frosting on an oversize pastry.

At the bottom of this sea of sandstone, there is a shallow natural reservoir that has been dammed by ranchers. Right across from that is a tall sandstone formation. Looking to the south from the top of this formation in late afternoon, there is a great panoramic shot. A little bit further to the northeast is a strikingly colorful mound with shades of white, gold and pink and a ribbon of deep red crossbedding at its base. The

Crossbedded Cliff

sandstone mass ends abruptly in a series of brainrocks, just a couple of hundred yards below this mound. From here, the view stretches far across the Paria Plateau. On a clear day, you'll be able to spot the pink cliffs of Bryce Canyon and the tall silhouette of Powell Point.

Walking back toward your car, you'll find some deep natural reservoirs to the southeast, close to the divide, hidden inside the phenomenal crossbedding. As you cross the divide, there are some shallow pools that fill with water during rains providing good opportunities for reflections. Some cow trails leading to the pools can be seen on the slickrock.

There are also some good brainrocks to the west in the direction of the White Pocket Butte. This is where you want to be to watch sunrise on the White Pocket Butte if you can spend the night where you parked.

Photo advice: The whitish sandstone and all the other subtle colors will not look their best at midday. Try to be there until late afternoon. Lenswise, anything goes, although you'll predominantly use a wide-angle lens. Above all, take plenty of time to enjoy the spectacular crossbedding and swirls. Be sure you have plenty of film or storage: Shapes, color, texture, and intricate details all contribute to an extraordinary sensory experience that you'll want to capture again and again with your camera.

Getting there: There are two ways to get to the White Pocket. One is to come via Poverty Flat following one of the two options described in the *Getting there* of the Cottonwood section (via Paw Hole or via BLM 1017 and 1066). You'll follow this way if you've visited Coyote Buttes South and camped there the night before. At Poverty Flat, take the sandy dirt road heading northeast and follow it for almost 6 miles to the White Pocket. Don't let yourself be fooled by the USGS map, which shows this road stopping at a corral not far from Poverty Flat. This road does go on until the White Pocket. Almost 4 miles from Poverty Flat, the road ascends a hill then descends on the other side, both in deep sand. Under dry conditions, this section may be difficult to negotiate, especially on the way back. To avoid getting stuck, you might want to park on the side and walk the rest of the way to the White Pocket (about 2 miles). As you reach a wooden fence, only a few hundreds yards from the White Pocket, note the track coming from the right. This is where you arrive if you choose the second alternative.

For the second option, leave House Rock Valley Road about 20 miles south of US 89 and turn east on BLM 1017, which is a good dirt road heading toward Corral Valley. Coming from the south on House Rock Valley Road, this turnoff is about 10 miles from US 89 A. Follow BLM 1017 eastward for 6.1 miles until Pine Tree Pockets and turn left on the road going north-east. After 3.9 miles, locate a faint side road heading north, forming the left branch of a Y. You can easily miss this turn because the track is very

Sunrise on the White Pocket

Waves (photo by Philippe Schuler)

faint. If you're not sure about your car's odometer or if you forgot to reset it, the coordinates for this turn are 36°53'03" 111°55'13". From here on, the sand gets extremely deep and I suggest you get out and test it over the next hundred feet or so. Be sure you are in "granny low", with tires deflated for better flotation and that you have adequate clearance to ride the ruts without getting your undercarriage encased in the deep sand. Since the area is rather flat overall, it is normally negotiable, unless it hasn't rained in months.

The distance from US 89 to the White Pocket is about 36 miles either way. Count on at least 2 hours to get there under the right conditions. Ask the rangers at the Paria Contact Station before choosing one of the two ways, as they usually know their respective condition. The first alternative via BLM 1017/1066 and Poverty Flat is normally less difficult, except for the sandy hill on the way back. However, you can avoid it by walking. You're also more likely to encounter other folks going to Cottonwood or to the White Pocket if you get stuck and need assistance.

Time required: At least 3 hours to scout the entire area and take photographs, much longer if you can take the time. Like the Coyote Buttes South, this visit is best done as an overnighter to take advantage of the golden hour before sunset and after sunrise the next morning.

Taking into consideration the respective remoteness but close proximity of Coyote Buttes South and White Pocket, it's a good idea to visit both locations during the same trip. One possible scenario would be to arrive at the White Pocket in mid-afternoon, visiting the area and camping on location that first evening. The early part of the next day would be devoted to additional exploration and photography of the White Pocket. You would then travel to Coyote Buttes South in mid-morning, which would give you the better part of a day to explore the area. You would spend a second night camping—this time near the Cottonwood trailhead (outside the wilderness boundary)—devoting the next morning to the Cottonwood area, before returning to civilization after paying a visit to Paw Hole along the way. ✿

Fire Cave

Chapter 18
A FORAY INTO NEVADA

Arch Rock in Valley of Fire

A FORAY INTO NEVADA

As a bonus, in this final chapter we will wander through a few remarkable sites located at the southern tip of Nevada, adjacent to the Arizona Strip. Not only are these sites in close proximity to the Arizona border, they are also located near I-15 on one of the main thoroughfares from the West Coast. If you happen to be coming or going from Las Vegas to visit Northern Arizona or Southern Utah, you'll easily pass by these locations and it would be sad to miss them. We'll begin this foray at the border with Arizona on I-15, heading southwest and finishing just west of Las Vegas.

The Gold Butte Byway

Gold Butte Road is a backcountry byway traversing rugged desert country similar to the Arizona Strip, south of I-15 and Mesquite. From NV 170, the road is paved for the first 21 miles to Whitney Pocket. Then it is well-graded for the next 20 miles to Gold Butte ghost town. Beyond that, the road turns into a rough track to reach the eastern shore of Lake Mead.

Whitney Pocket makes a good base for exploring the region with its numerous undeveloped campsites tucked at the bottom of striking red sandstone buttes. One of the main features of Whitney Pocket is the small dam built by the CCC for local cattle grazing. Although exploring the easily-climbed heights of the buttes to the south reveals some finely eroded red sandstone walls, Whitney Pocket has little photographic potential. From Whitney Pocket, a broad, usually well-graded road, leads eastward toward Arizona and Parashant Nat'l Monument. About 1.5 miles northwest of Whitney Pocket on Gold Butte Road, a narrow high-clearance road leads southwestward toward some interesting white sandstone outcroppings harboring many petroglyphs.

To the south of Whitney Pocket, the pavement turns to graded gravel and dirt. Except after severe flooding, the road is usually passable for passenger cars. About 7.5 miles south of Whitney Pocket, you'll find a turnoff to your right leading in 0.5 mile to the Devil's Throat, a 100-foot deep sinkhole surprisingly dug in the middle of a flat plain. It is unfortunately too big to photograph at ground level.

After observing the Devil's Throat, adventurous travellers with a high-clearance 4WD vehicle can continue westward on the dirt road to investigate a remarkable area of sandstone known as the Hobgoblins' Playground or Little Finland. I'll use the latter moniker for the description and directions. Little Finland is a place of extraordinarily twisted sandstone formations, sculpted into haphazard shapes by the forces of erosion. There is an endless amount of monsters, gargoyles, skulls, and other fantastic shapes which seem to come eerily alive in the evening light.

Not far from Little Finland is a short but very interesting and photogenic slot canyon known as the Seven Keyholes.

Photo advice: A wide angle to short telephoto will be your tool of choice to photograph the goblins. Little Finland's incredible formations are best photographed in the golden hour befor sunset. This makes logistics difficult due to the remoteness of the location. Driving at night is not advisable unless you backtrack your way with your GPS, following your track log. Little Finland is truly a fantastic photographer's playground. Enjoy it, but tread with caution as the

Hobgoblin on the prawl

formations are extremely fragile and degradation is noticeable over a period of just a few years.

Getting there: From Mesquite, follow NV 170 for about 9 miles toward Bunkerville/Riverside. Proceed left at the Y on unmarked Gold Butte Byway, just before the Virgin River bridge. Coming from the west I-15, 8 miles southwest of Mesquite, take Exit 112 toward Riverside/Bunkerville following NV 170 for 3 miles. Make a sharp right on the Byway shortly after the Virgin River bridge.

Do not attempt to visit Little Finland without a high-clearance 4WD vehicle—a necessity to avoid getting high-centered in the sandy washes. You'll also need a printout of the area's 7.5' topographic map and a GPS unit. It is advisable to go with a partner. A second vehicle will offer better security if the track is in bad shape. Track conditions are very unpredictable. I had no difficulty during my first trip; but, on my second trip, I found the track badly washed out. As it is difficult to find Little Finland without GPS coordinates, I'm including a series of waypoints for a few strategic spots along the route.

Gods & Monsters

There are two ways to reach Little Finland from Gold Butte Byway. If you decide to go there straight from Mesquite without seeing the Devil's Throat or Gold Butte Ghost Town first, take the sandy shortcut leaving Gold Butte Byway on the west side (right) at waypoint #1 36°28'31" 114°09'50". From here the track follows a sandy wash southwestward, until waypoint #2 at 36°26'35" 114°11'16". Continue straight ahead, heading west/southwest, noting the wash and track coming from your left. This is Mud Wash and the track coming from Devil's Throat, which I'll describe below. In a little while, you reach waypoint #3 at 36°26'10" 114°12'23" with a smaller wash coming from the left and the road leading to the Seven Keyholes. Continuing northwest inside the broad bed of Mud Wash, you'll pass a corral to your right. From here, make your way as best you can inside the wash as the track is oftentimes washed out. At waypoint #4, 36°27'49" 114°14'02", make a very sharp turn to the east/southeast for the final leg of your 9-mile journey from Gold Butte Road, ending up at the last waypoint at 36°27'09" 114°12'53". You'll know you've arrived when you see the lone palm tree at the base of the cliff on top of which the goblins are located. Cross the fence, turn right and walk along the rim. Coming from the Devil's Throat car park, turn on the dirt road paralleling Mud Wash westward, and you'll reach waypoint #2 in about 2.5 miles. Continue west/southwest to follow the above-described route.

To reach the Seven Keyholes, instead of continuing inside Mud Wash at waypoint #3, drive into the small wash to your left and almost immediately take the road going northwest parallel to Mud Wash. After about 1.8 miles, turn south, going up the plateau and down to the car park at 36°25'51" 114°13'17". The total driving distance from waypoint #3 is about 3.4 miles, with a very steep incline near mile 3 requiring low-range.

Time required: The better part of a day for a comprehensive exploration of Gold Butte Byway from I-15. About 5 hours from I-15 for Little Finland alone.

Nearby location: From Mesquite, you are only 20 minutes away from the heart of the spectacular Virgin River Gorge located in Arizona. The gorge has beautiful narrows in its southern part as I-15 crosses the Beaver Dam Mountains southwest of St. George. There is a rest area/campground about halfway through the gorge, which is the only point where you can take pictures.

Valley of Fire

This spectacular Nevada State Park is only 50 miles northeast of Las Vegas and thus sees large numbers of visitors. Most people spend only a few hours in the park. Photographers will want to plan at least a full day and preferably an overnighter to thoroughly enjoy the rich geological features of the park and shoot them under the best light. Arguably, the best way to visit the park is to see it in chunks. Over the years, I have stopped here many times on my way to and from my home in the L.A. area and Northern Arizona or Utah, taking advantage of the best light at such or such location at the time of my passage. I suspect that many readers will find this approach well adapted to their own travels, as Las Vegas' McCarran Airport is a major gateway for trips to the Southwest.

In the west side of the park, you'll find a short scenic loop, which can be done with your car, around the park's two nice campgrounds. This 2-mile loop—half graded, half paved—has many photogenic points of interest: a jumble of extraordinarily eroded red rocks, some petroglyphs and a few beautiful arches. All these sights are easy to photograph, preferably in the morning. I suggest starting with Atlatl Rock, then moving on to Arch Rock before exploring the west side of the Jumble of Rocks.

Atlatl Rock is located above a large car park, close to the campground of the same name (aka campground A). It is a tall sandstone wall with a large rock art panel about 60 feet above the ground. A metal staircase allows you to climb just below the panel. Atlatl Rock is named for the wooden dart thrower used by Basketmakers, Ancestral Puebloans and other Pre-Columbian Native American groups. One such weapon is depicted on the panel. In winter, shortly after sunrise, the sun forms a shadow on the petroglyph panel mim-

Sunrise casts an Indian silhouette on Atlatl Rock

Nighttime photography at Valley of Fire (photo by Vic Beer)

icking the profile of a Native American Indian. You'll have plenty of time to photograph Atlatl Rock as nearby Arch Rock is in shadow for quite a while after sunrise.

If you arrive at Arch Rock approximately 30 minutes after sunrise, you'll benefit from the best light. The arch is only a couple of minutes walk from the less developed campground of the same name (aka campground B), or you can park at one of the close pullouts. You can then shoot the arch from behind in rich direct light or photo-graph it from the front and slightly below, taking advantage of reflected light for a wonderful glow under its span. The arch also has good frontal light in late-afternoon.

After photographing Arch Rock, I suggest you stay until mid-morning to explore the Jumble of Rocks, particularly the west side, which has dozens of little arches and caves making great intimate landscapes when photographed in indi-rect light. The Jumble of Rocks has other named formations such as Piano Rock and Poodle Rock, but this is just the tip of the iceberg. Just explore at your whim and you'll find many possibilities for photography. If you can spend the night at one of the campgrounds during a full moon, I highly recommend doing some nighttime photography, experimenting with long exposures and/or doing some

Moonrise & Sunset

rock painting with a flash-light. Arch Rock is probably the easiest and most reward-ing formation for that.

The spectacular White Domes scenic road starts close to the Visitor Center and goes north for about 7 miles before ending up in a cul-de-sac at the White Domes car park. Along the way, it passes through some of the most strikingly colorful landscape you'll ever see. It is particularly well lit from late afternoon until sunset. You'll be stopping many times to admire and photograph the views, as well as to take short but very rewarding hikes.

The White Domes road's first landmark is Petroglyph Canyon, with Mouse's Tank at the end. This is a widely popular trail, probably so because of its short length and appeal to families. You'll pass several groups of petroglyphs on the left side of the trail before reaching Mouse's Tank, a deep natural depression collecting rainwater and retaining it for months. It is named after Mouse, an alleged "renegade Indian" who hid there. Mouse's Tank is only mildly interesting and certainly not a prime location for photography. Move along to your next stop at Rainbow Vista.

Rainbow Vista is an undeniable jewel and you'll want to spend plenty of time in its vicinity. I highly recommend that you visit it in late afternoon and until after sunset. However, you'll be faced with a tough choice, as the White Domes Trail (*see below*) is also at its best at the same time. The area around Rainbow Vista is particularly colorful and has a lot of photographic potential. Across the road from the car park, you have a very nice panoramic view of the area below with a medium to long telephoto. After taking in this must see view, follow the sandy trail for a few hundred yards. Before reaching the beginning of the red rocks, leave the trail and climb the pastel-colored slickrock slope to your left between the last two fins. Explore the area, looking for miniature arches, caves and other bizarre formations and striations. Great panoramic views of the back towards the east and northeast show the colorful beige and red rocks at close range. A wide angle lens will be your tool of choice here. Returning to the trail and continuing to its dead-end, you arrive at a viewpoint over an amazing

Rainbow sunset

jumble of dark red rocks, which are not easily photographed.

The short gravel road to Fire Canyon/Silica Dome brings you to a high vantage point overlooking the same colorful rocks seen from the Rainbow Vista Trail.

At the end of the White Domes road, the 1.2-mile White Domes Loop Trail is short, easy and extremely rewarding. After going down some slickrock steps through highly colorful sandstone, the trail passes by a couple of dilapidated wooden structures from an old movie set. There is nothing of photographic interest to the set. Instead, leave the trail and ascend the small orange-colored mound to your left or climb onto the slickrock area to the right. Both offer ample opportunities for photographing spectacular crossbedding.

Ephemeral Arch

Shortly after the movie set, you'll wander through a very short but photogenic slot canyon. If you haven't had the opportunity to visit the narrows and slot canyons of Southern Utah (*see Photographing the Southwest Volume 1 Chapter 5 – Along the Cockscomb*), this is your chance to get a feeling for what they look like. After particularly hard rains, the slot canyon may be flooded under several feet of water and you may need to retrace your steps and do the rest of the hike from the other end of the loop. In most cases it will be dry, or you'll only need a bit of shallow wading.

As you exit the slot canyon, the trail gradually ascends sand and slickrock. Continue on the path for a little while. You can then leave it and climb the slickrock slope to the right to find other colorful rocks and good viewpoints at sunset, before completing the loop back to your car. The White Domes Loop Trail is without a doubt the best hiking trail in the park and shouldn't be missed. It is best photographed from late afternoon on.

Back on NV 169, two interesting locations stand out among the various sights of the east side of the park: Elephant Rock and Ephemeral Arch. Elephant Rock is arguably the most famous landmark of the park. The arch is located alongside the park road, close to the east entrance. From the car park, a short trail leads to this remarkable feature that strikingly resembles the shape and proportions of

Elephant Rock

a pachyderm. It can be photographed from below as well as from above with equally good results. I tend to prefer the mid-afternoon view from above; but, it's just a matter of taste. Don't come too late, as the Elephant tends to "disappear" early in the shadow of the ridge.

Ephemeral Arch is not well known and there is no official trail to reach it. This small arch is extremely original, very delicate and well lit in late afternoon. It is worth the hike, although it can get very hot during the summer months. To get there, stop at the Cabins car park, climb the small hill to the right of the car park and descend into a side canyon leading in a short distance to the sandy north fork of Fire Wash. Follow the wash in a northerly direction until you find the arch to your right (36°26'26" 114°28'50"). It is about 1 mile from your car. The wash has no major obstacles and is easy to follow. There are small arches and interesting formations along the way. Another way to reach the arch is to park along NV 169 where it crosses Fire wash and follow the latter northward for about 1.3 miles. The only benefit is to avoid the descent into the wash from the Cabins car park.

Getting there: Valley of Fire's west entrance station is about 15 miles from Exit 75 on I-15 via NV 169. The east entrance fee station is about 22 miles from Exit 93 on I-15 via Logandale and Overton. By virtue of being closest to Lake Mead, the east entrance is a good place to start for visitors coming from Henderson, Boulder city and Southern Arizona via North Shore Road (*see next section*).

Lake Mead's North Shore

Several interesting sites can be found along NV 167, aka North Shore Drive, which runs on the left bank of the Colorado River as it forms Lake Mead. The road runs for about 45 miles from Valley of Fire to the town of Henderson, southeast of Las Vegas. Despite the name, North Shore Drive doesn't follow the shore of Lake Mead and, in fact, offers only sparse and distant vistas of the lake. The interest lies along the highway and to the north of it.

Coming from Valley of Fire and following NV 167 southwest, three picnic areas dot the road and are worth a stop: Blue Point Spring, Rogers Spring, and Redstone. Blue Point and Rogers springs, respectively about 4 miles and 5 miles from the Valley of Fire turnoff, are small oasis with hot springs flowing into Lake Mead. They are very different from the rest of the landscape, with their Washingtonian palm trees surrounding small ponds and streams. At Rogers Spring, a short 0.7-mile round-trip leads to an overlook with views of the lake.

Almost 7 miles further, you'll find the turnoff for the Bitter Springs Trail on your right. It is a 28-mile BLM backcountry backway reaching NV 169 about 3 miles from I-15. It passes through desert valleys, abandoned mines, rugged mountains and colorful sandstone

The Winding Road (photo by Philippe Schuler)

hills, such as the Buffington Pockets. Due to stretches of deep sand, you'll need a high-clearance 4WD for this dirt road.

About 6 miles from this turnoff, Redstone consists of several red sandstone outcrops very similar to what I described as the Whitney Pocket and the Jumble of Rocks in the west side of Valley of Fire. A short 0.5-mile loop trail winds its way through the buttes. Although quite striking by itself, Redstone is much smaller and not as spectacular as the Valley of Fire.

About 6.5 miles past Redstone, look for a large car park on the right side of the road. This is the trailhead for the North Shore Summit Trail, a short 0.5-mile climb to a round hilltop offering great views of the area, in particular the Bowl of Fire, which will be our next stop.

About 4.7 miles past the North Shore Summit Trail car park, look for a paved road to the right, going down at an angle. Slow down early as this road is masked by a butte and is only seen at the last moment. The pavement stops almost immediately at a vast car park where passenger cars should stop. High-clearance 4WD vehicles can continue and descend into Callville Wash. After 0.2 mile, the wash splits with main Callville Wash continuing straight ahead toward the Bowl of Fire and a smaller wash branching off to the left almost at a right angle and leading to Lovell Wash. To explore the Bowl of Fire, continue straight into Callville Wash for almost 1.8 miles to where the wash widens. Find a suitable place to park your vehicle. Although very sandy in places, the road is flat and without any obstacles. From here, walk north for about a mile into a smaller wash to reach the Bowl of Fire. The Bowl is quite similar to Valley of Fire, with a lot of red sandstone and some nice arches that photograph best during the golden hour. You're most likely to have the place to yourself.

Driving back to the junction with the previous wash close to NV 167, turn right into this smaller wash to visit the Lovell Wash Narrows. This site is quite spectacular and relatively easy to reach with a high-clearance 4WD vehicle. The road soon splits into three. Take the middle fork going uphill. The road continues to climb gently northwest with minimal obstructions and the broad Lovell Wash soon appears far below to your left. Park near the rim and walk down the washed-out road into the wash. After passing the remnants of a mine and a couple of bends, you arrive at the narrows proper. The narrows are only 0.3-mile long. They are superb, with spectacular veins of pastel colors. To find such beautiful narrows so close to Las Vegas comes as a real surprise. In the afternoon, the narrows will tend to be

Lovell Narrows

flooded with direct sunshine due to their southwest orientation. I recommend visiting in the early to mid-morning for best reflected light.

Your last stop should be the Callville Trail, whose trailhead is located at the entrance of the Callville Bay Campground. It is 4.7 miles past the Bowl of Fire/Lovell Wash turnoff on North Shore Drive, then 4 miles southeast on the Calville Marina road. The short trail offers an excellent panoramic view of the lake from the summit.

Red Rock Canyon

Any visitor to Las Vegas with an interest in the natural world should set aside some time for a visit to Red Rock Canyon National Conservation Area. This small park has several spectacular features and is a nice photographic location. It is so close yet so far from the hustle and bustle of Vegas.

A 13-mile one-way scenic loop takes you through the best places. From a geologic and photographic perspective, the park's main attraction is the colorful red sandstone outcrops, on a background of gray limestone and sheer cliffs. This is found essentially near the Calico area of the scenic loop and by the Sandstone Bluffs that form the base of the Spring Mountains. The rest of the park is typical Mojave Desert habitat with yuccas and Joshua trees.

If you only have time for a short visit, start with the Visitor Center. There is an excellent panoramic view of the Calico Hills from the back. If you're not hiking, you can take good photos from the Calico I and Calico II car parks at the beginning of the scenic loop. With a little more time, there are

Soft light on the Calico Hills

many good viewpoints from the easy Calico Hills Trail. It is just a short way from both car parks and can be entered from either, avoiding the less interesting section from the Visitor Center. The Calico Hills Trail continues northwest toward the Sandstone Quarry trailhead. It has more interesting views along the way, including a large boulder with petroglyphs.

The Sandstone Quarry, about 3 miles past the park entrance, is the trailhead for two popular hikes: the Calico Tanks and Turtlehead Peak. The latter is strenuous, involving a 1700-foot climb. The Calico Tanks Trail is only a moderate 1.2-mile climb through colorful sandstone to a fairly large natural reservoir. For a bird's eye view of the Calico Basin and Las Vegas in the distance, a 0.3-mile scramble

Storm over the Sandstone Bluffs

leads to a saddle near the top of the Calico Hills.

For a more in-depth discovery of Red Rock Canyon, hike to Icebox Canyon or Pine Creek Canyon, at the base of the Sandstone Bluffs.

Outside of the scenic loop and further south on NV 159, the Bonnie Springs Ranch area offers excellent views of the Sandstone Bluffs, Mt. Wilson and Rainbow Mountain from a number of dirt roads. There are good opportunities to photograph wild burros.

I particularly enjoy this area, having spent quite a number of days here, hiking and riding my horse, through unusual circumstances. As you may have read in my bio at the end of this book, I spent almost two decades as a software executive, which led me to spend much time at computer conventions held in Las Vegas. If I were to put all the days together, I estimate that I spent almost three months of my life here, either as an exhibitor or an observer. One year, my wife Patricia and I decided to break the routine by driving to Las Vegas with our two horses in tow. We settled in for the week at the Bonnie Springs Ranch Motel. One amenity of this motel is that it has corrals. In the morning, my wife would drive me down to the Convention Center in my suit and tie. She would pick me up again at the show in late afternoon and we would drive back to the motel, I would trade my business attire for riding gear and we would ride in the park until after sunset. During business meetings, I greatly enjoyed telling people that I was "horsing around in Vegas."

Photo advice: The Calico Hills are best photographed at sunrise, when the side light accentuates the contrast between the colorful red sandstone and gray limestone under sheer cliffs. Early morning light brings out texture in the cross-bedding. Late afternoon light enhances the nice hues of the red sandstone. The Sandstone Bluffs look best at sunrise and in mid- to late-afternoon.

Getting there: From I-15 (Exit 41) in Las Vegas, take West Charleston Blvd., which turns into NV 159. Follow it west for about 16 miles to the park entrance.

Time required: About 3 hours, including travel time from Las Vegas, for the briefest of visits, without any hiking. 4 to 5 hours for a more relaxed pace, including the Visitor Center and some hiking. ✿

Stormy sunset on the bluffs

APPENDIX

APPENDIX

A Glossary of not-so-obvious Terminology

Alcove: a shallow cave formed by the breakup of a sandstone layer weakened by water percolating from the top. Best examples: Grand Canyon NP, Canyon de Chelly NM.

Anthropomorph: a stylized figure with human-like attributes, as seen on rock art all over the Southwest.

Arch: a natural opening eroded by the action of the wind or rain. Best examples: Monument Valley, Valley of Fire.

Arroyo: Spanish term used in place of "wash" throughout the Sonoran desert region; see wash. Best examples: Organ Pipe Cactus NM, Saguaro NP.

Badlands: desert terrain forming strongly eroded shale or limestone hills, frequently striped with spectacular colors. A translation of the French "mauvaises terres", as named by French Canadian trappers. Best examples: Petrified Forest NP, Little Painted Desert, Coal Mine Canyon.

Bajada: a slope formed of multiple alluvial fans (fan-shaped deposits of sediments and debris found at the base of stream channels.) Best examples: Organ Pipe Cactus NM, Saguaro NP.

Balanced rock: a rock of hard material resting on top of a softer formation that has been eroded away, leaving the former balanced on top of the latter. Best examples: Around Page, Chiricahua NM.

Bedrock: the solid rock of the earth's crust underlying sandstone layers.

Butte: a small, deeply cut mesa that has been protected from erosion by a hard sedimentary layer on its summit. Best examples: Monument Valley, Lukachukai Mountains.

Cairn: a human-made conical pile a stones marking a footpath.

Canyon: a deep gorge formed by the course of a river. Found throughout the Southwest. Best examples: Grand Canyon, Little Colorado River.

Cave: a hole in a thick wall of sandstone formed by a spring-seep breaking up the sandstone. Best examples: Grand Canyon NP, Canyon de Chelly NM.

Confluence: the points where two rivers or canyons meet. Best examples: Colorado River and Little Colorado River in Grand Canyon NP.

Cross-bedding: intricately overlapped layers of sandstone. Best examples: The Wave, the White Pocket.

Cryptobiotic soil: aka cryptogamic soil or simply "crypto", Greek term for "hidden life", a blackish crust inhabited by micro-organisms whose activity creates a network of fibers holding soil particles together. Unfortunately, crypto is easily crushed by footsteps and car tires and takes decades to regenerate.

Desert varnish: dark stripy patina on sandstone, formed by iron or manganese oxide processed by micro-organisms. Best examples: Canyon de Chelly NM, Grand Canyon NP.

Diatreme: gaseous eruption during which the shattered rock falls back into the pipe. Magma often flows upward through the weakened crust to create a dike around the diatreme. Also known as volcanic plug or neck. Best examples: Agathla Peak, Church Rock.

Dike: intrusive magma rise created when a crack occurred in the earth's crust. Best examples: Agathla Peak.

Fins: a group of individually eroded rocks similar in shape to the fin of a shark and following vertical fracture lines.

Flash flood: a torrent of water suddenly formed by a violent rainstorm falling on non-porous soil. In the Southwest, these torrents naturally gravitate towards fissures in the rock, forming narrows and slot canyons.

Fold: a rise formed by the irregular uplift of sedimentary layers of rock. See also Monocline. Best examples: The Cockscomb, Comb Ridge.

Hogan: the traditional Navajo dwelling, built of wooden logs.

Goblin: a variation of the Hoodoo; exclusively in soft sandstone. Evokes images of mythological creatures of a grotesque shape. Best example: Little Finland.

Gooseneck: bend in a river in the form of a loop. Best examples: Goosenecks of the San Juan, Colorado River at Horseshoe Bend.

Hoodoo: pillar of eroded rock or sandstone, capped at the top by a more highly resistant layer. Best examples: Around Page, The Paria.

Kiva: underground ceremonial chamber built by Ancestral Puebloans and other native cultures of the Southwest.

Kokopelli: the ubiquitous anthropomorph, with its hunch back and flute. Common on rock art all over the Southwest.

Laccolith: mountain formed by magma uprisings pushing horizontally and vertically through the thick layers of sandstone. Best examples: all the most prominent mountains of the Colorado Plateau.

Mesa: a flat-top remnant of a plateau rising above the surrounding plain. Its name means "table" in Spanish. Best example: Monument Valley.

Moki steps: small steps carved in the sandstone to climb steep inclines and access dwellings, granaries or canyon rims.

Monocline: a spectacular fracture in the ground, resulting in layers of sedimental rock exposed at a steep angle. Also known generically as "Fold" and "hogback" when it's shorter in length. Best examples: The Cockscomb, Comb Ridge.

Natural Bridge: a natural opening formed by water action piercing through thin rock at the bend of a river. Best example: Rainbow Bridge.

Narrows: extremely narrow canyon formed by a watercourse that is often dry. Best examples: Paria Narrows, Buckskin Gulch.

Petrified dunes: ancient sand dunes turned to rock after being buried, then rounded and polished by erosion. Best examples: Coyote Buttes, Around Page.

Petrified wood: remnant tree trunks from ancient forests submerged by volcanic ash, then exposed by soil erosion. Best examples: Petrified Forest NP.

Petroglyph: rock art done by pecking, scratching or carving.

Pictograph: rock art painted on the surface of the stone.

Playa: Spanish for "beach", a dry lake bed formed by evaporation and consisting of dissolved minerals.

Pothole: aka *Tinaja* in Spanish. A shallow pool formed in slickrock or limestone, sometimes even bedrock, by water dissolving the sand or rock particles, which are then washed away during storms.

Rincon: short abandoned loop in a river gorge or any short tributary in a canyon or valley.

Reef: a natural rock barrier in the form of a ridge, formed by an almost vertical uplift of sedimentary layers. Best examples: San Rafael Reef, Capitol Reef.

Slickrock: generic term used to describe exposed masses of hard sandstone polished by the elements. This sandstone becomes extremely slippery under rain, ice and snow. Found all over the Southwest.

Slot canyon: a narrow passage with smooth walls, formed not by constantly flowing water, but by the repeated action of flash floods. Best examples: Antelope Canyon, Wire Pass.

Spires: rock capped by a hard uppermost slab and eroded by rain into vertical towers.

Tank: a large pothole. Best example: The White Pocket.

Travertine: layered calcium carbonate formed by deposition from spring waters or hot springs. Best examples: Havasu Canyon.

Volcanic plug: see diatreme. Best examples: Agathla Peak, Church Rock.

Wash: a dry watercourse channeling runoff water after thunderstorms.

Window: a hole trough a wall of rock, with edges not quite as defined as an arch. Best example: Canyon de Chelly.

Maps

The maps are classified by scale, beginning with the largest and most general.

Large scale road maps: The best general road map is without doubt the Indian Country Guide published by the American Automobile Association (AAA). This remarkable guide/map is a sheer pleasure to read and use. It contains a surprising amount of dirt and gravel roads, with very accurate mileage and it does an excellent job of referencing little-known locations. Unless you intend to do some heavy-duty hiking or four-wheeling, this map is quite sufficient for an ordinary car-based tour of the Colorado Plateau. Unfortunately, coverage doesn't extend to southern Arizona and Nevada. Sites located in that area are adequately covered by the AAA Arizona–New Mexico map and park mini-guides. You can obtain these maps from any AAA office and many of the bookstores in the National Parks and Monuments.

Other road maps: Rand McNally Road Explorer software allows you to print express maps of Arizona and Nevada and generate detailed roadbooks for your own use or for the benefit of friends or groups.

National Park and Monument miniguides: These wonderfully concise miniguides are packed with all the essential information about the parks, their history, geology and fauna. You can get them at the park entrances or at Visitor Centers. They will help you find your way around on roads and trails. To visit some sites north of Page (such as Alstrom Point), you'll benefit greatly from the Grand Staircase Visitor Information brochure which includes a map with a very convenient numbering system that greatly helps identifying and navigating the numerous dirt roads of the area.

National Park topographic maps: If you plan on adventuring along the trails and roads in distant parts of the national parks, the topographic maps of the Trails Illustrated series, printed on waterproof paper, are extremely well made and highly recommended. I always use them for hiking in the parks.

USGS, BLM and Forest Service topographic maps: These maps are essential for navigation in the backcountry. The BLM Arizona Strip Visitor Map, in particular, is essential if you plan to do any driving and hiking in the Arizona Strip.

Topo maps on CD-ROM: A fantastic resource to plan your trip beforehand. The maps print spectacularly well and you can mark your intended route. Great to enter way points in your GPS. Delorme, Maptech and National Geographic make topo mapping software on CD-Rom. National Geographic's Topo! State Series is particularly good. On the web, topozone.com allows you to display at no charge small portions of topographic maps using GPS coordinates and to print them on your own equipment. This site and others, such as backpacker.com, offer a paying service allowing you to download and print personalized maps.

Topographic atlas: DeLorme Atlas & Gazetteer Series.

Selected Bibliography - Guidebooks

You have a wide selection of materials from which to choose among the traditional guidebooks. Here are some of my favorites:

National Geographic's Guide to the National Parks of the USA, published by the National Geographic Society, ISBN 0-792269-72-1: an excellent general reference work, very well illustrated with many photographs.

Journey to the High Southwest by Robert Casey, published by Globe Pequot Press, ISBN 0-762704-99-3: a remarkably endearing and thoroughly documented travel guide to the Four Corners.

Hiking the Southwest's Canyon Country by Sandra Hinchman, published by The Mountaineers Press, ISBN 0-89886-492-5; an excellent hiking guide to the Southwest, very complete, with great maps.

Canyon Hiking Guide to the Colorado Plateau by Michael Kelsey, published by Michael R. Kelsey Publishing, ISBN 0-944510-16-7; a remarkable resource for fit people wanting to explore canyons and remote places of the Colorado Plateau. To be used responsibly and according to the author's warnings and disclaimer. Hiking times are seriously underestimated for the great majority of people. Use maps with caution and not as your primary source of information.

Hiking and Exploring the Paria River by Michael Kelsey, published by Michael R. Kelsey Publishing, ISBN 0-944510-21-3; the comments for the previous book apply to this one too.

Canyon Country Geology for the Layman and Rockbound by F.A. Barnes, published by Arch Hunter Books, ISBN 1-891858-18-1: one of many highly informative and easy-to-read guidebooks by Mr. Barnes. Highly recommended.

Hikers Guide to the Superstition Wilderness by Jack Carlson, published by Clear Creek Pub, ISBN: 1-884224-05-9; a must for hiking the Superstitions.

Scenic Driving Arizona by Randy Johnson & Stewart Green, published by Falcon Press, ISBN 1-56044-449-5: excellent for driving around Arizona.

Sedona hikes: 130 day hikes & 5 vortex sites around Sedona by Richard & Sherry Mangum, published by Hexagon Press, ISBN 1-891517-07-4. Often updated hiking guide to the Sedona area. Well-done and very practical.

Sedona Calling: A Guide to Red Rock Country by Lawrence W. Cheek, published by Arizona Highways, ISBN: 0-916179-81-8: excellent resource on Sedona and surroundings.

Sedona's Top 10 hikes by Dennis Andres, published by Meta Adventures, ISBN 0-972-1202-2-x. A well-done resource if you have little time to spend in Sedona and want to hike some of the most popular trails.

Backcountry Adventures: Arizona by Peter Massey and Jeanne Wilson, published by Swagman Publishing, ISBN 0-966567-50-1: a 4lbs monster of a book, full of remarkable advice for driving around Arizona's backroads.

Rock Art and Ruins for Beginners and Old Guys by Albert Scholl Jr., published by Rainbow Publishing, ISBN 0-9704688-0-6: a fun guide to the major rock art sites.

Route 66 Traveler's Guide and Roadside Companion by Tom Snyder, published by St. Martin's Griffin, ISBN 0-312254-17-2: a fun and informative guide for driving Route 66.

Selected Bibliography - Other Recommended Reading

I cannot recommend too highly the following works, which I consider quintessential to a good understanding of various aspects of the Southwest. Reading these books during a trip in the American West reinforces the pleasure of discovery.

Standing Up Country by Gregory Crampton, published by Rio Nuevo Publishers, ISBN 1-887896-15-5: a wonderful resource on the human history of the Colorado Plateau, richly illustrated with outstanding photography.

Desert Solitaire by Edward Abbey, published by Ballantine Books, ISBN 0-345326-49-0: the classic among the numerous books by Abbey, the rebel ranger, at once liberal and redneck. Abbey depicts his love of the desert with a fine sensibility. It's the great accompaniment for a trip to Havasupai.

The Southwest Inside Out by Thomas Wiewandt and Maureen Wilks, published by Wild Horizons Publishing, ISBN 1-879728-03-6: a highly-innovative and approachable presentation of the natural features of the Southwest. Remarkably illustrated. Outstanding photography.

Architecture of the Ancient Ones by A. Dudley Gardner and Val Brinkerhoff, published by Gibbs Smith, ISBN 0-87905-955-9: Outstanding photography.

The Exploration of the Colorado River and Its Canyons by John Wesley Powell, published by Penguin USA, ISBN 0-140255-69-9: Powell's extraordinary journals of his expedition, prefaced by Wallace Stegner.

The Dark Wind by Tony Hillerman, published by Harper, ISBN 0-061000-03-5: a novel with a cool Navajo cop as its reluctant hero. An excellent introduction to Navajo culture in the guise of a lively story. A must-read when crossing the Big Rez! Don't be ashamed of the "white guy" syndrome. If you get hooked on Navajo and Hopi culture, you'll naturally step up to serious works.

Centennial by James Michener, published by Fawcett Books, ISBN 0-449214-19-2: a remarkable book, even though it's not really about the Southwest. It's an absolutely fascinating saga of the West and a shock for those who have never read Michener.

Needless to say, there are numerous coffee table books depicting the Southwest. These books by well-known photographers such as Ansel Adams, Jack Dykinga, Joseph Lange, David and Marc Muench, Eliot Porter, Lynn Radeka, Galen Rowell, Anselm Spring, Tom Till, Linde Waidhofer, Art Wolfe and many more are a pleasure to look at. They are also an excellent source of locations as well as a great way to improve your photographic skills through emulation.

On the Go Resources

These resources are intended as a quick way of finding further information while you're on the road, by calling the appropriate agency. The phone numbers have been verified shortly before we went to press; however, phone numbers can change and this information may be obsolete by the time you read it. I hope you find this list useful in your travels. It is just a convenient way to call from the road and I have purposely avoided presenting a formal list of web sites.

National Parks & Monuments
Agua Fria NM (623) 580-5500
Canyon de Chelly NM (520) 674-5500
Casa Grande NM (520) 723-3172
Chiricahua NM (520) 824-3560
Glen Canyon NRA (928) 608-6404
Grand Canyon NP (520) 638-7888
Grand Canyon NP Trail Information (520) 638-7888 (press 1-3-1)
Montezuma Castle NM (928) 567-3322
Navajo NM (928) 672-2700
Organ Pipe Cactus NM (520) 387-6849
Parashant NM (435) 688-3246
Petrified Forest NP (928) 524-6228
Red Rock Canyon NRA (702) 363-1921
Saguaro NP Mountain District (520) 733-5153
Saguaro NP Rincon District (520) 733-5153
Sunset Crater NM (520) 526-0502
Tonto NM (520) 467-2241
Tuzigoot NM (928) 634-5564
Vermilion Cliffs NM (435) 688-3200
Walnut Canyon NP (928)526-3367
Wupatki NM (520) 679-2365

State Parks
Alamo Lake SP (928) 669-2088
Kartchner Caverns SP (520) 505-536-2800
Lost Dutchman SP (480) 982-4485
Valley of Fire SP (702) 397-2088

Other Parks & Organizations
Antelope Canyon Navajo Tribal Park (520) 698-2808
American Rock Art Research Association (888) 668-0052
Archeology Vandalism Hotline (800) 722-3998
Arizona Road Conditions (888) 411-ROAD

BLM of Kanab (435) 644-4600
BLM office of St. George UT and the Arizona Strip (435) 688-3200
Cabeza Prieta National Wildlife Refuge (520) 387-6483
Cameron Visitor Center (928) 679-2303 voice (928) 679-2017 fax
First Mesa Consolidated Villages Tourist Office (520) 737-2262
Grand Canyon National Park Lodges (303) 29-PARKS, or (303) 297-2757
Havasupai Reservation (520) 448-2121
Hopi Cultural Center (520) 734-2401
Hualapai Tribe Reservations (888) 255-9550 or (520) 769-2230
John Wesley Powell Memorial Museum (928) 645-9496 or (888) 597-6873
Navajo Parks and Recreation at Window Rock (602) 871-4941
Paria Canyon-Vermilion Cliffs Wilderness (435) 688-3246
Rock Art Ranch, Brantley Baird (928) 288-3260
Sedona Chamber of Commerce (800) 288-7336
Sedona Ranger Station (928) 282-4119
Sedona Visitor Center (928) 282-7722
Sedona Palatki Reservations (928) 204-5818
Superstition Wilderness (602) 225-5200
V-Bar-V Ranch Petroglyph Site (520) 282-4119
Wildflower bloom web site: www.desertusa.com/wildflo/wildupdates.html

Note: all National Parks and Monuments and most travelers' bureaus will send you free documentation anywhere in the world to prepare your trip.

Permits for Coyote Buttes (including the Wave)
https://www.blm.gov/az/paria/obtainpermits.cfm?usearea=CB

Antelope Canyon Concessionaires
Antelope Canyon Adventures (928) 645-5501
Antelope Canyon Navajo Tours (928) 698-3384
Antelope Canyon Tours (928) 645-9102
Grand Circle Adventures (928) 645-5594
Overland Canyon Tours (928) 608-4072
Ken's Tours (928) 660-2844
Lower Antelope Corkscrew Canyon (480) 560-9965

RATINGS

Using a scale of 1 to 5, the following ratings attempt to provide the reader with an overall vision of each location, in order to facilitate comparisons and choices. Obviously, the ratings alone don't tell the whole stoty about a location and should be used only in cunjunction with the explanations of each section.

The ratings are assigned on the basis of four different criteria: overall interest of a location, based mostly on its scenic value (or its beauty and interest in the case of rock art and ancestral dwellings), photographic potential for those of you who happen to carry a camera :-) and level of difficulty to access each location with your vehicle and/or on foot.

The objectivity of ratings done by an author tend to be somewhat tainted by the individual's personal preferences. To minimize personal bias, I arrived at the ratings through a concensual process with a team of knowledgable friends and photographers. We based our assessments on the criteria below and I think we achieved even-handed results. I hope you'll find the ratings helpful in preparing your trip(s) to the Southwest.

Rating	Scenic Value
–	Of no particular interest
♥	Mildly interesting, visit if nearby and/or time permitting
♥♥	Scenic location, worthy of a visit
♥♥♥	Very interesting, scenic or original location
♥♥♥♥	Outstandingly scenic or rewarding location - a highlight
♥♥♥♥♥	World-class location - absolutely tops

Rating	Photographic Interest
♥	Of no particular photographic interest
♦	Worthy of a quick photo
♦♦	Good photo opportunity
♦♦♦	Good photographic potential and scenic subjects
♦♦♦♦	Outstanding photographic potential, highly original or scenic subjects
♦♦♦♦♦	World-class photographic location, "photographer's dream"

Rating	Road Difficulty
♦	Paved road, accessible to all normal-size vehicles
♠	Dirt road accessible without difficulty by passenger car (under normal conditions)
♠♠	Minor obstacles; accessible by passenger car with caution (under good conditions)
♠♠♠	High-clearance required, but no major difficulty
♠♠♠♠	High-clearance 4WD required, some obstacles, no real danger
♠♠♠♠♠	High-clearance 4WD required, some risk to vehicle & passagers, experienced drivers only

Rating	Trail Difficulty
♠	No or very little walking (close to parking area)
♣	Easy short walk (<= 1h r/t), for everybody
♣♣	Moderate hike (1 to 3h r/t) with no major difficulty or short hike with some minor difficulties
♣♣♣	Moderate to strenuous (3 to 6h r/t) and/or difficulties (elevation gain, difficult terrain, some risks)
♣♣♣♣	Strenuous (> 6h r/t) and/or globally difficult (elevation gain, difficult off-trail terrain, obstacles, risks)
♣♣♣♣♣	Backpacking required or for extremely fit dayhikers

Location	Page	Scenic Value	Photogr. Interest	Road Difficulty	Trail Difficulty
3 Grand Canyon - South Rim					
Mather & Havapai Points	53	♥♥♥♥♥	♦♦♦♦	—	—
Hopi Point & Hermit's Rest Road	53	♥♥♥♥	♦♦♦♦	—	—
Yaki Point	54	♥♥♥♥	♦♦♦♦	—	—
South Kaibab Trail (to Cedar Ridge)	55	♥♥♥♥	♦♦	—	♣♣♣
South Kaibab + Bright Angel loop via the Colorado River	56	♥♥♥♥♥	♦♦♦	—	♣♣♣♣♣
Desert View Road & Viewpoints	59	♥♥♥♥	♦♦♦♦	—	—
Little Colorado River Viewpoints	59	♥♥	♦♦	—	—
Blue Spring Trail	59	♥♥♥	♦♦	▲▲▲	♣♣♣♣
Salt Trail	60	♥♥♥♥	♦♦♦♦	▲▲▲	♣♣♣♣♣
4 Grand Canyon - North Rim					
Bright Angel Point	63	♥♥♥♥	♦♦♦♦	—	♣
North Kaibab Trail (to Redwall Bridge)	63	♥♥♥	♦♦	—	♣♣♣
Point Imperial	64	♥♥♥	♦♦♦♦	—	—
Cape Royal	65	♥♥♥	♦♦♦	—	♣
Point Sublime	65	♥♥♥	♦♦	▲▲▲	—
Deer Creek + Thunder River Trails	66	♥♥♥♥	♦♦♦	▲▲▲	♣♣♣♣♣
Toroweap Viewpoint	68	♥♥♥♥	♦♦♦♦	▲▲▲	—
Trumbull Pioneer Schoolhouse	70	♥	♦	▲▲▲	—
Kanab Point	70	♥♥	♦♦	▲▲▲	—
Whitmore Trail	71	♥♥♥	♦♦	▲▲▲	♣♣
Nampaweap Rock Art Site	71	♥	♦	▲▲▲	♣
Snake Gulch	72	♥♥♥	♦♦	▲	♣♣♣
5 Grand Canyon - Colorado River					
North Canyon	78	♥♥	♦♦♦	—	♣
Vasey's Paradise	78	♥♥♥	♦♦	—	—
Saddle Canyon	79	♥♥♥	♦♦	—	♣♣
Nankoweap Granaries	79	♥♥♥♥	♦♦♦♦	—	♣♣
Little Colorado Confluence	79	♥♥♥	♦♦	—	♣
Elves Chasm	82	♥♥♥	♦♦♦	—	♣
Deer Creek	82	♥♥♥	♦♦♦	—	♣♣
Matkatamiba Canyon	82	♥♥	♦♦	—	♣♣
Havasu Creek (to swimming holes)	83	♥♥	♦♦	—	♣
Havasu Creek (to Beaver Falls)	83	♥♥♥	♦♦	—	♣♣♣
National Canyon	83	♥♥	♦♦	—	♣♣
6 Grand Canyon - Havasupai					
Hualapai Top to Supai Village (one way)	86	♥♥♥	♦♦	—	♣♣♣
Navajo Falls (from Supai)	87	♥♥	♦	—	♣
Havasu Falls (from Supai)	87	♥♥♥♥♥	♦♦♦♦♦	—	♣♣
Mooney Falls (from Supai)	88	♥♥♥	♦♦♦	—	♣♣♣
Beaver Falls (from Supai)	90	♥♥♥	♦	—	♣♣♣
Seligman	91	♥♥	♦♦	—	—
Grand Canyon West	92	♥♥	♦♦	▲▲	—
7 Around Sedona					
Tlaquepaque	96	♥	♦	—	—
Chapel of the Holy Cross	97	♥♥	♦♦	—	—
Airport Mesa Vortex	97	♥♥♥	♦♦	—	♣
Red Rock Crossing / Crescent Moon	97	♥♥♥♥	♦♦♦♦	—	♣
Red Rock SP	98	♥♥	♦♦	—	♣♣
Saddle of Cathedral Rock	99	♥♥♥	♦♦♦	—	♣♣
Schnebly Hill Road & Vista	99	♥♥♥	♦♦	▲▲▲	—
Schnebly Hill Road - Trail to Munds Jack Hot Loop	100	♥♥♥	♦♦♦	▲▲▲	♣♣
Huckaby Trail	100	♥♥	♦♦	—	♣♣
Broken Arrow Trail	100	♥♥♥	♦♦	—	♣♣
Bell Rock & Courthouse Butte	101	♥♥♥	♦♦	—	♣♣
Oak Creek Canyon Road	102	♥♥♥	♦	—	—
Slide Rock SP	102	♥♥	♦♦	—	♣

Location	Page	Scenic Value	Photogr. Interest	Road Difficulty	Trail Difficulty
West Fork of Oak Creek Trail (from Call of the Canyon)	102	♥♥♥♥	♦♦♦	—	♣♣
West Fork of Oak Creek Canyon (from top to trailend)	104	♥♥♥	♦♦	♠♠♠	♣♣♣♣♣
Dry Creek Road	104	♥♥	♦♦	—	—
Devil's Bridge	104	♥♥♥	♦♦♦	♠♠	♣♣
Brin's Mesa Trail	104	♥♥♥	♦♦	♠♠	♣♣
Vultee Arch Trail	105	♥♥	♦♦	♠♠	♣♣
Boynton Canyon Trail	106	♥♥♥	♦♦	—	♣♣
Fay Canyon Trail + spur trails	106	♥♥♥	♦♦	♠♠	♣♣
Doe Mountain Trail	107	♥♥	♦♦	♠♠	♣♣
Bear Mountain Trail	107	♥♥♥	♦♦	♠♠	♣♣♣♣
Palatki Heritage Site	108	♥♥	♦♦	♠♠	♣
Soldier's Pass Arches Trail	109	♥♥	♦♦♦	—	♣♣
Sycamore Canyon - Parson's Trail	110	♥♥♥	♦♦	♠♠	♣♣♣
Tuzigoot NM	111	♥♥	♦♦	—	♣
Jerome	111	♥♥	♦	—	—
Granite Dells - Watson Lake	112	♥♥♥	♦♦	—	♣
Montezuma Castle	112	♥♥♥	♦♦	—	♣
Montezuma Well	113	♥♥	♦	—	♣
V-Bar-V Ranch	113	♥♥	♦♦	—	♣
Agua Fria NM	114	♥	♦	♠	♣♣
8 Superstition Mountains					
Lost Dutchman - Siphon Draw Trail	117	♥♥	♦♦♦	—	♣♣
Lost Dutchman - Top of the Flatiron	117	♥♥♥	♦	—	♣♣♣♣♣
Lost Dutchman - Prospector' View to Treasure Loop Trail	117	♥♥♥	♦♦♦♦♦	—	♣
Peralta Canyon Trail & Weavers Outlook Ridge	118	♥♥♥	♦♦	♠	♣♣
Bluff Spring & Upper Barks Canyon Trails	119	♥♥	♦♦	♠	♣♣♣♣
Apache Trail Road	120	♥♥	♦♦	♠	—
Tonto NM - Lower Cliff Dwelling	121	♥♥	♦♦	—	♣
Tonto NM - Upper Cliff Dwelling	121	♥♥	♦	—	♣♣♣
Casa Grande NM	122	♥♥	♦♦	—	—
9 Southwest Arizona					
Kofa Mountains - Palm Canyon	124	♥♥	♦♦	♠	♣♣
Kofa Mountains - Kofa Queen Canyon Road	125	♥♥	♦♦	♠♠♠♠	—
Kofa Mountains - King of Arizona Mine District	125	♥	♦	♠♠♠	—
Kofa Mountains - Castel Dome Mine District	125	♥♥	♦	♠♠♠	—
Kofa Mountains - Red Rock Pass Road	126	♥♥	♦♦	♠♠♠	—
Alamo Lake (wildflower season)	126	♥♥	♦♦♦	—	—
Painted Rocks	127	♥♥	♦♦	—	—
Organ Pipe Cactus NM - North Puerto Blanco Drive	127	♥♥	♦♦	♠	—
Organ Pipe Cactus NM - Senita Basin	128	♥♥♥	♦♦♦	♠	♣♣♣♣
Organ Pipe Cactus NM - Ajo Mountain Loop	128	♥♥♥	♦♦♦	♠	—
Organ Pipe Cactus NM - Palo Verde Loop Trail	129	♥	♦	—	♣
Cabeza Prieta National Wildlife Refuge	129	♥♥	♦	♠♠	—
Ajo Plaza & Cornelia Mine	130	♥♥	♦	—	—
Puerto Penasco / Rocky Point	130	♥♥♥	♦♦♦	—	—
Gran Desierto de Altar	130	♥♥♥♥	♦♦♦	♠♠♠	—
Picacho Peak - Calloway Trail (wildflower season)	132	♥♥♥	♦♦♦	—	♣♣♣
Picacho Peak - Hunter Trail (wildflower season)	132	♥♥♥	♦♦♦	—	♣
Ironwood Forest & Sonoran Desert NM	132	♥♥	♦♦	♠	♣
10 Southeast Arizona					
Saguaro NP West - Bajada Loop Drive	134	♥♥♥	♦♦	♠	—
Saguaro NP West - Valley View Trail	135	♥♥	♦♦	♠	♣
Saguaro NP West - Signal Hill	135	♥♥	♦♦	♠	♣
Saguaro NP West - King Canyon + Sendero Esper. Loop	135	♥♥♥	♦♦	—	♣♣♣
Gates Pass	136	♥♥	♦♦	—	—
Saguaro NP East - Cactus Forest Drive	137	♥♥♥	♦♦♦	—	—
Saguaro NP East - Freeman Homestead Loop Trail	137	♥♥	♦♦	—	♣

Location	Page	Scenic Value	Photogr. Interest	Road Difficulty	Trail Difficulty
Sabino Canyon Recreation Area	137	♥ ♥	♦ ♦	–	♣ ♣
Kartchner Caverns SP	138	♥ ♥	♦	–	♣
San Xavier Del Bac & Tumacacori Missions	138	♥ ♥	♦ ♦	–	–
Chiricahua NM - Bonita Canyon Drive	140	♥ ♥	♦ ♦	–	–
Chiricahua NM - Massai Point Trail	140	♥ ♥	♦ ♦ ♦	–	♣
Chiricahua NM - Echo Canyon Loop	140	♥ ♥ ♥	♦ ♦ ♦	–	♣ ♣
Chiricahua NM - Heart of Rocks Trail	140	♥ ♥ ♥	♦ ♦ ♦	–	♣ ♣ ♣ ♣
Cave Creek Canyon (via Pinery Canyon Road)	142	♥ ♥	♦	♠ ♠ ♠	♣
Tombstone	142	♥ ♥	♦	–	–
11 Around Interstate 40					
Sunset Crater NM - Lava Flow Trail	144	♥ ♥	♦ ♦	–	♣
Wupatki NM - Wukoki Pueblo	145	♥ ♥	♦ ♦ ♦	–	♣
Wupatki NM - Wupatki Pueblo	145	♥ ♥ ♥	♦ ♦	–	♣
Wupatki NM - Doney Mountain	146	♥	♦	–	♣
Wupatki NM - Lomaki Pueblo	146	♥	♦	–	♣
Wupatki NM - Citadel Pueblo	147	♥ ♥	♦	–	♣
Walnut Canyon NM - Rim Trail	147	♥	♦	–	♣
Walnut Canyon NM - Island Trail	147	♥ ♥ ♥	♦ ♦	–	♣ ♣
Grand Falls	148	♥ ♥ ♥	♦ ♦	♠ ♠ ♠	–
Little Painted Desert	149	♥ ♥	♦ ♦ ♦	–	–
Coal Mine Canyon	150	♥ ♥	♦ ♦	♠ ♠	–
Hopi Mesas & Villages	151	♥ ♥ ♥	–	–	–
Petrified Forest NP - Giant Logs	152	♥ ♥ ♥	♦ ♦	–	♣
Petrified Forest NP - Long Logs & Agate House	152	♥ ♥ ♥	♦ ♦ ♦	–	♣ ♣
Petrified Forest NP - Crystal & Jasper Forest	152	♥	♦	–	♣
Petrified Forest NP - Blue Mesa	152	♥ ♥ ♥	♦ ♦ ♦	–	♣
Petrified Forest NP - Newspaper Rock & Puerco Blanco	153	♥	♦	–	–
Petrified Forest NP - Painted Desert Viewpoints	153	♥ ♥	♦ ♦	–	–
Petrified Forest NP - Black Forest Wilderness	153	♥ ♥ ♥	♦ ♦	–	♣ ♣ ♣
Holbrook - Old West Museum	156	♥ ♥	–	–	–
Rock Art Ranch	156	♥ ♥	♦	–	–
12 Canyon de Chelly					
Canyon de Chelly NP - South Rim Road Viewpoints	160	♥ ♥ ♥ ♥	♦ ♦ ♦ ♦	–	♣
Canyon de Chelly NP - White House Trail & Ruins	160	♥ ♥ ♥	♦ ♦ ♦	–	♣ ♣
Canyon de Chelly NP - North Rim Road Viewpoints	161	♥ ♥	♦ ♦	–	♣
Canyon de Chelly NP - Inner canyon guided tour (full day)	161	♥ ♥ ♥ ♥	♦ ♦ ♦	♠ ♠ ♠ ♠	–
Canyon de Chelly NP - Inner Canyon - The Window	164	♥ ♥	♦ ♦ ♦	♠ ♠ ♠ ♠	♣ ♣
Hope Arch	165	♥ ♥	♦ ♦	♠ ♠ ♠	–
Lukachukai Mountains - Los Gigantes Buttes area	166	♥ ♥	♦ ♦	♠ ♠ ♠	–
Lukachukai Mountains - Dancing Rocks	167	♥ ♥	♦ ♦	–	♣
Window Rock - Navajo Museum & Arch	167	♥ ♥	♦ ♦	–	–
Hubbel Trading Post National Historic Site	168	♥	♦	–	–
13 Monument Valley					
Visitor Center Viewpoint & Valley Drive (self drive loop)	171	♥ ♥ ♥ ♥ ♥	♦ ♦ ♦ ♦	♠ ♠	–
Valley Drive + spurs (complete extended guided tour)	172	♥ ♥ ♥ ♥ ♥	♦ ♦ ♦ ♦ ♦	♠ ♠ ♠	–
Tear Drop Arch (guided tour)	174	♥ ♥ ♥	♦ ♦ ♦	♠ ♠ ♠ ♠	–
Mystery Valley (guided tour)	175	♥ ♥ ♥	♦ ♦ ♦	♠ ♠ ♠ ♠	–
Hunt's Mesa by 4WD (guided tour)	176	♥ ♥ ♥ ♥ ♥	♦ ♦ ♦ ♦ ♦	♠ ♠ ♠ ♠	♣
Hunt's Mesa backpack (guided tour)	176	♥ ♥ ♥ ♥ ♥	♦ ♦ ♦ ♦ ♦	♠ ♠	♣ ♣ ♣
Agathla Peak	178	♥ ♥	♦ ♦	–	–
Church Rock	178	♥ ♥	♦ ♦	–	–
Baby Rocks	179	♥	♦	–	–
Navajo NM - Sandal Trail & Viewpoint	179	♥ ♥	♦ ♦	–	♣
Navajo NM - Aspen Forest Overlook	179	♥ ♥	♦	–	♣
Navajo NM - Betatakin	179	♥ ♥ ♥	♦ ♦ ♦	–	♣ ♣ ♣
Navajo NM - Keet Seel	180	♥ ♥ ♥ ♥	♦ ♦ ♦	–	♣ ♣ ♣ ♣
Eggshell Arch	182	♥ ♥ ♥	♦ ♦ ♦	♠ ♠ ♠ ♠	♣

Location	Page	Scenic Value	Photogr. Interest	Road Difficulty	Trail Difficulty
14 Antelope Canyon					
Upper Antelope Canyon (guided tour)	185	♥♥♥♥♥	♦♦♦♦♦	♠♠♠♠	♣
Lower Antelope Canyon	188	♥♥♥♥♥	♦♦♦♦♦	–	♣♣
Canyon X / Peach Wash (guided tour)	190	♥♥♥♥	♦♦♦	♠♠♠	♣♣
15 Around Page					
Horseshoe Bend	193	♥♥♥♥	♦♦♦♦	–	♣
Water Holes Canyon	194	♥♥♥	♦♦	–	♣♣
Marble Canyon & Lee's Ferry	196	♥♥	♦♦	–	–
Cathedral Wash	197	♥♥♥	♦♦	–	♣♣
Alstrom Point	198	♥♥♥♥	♦♦♦♦	♠♠♠♠	♣
Nipple Bench & Kelly Grade	199	♥♥	♦♦	♠♠♠	–
Rainbow Bridge	202	♥♥♥♥	♦♦♦	–	♣
Stud Horse Point	204	♥♥	♦♦	♠♠♠	–
16 Coyote Buttes North					
The Wave	207	♥♥♥♥♥	♦♦♦♦♦	♠♠	♣♣♣
Arch & Lace rocks (on the way to The Wave)	212	♥♥	♦♦	♠♠	♣♣♣
Brain Rocks & Second Wave	213	♥♥♥♥	♦♦♦♦♦	♠♠	♣♣♣
Sand Cove	214	♥♥♥	♦♦♦	♠♠	♣♣♣
Top Rock (on the top & backside)	216	♥♥♥♥	♦♦♦♦	♠♠	♣♣♣♣
The Teepees	218	♥♥♥	♦♦♦	♠♠	♣♣♣
Wire Pass & a foray in Buckskin Gulch	219	♥♥♥	♦♦♦	♠♠	♣♣
17 Coyote Buttes South					
Paw Hole	224	♥♥♥	♦♦♦	♠♠♠♠	♣♣
Cottonwood Plateau, Teepees & Cove	225	♥♥♥♥♥	♦♦♦♦	♠♠♠♠	♣♣♣
White Pocket	231	♥♥♥♥	♦♦♦♦	♠♠♠♠♠	♣♣
18 A foray into Nevada					
Gold Butte Byway - Whitney Pocket	238	♥♥	♦	–	♣
Gold Butte Byway - Little Finland	239	♥♥♥	♦♦♦	♠♠♠♠	♣♣
Virgin River Gorge	241	♥♥	♦	–	–
Valley of Fire SP - West Side Scenic Road stops	241	♥♥♥	♦♦♦	♠	–
Valley of Fire SP - White Domes Scenic Road	242	♥♥♥	♦♦	–	–
Valley of Fire SP - Mouse's Tank	243	♥♥	♦	–	♣
Valley of Fire SP - Rainbow Vista area	243	♥♥	♦♦♦	–	♣♣
Valley of Fire SP - White Domes Loop	243	♥♥♥♥	♦♦♦	–	♣♣
Valley of Fire SP - Elephant Rock	244	♥♥	♦♦♦	–	♣
Valley of Fire SP - Ephemeral Arch	244	♥♥	♦♦	–	♣♣
Lake Mead North Shore - Picnic area & viewpoint stops	245	♥♥	♦♦	–	♣
Bitter Springs Trail	245	♥♥	♦♦	♠♠♠♠	–
Bowl of Fire	246	♥♥	♦♦	♠♠♠	♣♣
Lovell Wash Narrows	246	♥♥♥	♦♦	♠♠♠♠	♣♣
Red Rock Canyon - Scenic Road	247	♥♥♥	♦♦	–	–
Red Rock Canyon - Calico Hill Trail	247	♥♥	♦♦	–	♣♣
Red Rock Canyon - Calico Tanks Trail	247	♥♥	♦♦	–	♣♣
Bonnie Springs Ranch area	248	♥♥	♦♦	♠♠	♣

Warning: Road Difficulty ratings are for normal, dry conditions. Driving conditions can change dramatically during or after a rain, even more so on clay roads or roads that follow the course of a wash. As an example, the well-used House Rock Valley Road—which would rate a 2 in difficulty—can become impassable after a thunderstorm and stay so for days on end, even with 4WD. Severe weather can dramatically alter conditions for extended periods of time. When the road was last maintained also has a huge impact on its condition and can alter the rating by 1 level in either direction. Always check current road conditions with local authorities before you leave.

INDEX

A not so brief blip about the Author

I was born in Paris, France. Thanks to an open-minded family, I attended school in Paris, London, Barcelona and several cities in Germany. I hold degrees in modern languages and international business.

A couple of years after college, I did the best thing a young person can do to widen his or her horizons and gain an understanding of our world and its wonderful diversity: I set out on a 20-month trip around the world, photographing extensively.

From 1976-1981, I lived in Tokyo, becoming a permanent resident of Japan and teaching at Sophia University. During this time, I also worked as a freelance photographer and pursued my research on the origins of Sumo and its ties with the Shinto religion, resulting in *Sumo – Le Sport & le Sacré* published in 1984. My years in Japan have had a profound influence on my life, my philosophy, and my photography.

I immigrated to the United States in 1982, settling in Southern California and creating Graphie Int'l, Inc, specializing in software, multimedia and, later on, internet technologies. Constant exploration and photography of the Southwest resulted in the publication of *Land of the Canyons* in 1998. In 1999, I permanently switched my focus from the software industry to a full-time career as a fine-art photographer, author and publisher, spending a good deal of my time in the Southwest.

I have been photographing since the age of 11, paying my dues to the B&W chemical lab for many years before becoming an early adopter of Cibachrome. I prefer shooting 2¼" medium format. Although I have shot Hasselblad and Mamiya, I now do the majority of my photography with two Fuji 645 rangefinder cameras, which I find well-suited to my style of photography. In the past, I have also used a 35mm Olympus OM-4 system extensively, especially for extreme wide-angle and long-telephoto shots. Nowadays, I use Canon and Olympus dSLR cameras and Panasonic digicams regularly. When shooting film, I use Fujichrome Velvia and Astia. In my work, I seek to challenge the imagination with images characterized by bold colors, unique textures and a striking sense of depth, ranging from starkly minimalist compositions to complex abstracts. ❁

Intentionally left blank for notes